GOTH

Also by Lol Tolhurst:

Cured: The Tale of Two Imaginary Boys

GOTH

A HISTORY

LOL TOLHURST

QUERCUS

First published in Great Britain in 2023 by

QUERCUS

Quercus Editions Ltd
Carmelite House
50 Victoria Embankment
London EC4Y 0DZ

An Hachette UK company

Copyright © 2023 Laurence A. Tolhurst
Cover design by Timothy O'Donnell
Front cover photo: Laurence A. Tolhurst copyright © 2023
Cover copyright © 2023 by Hachette Book Group, Inc.

The moral right of Laurence A. Tolhurst to
be identified as the author of this work has been
asserted in accordance with the Copyright,
Designs and Patents Act, 1988

All rights reserved. No part of this publication
may be reproduced or transmitted in any form
or by any means, electronic or mechanical,
including photocopy, recording, or any
information storage and retrieval system,
without permission in writing from the publisher.

A CIP catalogue record for this book is available
from the British Library

HB ISBN 978 1 52942 427 0
TPB ISBN 978 1 52942 428 7
Ebook ISBN 978 1 52942 430 0

Every effort has been made to contact copyright holders.
However, the publishers will be glad to rectify in future
editions any inadvertent omissions brought to their attention.

Quercus Editions Ltd hereby exclude all liability to the extent
permitted by law for any errors or omissions in this book and for any loss,
damage or expense (whether direct or indirect) suffered by a
third party relying on any information contained in this book.

10 9 8 7 6 5 4

Print book interior design by Amy Quinn

Printed and bound in Great Britain by Clays Ltd, Elcograf S.p.A.

Papers used by Quercus are from well-managed forests and other responsible sources.

For those outside the walls who finally found a home

"Don't try to understand! It's enough if you do not misunderstand."

—Nisargadatta Maharaj

The author in 2020
Credit: Cindy Tolhurst

CONTENTS

	Foreword	ix
	Author's Note	xi

PART ONE: ORIGINS

Introduction:	From Punk to Poignancy	3
	August 16, 1977, Nighttime	4
Chapter One:	Gothic Psychic Geography	9
	Joe Strummer: *The Firebrand of Punk*	16
Chapter Two:	The Poetry of Pain	21
	Goth in Literature	21
	T. S. Eliot: *Modernist Goth*	28
	Camus & Sartre: *The Brothers Absurd*	30
	Sylvia Plath: *Through a Bell Jar Darkly*	33
	Anne Sexton: *Suicide and Transformations*	38
Chapter Three:	Prototypes	41
	The Doors of Perception	41
	Suicide: *Suicide Times*	46
	Nico: *Nothing*	50
	Alice Cooper: *Snakes Alive!*	54
	Scott Walker: *Drifting*	58
	Marc Bolan: *Life's a Gas*	60
	David Bowie: *Low Level*	63

PART TWO: ETERNALS

Chapter Four:	Architects of Darkness	71
	Joy Division: *This Is the Way, Step Inside*	71

	Bauhaus: *Undead*	90
	Siouxsie and the Banshees: *Liberation and Lament*	100
	"Phil Spector in Hell": *The Cold Psychedelia of The Cure*	119
	The Four Drummers of Destiny	146

PART THREE: LEGION

Chapter Five:	Spiritual Alchemists	151
	Cocteau Twins: *Eternity's Song*	151
	Wire: *Wired*	156
	Sisters of Mercy: *Sisters Are Doing It for Themselves*	160
	The Mission: *Wayne Hussey's Mission in Life*	161
	The Damned: *Waiting for the Blackout*	165
	And Also the Trees: *Cut from the Same Cloth*	167
	All About Eve: *Goths with Grace*	171
Chapter Six:	Infinity's Window	181
	The Batcave and Beyond	181
	Depeche Mode: *The Priory*	191
	Deathrock, CA	197
Chapter Seven:	We Are Many	207
	Nine Inch Nails	207
	Drab Majesty	209
	Cold Cave	210
	Black Marble	211
	Molchat Doma	211
	Legionnaires	212
Chapter Eight:	Before and After Goth	213
	Visually Gothic	213
	Elder Goths and Fashion	216
	Why Goth Matters	221
	Afterword	225
	Acknowledgments	229
	Sources	233
	Index	235

FOREWORD

ENGLAND 1970. IT'S ONLY TWENTY-FIVE YEARS SINCE BRITAIN'S DADS-to-be came home from World War II. The youngest of the postwar babies are just discovering music beyond The Monkees and The Banana Splits, as Jimi Hendrix plays "Foxy Lady" live for the very last time at the Isle of Wight festival. The pirate radio stations, Caroline and Luxembourg, transmit illicit sounds from outside the BBC's radio broadcasting monopoly. Eager young ears listen from under the bedsheets of a postwar Britain falling deeper and deeper into recession. Ex-pirate DJ John Peel infiltrates the BBC and champions the esoteric, glamorous music of Marc Bolan, David Bowie, and Roxy Music.

England 1976. Global oil prices tumble, unemployment hits one million, Prime Minister Harold Wilson resigns, and John Peel discovers The Ramones. Regular listeners complain, Peel plays more Ramones, and within the month, the average age of his audience has decreased by ten years. Following the "Bill Grundy versus The Sex Pistols" TV incident of December 1, 1976, the *Daily Mirror*'s front page turns The Ramones' "Sheena Is a Punk Rocker" into "Siouxsie's a Punk Shocker" and lands the nineteen-year-old Siouxsie amongst the Cornflakes and Weetabix of Britain's teenage dreamers. As 1978 draws to a close, industry strikes plunge the United Kingdom into its Winter of Discontent. Siouxsie Sioux releases her debut *Scream*; Johnny Rotten, now John Lydon, releases Public Image Limited's *First Issue*. Ladies and Gentlemen, please rattle your safety pins for post-punk.

I was flung into punk as drummer with The Spitfire Boys, slipping into something a little more comfortable with Big in Japan, before leaving Liverpool to its own post-punkers, Echo and the Bunnymen and The Teardrop Explodes. If ever there was a time when "this town ain't big enough for the both of us," then that was it. In London, I drummed on The Slits' *Cut*, "made a veil" for a John Peel session with ex-Pistols bassist Glen Matlock, then made the recently bisected Siouxsie and the Banshees into a trio. It was whilst touring as drummer for Siouxsie's WWI-inspired album *Join Hands* that I met drummer and writer Lol Tolhurst. The Cure opening for Siouxsie in 1979 was the original imaginary trio of Lol, Michael, and Robert.

Lol and I would remain distant partners in the drummer's dance for forty years. Then in 2019 we met for breakfast in a downtown LA diner, to talk about the future and to plan our past. As solid as elephants, drummers never forget, and if we do, it wasn't true. Lol has proved his elephantine powers of recall and his incisive mind as the celebrated author of *Cured*. A lucid personal memoir by a pioneer of mesmerizing motoric beats that left drum machines blinking for mercy.

Cured also alluded to a myriad of unsung heroes, heroines, and ghost notes left unplayed. All are brought out of a forest, into the light, together here for the first time in this comprehensive and definitive Goth opus: *Goth: A History*.

Budgie
Berlin, 2023

Budgie
Credit: Louis Rodiger

AUTHOR'S NOTE

Before Goth there was anarchy and the mystery of anarchy begat Goth. What was the mystery of anarchy? Isn't Goth just the mysterious part of a nihilistic rebellion called punk?

Or is Goth the true golden thread weaving its way from the past until now and ever onwards to outsider infinity?

What interests me is the why and the wherefore. The rest is mere detail. From The Doors (of perception) to The Cure and further I'm searching for the essence that has always resonated with dark seekers. Some identify as Goths, others do not; but we are all the same tribe. These are my people.

Victorian ladies would carry a small black-and-white photo or miniature portrait in a locket as a remembrance of love lost. This book should fulfill that same melancholy longing...

PART ONE

ORIGINS

INTRODUCTION

FROM PUNK TO POIGNANCY

"Jumping someone else's train" in Crawley, 1985
Credit: Richard Bellia

AUGUST 16, 1977, NIGHTTIME

I am in a darkened bedroom in my hometown of Crawley, listening to the radio in the late-night gloom with a girl called The Raven. She has long, straight black hair and all black clothes. I am eighteen years old.

The Raven turns the radio's tuning knob, trying to find something in the airless room to listen to. A crackle of static and a breathless voice eerily intones, "The king is dead. Elvis Presley, the king of rock and roll, died tonight in Memphis, Tennessee."

To us, Memphis might as well have been the moon. It was that far from our experience of growing up in the ever-present doom of Thatcher's postwar Britain. We knew Elvis's death meant something, but what? The changing of the guard? A way forward?

Elvis's journey may have come to an end, but mine was just beginning. Together with my friends Robert Smith and Michael Dempsey, we started on the path to recording The Cure's first album, *Three Imaginary Boys*.

The songs were sparse and angular, somewhere between punk and pop, but the title track provided an indication of where the band was headed. Its dark lyric of longing and shadow came from a dream I had that haunted me for days. Robert perfectly melded the words with his guitar and melancholy vocal suspended on the minimalist framework of my spartan drums and Michael's melodic pulse.

I think we knew it was the right way for us even before we really understood it. That year among the books I read were Camus's *The Stranger*, Plath's *The Bell Jar*, and Sartre's *Nausea*. They all spoke to something darker within me, but also something more beautiful, and it inspired my playing. All of us channeled the pensive yearning of our souls into the music we were making that summer of '77 and discovered the blueprint for The Cure's oeuvre.

We had seen the disease. The Cure was inevitable.

Did we realize what we were on to at the end of the seventies?

We did not. In fact, we resisted it. Despite our passionate insistence that The Cure was not a Goth group, The Cure was very much a Goth group. We were like the famous quote by Groucho Marx and we didn't want to belong to any club that would accept us as members. We were also against the idea of following anything or anybody. That was the raison d'être for our third single,

"Jumping Someone Else's Train," which was specifically against joining any bandwagons that happened to be passing by at the time.

We were very serious young men and leery of being pigeonholed by our many critics who didn't care for our dark music. Yet notwithstanding that idea we became the fertile ground on which the movement flourished.

Somehow everything The Cure did between 1980 and 1984 became hallmarks of this elusive subculture. Call it the enigma of post-punk. Gloomy action glimpsed at a distance in a mushroom cloud of teased black hair.

Consider the songs from what many of our most diehard fans regard as our three early dark albums, our "Goth phase," if you will: *Seventeen Seconds*, *Faith*, and *Pornography*. They remain the foundation for not just a new kind of music, but a way of being in the world. The only thing we lacked was a name for it, but that came soon enough. My investigation into this led me to understand the subculture in a deeper way. This was the occasion for a startling epiphany: it's almost unheard of in modern music for something so completely amorphous to have endured for so long.

The Cure did not have a particular style; rather, we were the essence of a melancholy spirit. That's what struck a chord with our fans—not just in dreary old England, but around the world, where people perceived the view to be just as dim and grim as we did. It guided us on our adventure to the other side of our looking-glass future. We'd seen the futility of existence in Britain's long postwar malaise, and we clamored for something more.

Paradoxically, Goth is often portrayed in a comical way by the media. It probably needs to be so to make it overtly two-dimensional and easily digestible for those who will never comprehend it. As with punk before it, if you can identify the main components, then you can précis the understanding of what it is.

Critics of punk rock saw the spiky hair and angry lyrics and assumed that's what punk was all about, missing the point entirely. The choices by early punks were directed by a nonconformist impulse to go against the grain of society. That's what the punk movement was about, not just the music they made or the clothes they wore.

As a young punk on the outskirts of London, I also understood it to be many other things: a credo, a posture, a two-minute manifesto I could wave in the face of my fear to banish uncertainty and despair, and to give me hope in a dark and diminished Britain. Our detractors never understood that, but the dark-haired boys and girls did. The Raven knew it deep in her bones. That otherworldly beauty made sure we never forgot it.

Descartes's famous phrase—*Cogito, ergo sum:* I think, therefore I am—has led Western man to equate his identity with his mind, instead of with his whole organism. I think we can equate the origins of Goth, and its close cousin post-punk, with the quest to find what's beyond the Cartesian mode of thought. If punk was pure, instinctual nihilism, Goth searched for meaning—even if we didn't quite realize it back then. Its sources varied. They were not always music. Literature, cinema, and other visual art inspired us. The comic book version has Goths sleeping in coffins and bats flying about, too trite and easy I'd say (although I know a man in Portland that does indeed sleep like that). There's a duality at the heart of Goth that's beautiful and human and unearthly all at the same time, which assures its continued relevance today.

There are obvious connections with Byron and Poe and other roots macabre, but I think that is just the externalization of the impulse that drove Goth.

Most thinking and feeling teens in the UK after the first explosion of punk felt liberated from a desperate survival mode, thinking that had existed in Britain since the end of World War II. Punk came and kicked down the doors and strangely let in the light so the black heart of something like Goth could exist. It showed a whole generation that anything was possible, and it could be closer to the dark impulse, that anxious parent of the soul, that shell-shocked teens kept under cover.

Goth and post-punk allowed us as teenage boys and girls to reveal our dreads and desires, bubbling under the intense surface. So where are the roots, where are the seeds we grew from?

Goth is not really a subculture I've come to understand. It's a way to understand the world. It's the essence of a deeper metaphysical journey. If you live in England, it's all around you, especially in London. It's in the Victorian buildings of old London town, in beautiful mystical Gothic palaces like Strawberry Hill. It's in Westminster Abbey, the Valhalla of British heroes: a large Gothic abbey church, a thousand years old. It's farther out in the Kent countryside at Canterbury Cathedral. It's in every downpour of constant rain and gloomy, grey skies. It's in the dark alleys and foggy Thames banks. In the walls of ancient pubs and still-cobbled Dickensian streets. It is, in fact, everywhere.

We just had to locate its meaning.

The Cure in Bourges, France
Credit: Richard Bellia

CHAPTER ONE

GOTHIC PSYCHIC GEOGRAPHY

Our story starts in a time not unlike the time we find ourselves in now. Polarization was the order of the day in late seventies England. People of worth felt worthless, and nothing seemed meaningful except the crashing sounds of boredom and fermenting anger. We were living through Thatcher's nightmare. The Iron Lady, together with her American counterpart Ronald Reagan, had cemented our future and it didn't look very appealing. Where were we to go? What were we to do? We didn't know but something told us deep inside that the old era, the old guard, had to go.

When The Clash's first record album came out in the UK in April 1977, the band was on the front cover. In typical Clash swagger Joe, Paul, and Mick stood there, daring you to hear them. Hand-painted slogans on thrift store shirts, the real deal, disaffected London youth. No surprise there then, but when you turned the album over there was an artily blurred picture of charging police officers.

This photo, shot by Rocco Macauley, was taken during the 1976 riot at the Notting Hill Carnival in London. The carnival was an annual Caribbean festival that had taken place since 1966. In 1976 simmering tensions between the police and the community boiled over, and there were clashes between the two parties due to the harassment felt by the local population. The photo on the back shows the police running under an overpass, and in the background are blurry images of other people and street vendors. That summer of '76 was the hottest in living memory in the UK and out of its fiery belly came the punk revolution.

This particular photo holds a special meaning for me in the psychic geography of my youth. I was at the carnival with my friend and bandmate Porl "Pearl" Thompson. We were in our late teens, not yet adults, and had decided to check out the carnival. A colorful cornucopia of sounds and sights of the Caribbean heart of West London. As the day wore on, we noticed the gradually increasing hostile atmosphere between the police patrolling the festival and the youth of the area milling about on the perimeters, both sides warily eyeing each other.

Suddenly, a bottle was lobbed from the crowd, tracing a perfect arc across the street from the side where the youth were assembled to the side where the police were gathered. The world stood still for a second with all eyes on the bottle as it appeared to spin through the air in slow motion and smashed onto the street in front of the police, shattering into a thousand small fragments, shocking us into reality with the unmistakable sound of the starting gun for the riot that was to ensue.

We took that as a sign that we should leave straightaway. We both ran toward the tube station as fast as we could. I was just seventeen, Pearl not yet twenty, and this was a little too real for sheltered young boys from the sticks. Together with hundreds of others having the same thought we squeezed down the stairs into the underground station and jumped on the next train that came through on the central line to Oxford Circus, down to Victoria, and then on to the Gatwick train to take us back home to the safety of the suburbs. For us, it was never to be that simple again.

Later that night we saw the melee on the TV and realized we had been at a pivotal moment in our personal history, a history marked by a specific place as well as time. I can never look or think about that area of London without recalling my experience that day. It has placed a permanent marker in my memory. That place and those events locked together forever. I think it is one of the strongest connections I have as it forged an association with The Clash that won't be broken by time or other circumstances. It is an indelible mark on my soul.

Today when I see that album in people's record collections, I turn the cover over and point to the photo and the image of people running about in the background. I point to them and say "You know that's me there!" because even if it wasn't actually me in the shot, I know I was there to witness the spiritual birth of punk in the UK.

I live, as we all do, in a place defined by imaginary lines and mythical times. For sure there are mountains and rivers that create boundaries marked on maps, but the borders are political and historical, and these oftentimes arbitrary demarcations define where I've lived for nearly thirty years, which is California. These random lines on the map do not really suit the purpose for which they are intended. They are boundaries to keep people in or out—and sometimes ideas as well—but as world events have shown, they do not hem in people's souls as much as some other people wish they might. In short, they do not define us as much as you would imagine. In my travels around the world, these last forty years, I've come to realize that what holds people together are beliefs and ideas and experiences and—dare I say it—a love of those things. Although these fanciful imaginary lines have been in place for many years, this is especially true in a day and age where information and its toxic corollary, disinformation, are widely available across the globe.

Most of what we will talk about here is defined in a recent era, the seventies and the eighties, with a brief sojourn into the future now, the present moment, where we all reside. There will be some other context that we will talk about, but by and large it's those two decades that our focus is on, and for good reason. Apart from the fact that it was where our protagonists germinated from, it was back then, if you conform to our map paradigm, a world presented in quite a different way than is now perceived.

Information was not widely available across the internet, which was not even a thing at all until the late sixties, when the fledgling ARPANET delivered its first message: October 29, 1969, a "node-to-node" communication from one house-sized computer to another behemoth machine. The first computer was at UCLA and the second at Stanford, both in California. At this point the internet was used for communication only among a few universities and government agencies. I imagine a computer mainframe version of Alexander Graham Bell's telephone (or Elisha Gray's or Antonio Meucci's versions, depending on where your sympathies lie) where academics and military men sent bitmap text in Digi Grotesk—a proto-Goth name if ever I heard one.

But I digress. By and large, none of this was useful until the late eighties. In fact, I first used email, probably AOL, in the early nineties. Unlike now, when it is ubiquitous, I knew only one other person that utilized it: my lawyer. I was the only other person he knew who had it because for about a year we only received messages from each other. A strange procession of non-love notes. No, it was not really a thing until most of what I am writing about here had been firmly established.

My younger readers might wonder how did we communicate our ideas in a coherent way? With a method that, as we shall see, was powerful enough to build a cultural framework and ensure that it would continue to make waves and define a generation of misfits and outsiders that still reverberates today. This to me is the heart of the mystery of where the long-lasting and ever-evolving influence of Goth and its post-punk cousin comes from.

This is a story of traveling across the globe's imaginary geographical lines to bring ideas through music and words to other people directly. It's similar to dharma transmission in that it moves from one person to another by playing the music or singing the ideas or celebrating those ideas together in a way that's almost intravenous in its spiritual directness.

Sure, there were records and the radio so that we could relive the experience of listening to the music and dissect its messages, and later some very basic host forums emerged where these ideas could be discussed, but in the beginning we had to play directly to others. It didn't just exist on the iTunes internet island or Spotify's music-world-domination servers.

Make no mistake, at the time I am talking about, the eighties to be specific, I had identified quickly that the lingua franca of the world was not English or Chinese or some other form of verbal communication, it was music. Everywhere I went from North America to Australia and all across Asia, I heard the same songs on pop radio in my hotel room. You might say, "Well, that's not the *true* experience of the place. What about the indigenous music of these countries that wasn't on the radio?"

It's still there and a source of interest to me now as it was then, but what I'm identifying here are the codes we the younger generation passed from one another to communicate our feelings in our limited capacity to understand our world. It was how we delineated our place in time and history, which tribe we really belonged to. This might sound a little pretentious nowadays, but make no mistake, pop, or if you prefer, youth music, was very powerful stuff back then. It defined us all. I feel it still does.

Our music was perceived as dangerous enough to make the powers that be in, say, Eastern Europe, try to ban it. As noted in Tim Mohr's excellent book *Burning Down the Haus: Punk Rock, Revolution, and the Fall of the Berlin Wall*, there were various ways the new revolution snuck in—quite literally under the wall.

Personally, when I was a teenager there were not many alternatives to the stodgy BBC radio—only John Peel's show, which we will come to. There were some pirate radio stations like Radio Caroline that generally avoided the laws of England by being broadcast—yes, you guessed it—like pirates, from a ship in the ocean outside the national boundaries set by the British government. Their clandestine radio waves seeped across national borders, and I was able to pick this up along with other noncommercial programming on my small portable transistor radio. Late at night, with the little earpiece planted firmly in one ear, it was my introduction to all the new and non–Top 40 music.

According to Mohr, another station, Radio Luxembourg, based in the Grand Duchy, was able to go even further and sneak across completely different ideological lines in Eastern Europe. Very subversive stuff, which is why, I suppose, it was hard to get those records out there. It's always been about the transfer of radical ideas for me. The fact of the matter is there were only two methods of direct transfer, and one of them—the radio—made our mission more difficult but was, in many ways, I believe, better.

Not for us the abstract counting of hits or followers on social media. No, we went somewhere—Boston, Brussels, Brisbane, Berlin—and then came back six months or a year later and did it all over again in a slightly different manner.

In those early years we were young men with the stamina needed to constantly circumnavigate the globe. We needed to transmit the fervor we found as we were in direct competition for souls with the controlled soporific drip of the media as The Clash's Joe Strummer sings on "London's Burning": "Everybody's sittin' round watchin' television" (Strummer/Jones).

There was the print press, of course, which we could access. In fact, when I was a teenager, apart from the radio, that was the only other way I could find out about music for two main reasons: I didn't have the money to buy many albums, and I couldn't get into the venue to see bands because I was too young. In grey old England, most places that had live music were pubs or clubs, so no one under eighteen was allowed inside.

That was the main reason I was so happy when the local newsagents in my town gave me a job as a teen. First, I delivered newspapers on my bicycle to people's houses on cold drizzly mornings. I soon graduated to "marking up," preparing the newspapers for other teens to deliver. It fulfilled the twin areas of my desire, as it gave me enough money each week to buy a new album from my extensive "must hear" list, which was constantly fueled by reading about bands in the print press at the newsagent's store. Three weekly music magazines—*Melody Maker*, *New Musical Express*, and *Sounds*—covered all the new music. Last but not least, we had the John Peel show on BBC Radio 1 every night from 10 p.m. to midnight. It cannot be overstated just how influential Peel was for a whole generation of ne'er-do-wells and misfits finding out about the really important stuff. The real music.

The Cure at the Rainbow Theatre in London on May 11, 1979
Supplied by JC Moglia

Sure, we could tune in and listen to the Top 20 stuff on the regular radio and once a week check the television with *Top of the Pops* on BBC One, which occasionally by some strange quirk of programming might have someone real on like Bowie or Bolan. No, it was the John Peel show that informed us of the true music of our hearts. He played everything that meant something, and sometimes if you sent him a tape of your band, he would even play that too.

It was unheard of at the time to be able to broadcast your music to the world that way. I recall the first time I heard us as The Cure on the Peel show, it was akin to a religious experience. I'm sure I was crying tears of joy. It meant that much to us as young punks. The nearest I can relate it to in America was someone like Rodney Bingenheimer's show on KROQ in Los Angeles. That was it. By and large, it wasn't until the advent of college radio that we as a young band had an opportunity to be heard in the US.

Touring was the best way to bring the sounds directly to other like-minded youth across the globe. In America, that meant six months driving around to every little college town and playing most of them. It must be said it was a reliable way of existing in the early eighties as colleges provided several of the necessities of touring as a financially challenged band. Colleges had money to pay bands, which was a revelation to us when we were new to touring. We were used to unscrupulous bar and club owners or, even worse, outside promoters who saw a quick buck from naive young musicians willing to play for nothing more than a few beers. That shit still goes on, I'm sure.

Colleges, however, generally had a social fund to provide the students with entertainment that was replenished each year. Thank you, Lord! As we became more well known, we could base our tours around a few well-appointed schools whose students loved us and use the windfall to fund the whole schedule. It's the story of my early twenties crisscrossing the US in a tour bus or a commercial plane to bring our brand of art to a whole different bunch of people directly. Although it took years to build a fan base of believers, it paid dividends and made a solid enough impression that many of those initial followers became lifelong fans, and over forty years later I still hear from them.

It's a lesson that I still remember, never underestimate the personal touch, especially in something as intimate as music where you can make your dreams and beliefs a real part of others' personal psychic geography.

JOE STRUMMER: THE FIREBRAND OF PUNK

Joe Strummer saved my life and made me who I am today. Not literally, you understand, but he and the punk movement showed me how to become a man.

Sir Joseph Strummer (né Mellor), late of Maida Vale, West London and the West Country, saved my life because undoubtedly without The Clash, the band Joe joined from the still-warm ashes of the 101ers, I would not have started on the path that led me here. That led me to music, art, literature, cinema, et al. To true manhood. The real trip.

He saved me from being down-and-out in Horley and the home counties. DOA in suburban desolation. As I look back, I see the signposts. How the times and the music were drawing me into what has become a lifelong journey into the angst and artistic arc of this world's truths.

Because of Joe, I chose a peripatetic life for my younger self. Punk rock educated me. The storm it threw me into was a vortex that I gladly embraced. I had seen The Clash play with Robert in our hometown and witnessed firsthand

"The man himself showing us the way"
Credit: Dina Douglass

the transformative power Strummer wielded over the violent and Neanderthal skins that wanted to dismember the opening act—Alan Vega's band Suicide from New York—for the crime of being from somewhere else. Strummer singlehandedly talked the bald beer monsters down and defused a very tense situation. Utterly awesome. I didn't try to go backstage after the show. I was too much in awe of the whole process back then to want to step into the royal palace.

But first . . . That night I saw The Clash with Robert, everything changed. We and a handful of others would help spearhead a new genre of music that, like punk, had its own style that continues to this day.

We were labeled new wave before anybody thought of the name Goth and, truth be told, we weren't quite punk or any old style of rock. We were evolving into something different. Post-punk.

Personally, I was looking for something with a more spiritual, perhaps even mystical, sense than the straight nihilism of punk. Art, specifically music, had taken hold of me, or perhaps I had a hold of it. It was my way of making sense of this confusing new world. I latched onto music the way a drowning man clutches at anything floating past to save his life. It was that important to me. For us, music wasn't just entertainment or a way to meet girls. Personally, I had to become wholly invested in it and its power to create purpose in my own world. Otherwise, I felt I might perish or, even worse, disappear in suburbia, lost forever in a happy crowd. I needed to believe in its power. In that way, what I saw that night at my first Clash show was more akin to one of Saint Augustine's ecstatic visions than a simple rock show.

Then there were Alan Vega and Martin Rev of Suicide, the opening band. Minimal, stark, and brutal. They had Goth in their dark hearts. They called it punk music. New York punk, to be precise, and we understood it at once.

In England, the punk explosion was a direct response to the austere times brought on by the crippling recession and the totalitarian political climate that Thatcher and her cronies inspired. Yes, we were bored teenagers as The Adverts sang, but we also agreed with the Sex Pistols: there was no future for us. We had to make our own future and, initially, punk was the only attractive alternative.

Growing up in the late sixties and early seventies, we had been taught that only exceptionally gifted people could be artists. This was especially true in the

Alan Vega of Suicide
Credit: Mick Mercer

class-ridden society of postwar England. We always felt the disapproval of our supposed "betters." There was no escaping it. Punk helped turn all that on its head. We finally had a way out. The doors of perception were flung wide open and we rushed headlong out into the new punk dawn. Only then did we realize we had left something behind that we might need.

Art, poetry, light, and darkness—especially darkness. I mean, punk was essential to our understanding of anarchy and nihilism, but once we kicked down the doors and broke the chains of repression, what was in our new Nirvana?

Not much actually. England had just joined the European community in the mid-seventies. However, we were yet to receive the benefits of such an association. Dark times indeed. We needed to believe in something. Art was a dangerous currency again. The paintings of artists like Francis Bacon served to illuminate our worldview. Whatever it was, it wasn't clean, and it wasn't pretty.

One of the things post-punk liberated was the sense of romantic longing that is inherent in teen lives. We were able to jump out of the misogynistic, musical quicksand of the seventies, cross over the bridge of punk, and give a voice to the thousand bedsit poets in love with the melancholy beauty of existence.

You could be a sensitive young man or woman without the chest-thumping machismo or sexism of old. You could be in touch with your unease—something that every teen intuitively understands.

Out of the firestorm of punk arose a different beast more suited to my personality and particular emotions. The ghosts of some distant spiritual alchemists rising once again.

CHAPTER TWO

THE POETRY OF PAIN

GOTH IN LITERATURE

While Goth as a style and a culture undoubtedly arose in the post-punk musical underground, one can also trace the prehistory of Goth through literary and artistic precursors.

While Goth as a musical genre has only been around for half a century, there are ample examples in other areas of arts and literature whose creators ruminate on the darker aspects of the human psyche.

Gothic literature began in the eighteenth century with Horace Walpole's novel *The Castle of Otranto*, which was first published in 1764. The second edition of the book contained the subtitle *A Gothic Story*. The novel is set in a ruined and haunted castle and was inspired by a nightmare that Walpole had in his Gothic Revival–style home, Strawberry Hill House in southwest London.

According to Dr. Tracy Fahey, Walpole's novels kicked off the Gothic genre, "sparking off a chain of other novels by Ann Radcliffe, Matthew Lewis, William Beckford, later Bram Stoker, and still later, Mary Shelley. These were novels filled with dramatic events, incest, murder, hideous deaths, and terrible secrets that inevitably came to light."

An Irish author and academic, Fahey holds a PhD in the Gothic in visual arts, and her nonfiction writing on the Gothic and folklore has appeared in Irish, English, Italian, Dutch, and Australian edited collections. The British

Fantasy Awards have short-listed her twice for Best Collection: in 2017 for *The Unheimlich Manoeuvre* and in 2022 for *I Spit Myself Out*. Since I first met Dr. Fahey in Ireland on my book tour for *Cured* in July 2017, we have kept in touch and corresponded occasionally in the years since. She is an impeccable source on all things Gothic.

I wondered if these books were a reaction to feelings of deep uncertainty that people were feeling at the time. This was how it was with our music, particularly in the UK during the late seventies. Goth as a musical direction was formed as a revolution. The initial spark came from punk, but the various themes of Goth music echoed those of Gothic works from previous centuries yet updated them for a new time. Did these older texts also emerge during times of political, social, and economic upheaval?

"Gothic as a mode never exists in a vacuum," Fahey explained. "This genre evolved in the wake of the Industrial Revolution, which saw seismic changes in new technologies, and a move from rural to urban living, and it comes of age in a period of revolutions—the American War of Independence which shook the British Empire to its foundation, and the bloody Reign of Terror in France, a tinder-spark for European revolution. Historically, formulations and re-formulations of the Gothic are associated with crisis and periods of uncertainty in history."

That makes a lot of sense to me. Conflict, which is so often the catalyst for personal change, can have larger cultural ramifications if enough people are committed to do something about it. Fahey believes that's what united these two very different forms of artistic expression—music and novels. "What stays the same is the use of the Gothic to respond artistically to periods of conflict and unrest. As art historian Gilda Williams has commented, 'The Gothic remains, in sum, as an enduring term particularly serviceable in times of crisis—today as it did in the late 18th century, as an escape valve for the political, artistic and technological crises underway.'"

Goth music is, first and foremost, evocative, but it's not just the somber music and brooding lyrics that make Goth so distinctive. It has a tradition of theatricality that comes directly from these novels and the way they've been repurposed by scores of artists working in various media over the years.

"Gothic literature represents the dark side of Romanticism," Fahey told me.

It is intensely theatrical, festooned with castles, dungeons, monsters, vampires, ghosts. It features staggering co-incidences and horrid ends. The turning point toward the sensational and the dramatic really started with Matthew Lewis' *The Monk* in 1796; a heady mix of eroticism, corruption, murder and religious transgression. The novel was publicly condemned as a scandal and privately and avidly consumed. Reading these theatrical, extraordinary novels was an illicit and subversive experience. Similarly, the subcultural phenomenon of the Gothic saw it gather force underground, in bars and clubs, before being recognized officially on the music scene.

Right! First it was under the radar in places like The Palace in Camden and The Batcave in Soho before becoming more mainstream. It was almost a sacred experience to be part of those scenes. It was baroque and heavily ritualized, a bit like going to church only a lot more fun. However, from the outside looking in, I suppose we looked outrageous to those narrow-minded souls who didn't understand why we were putting on makeup or wearing such peculiar clothes.

"All kinds of creatures of the night were drawn to The Batcave."
Credit: Mick Mercer

"Goth has a quixotic Grand Guignol quality," Fahey said,

which mingles diverse influences from German Expressionism to classic horror movies, is one we can trace back to the origins of Gothic literature. *Bela Lugosi's Dead*, released by Bauhaus in 1979, described by Gothic scholar Nick Groom as the first Gothic single, borrows freely from Hammer Horror and vampiric lore. The love-child of punk and rock, Gothic music became its own animal; anti-consumerist, nihilist, looking to the rich heritage of the Gothic visual and literary tradition to express itself. Bands like The Damned and Siouxsie and the Banshees introduced a distinctive funereal aesthetic of dark clothes and elaborate black and white make-up, a form that would later be adopted by Neil Gaiman in his re-imagination of the character of Death in the *Sandman* graphic novels. The Birthday Party's 1982 *Release the Bats* unleashed a flood of classic Gothic tropes from sex vampires to horror bats.

Literature inspired music and music inspired literature in an endless recursive loop, like a video of Wednesday Addams dancing into infinity. But some images and texts are so powerful, they are repeated and repurposed over and over again. Is culture a kind of Dr. Frankenstein piecing together bits and pieces that have been cast off from previous generations?

Dr. Fahey thinks so.

Mary Shelley's 1818 *Frankenstein; or, The Modern Prometheus*, is a Gothic novel that examines the idea of monstrosity and otherness in a way that questions the dark side of human nature and reflects the unease at contemporary scientific developments. In *Skin Shows: Gothic Horror and the Technology of Monsters*, Jack Halberstam says that Gothic novels use "the body of the monster to produce race, class, gender, and sexuality within narratives about the relation between subjectivities and certain bodies." Frankenstein is a story of monstrosity and otherness explored through the patchwork of dead flesh that constitutes the unnamed monster's body.

It's not just the story of Victor Frankenstein, the creator of this monstrous creature, that fascinated me, but the creator of the creator: the author Mary Shelley. It can even be argued that Mary Shelley wrote the first real science fiction story. In fact author Brian W. Aldiss said just that in his work, *The Detached Retina: Science Fiction and Fantasy*, in which he states that the central character, Victor Frankenstein, "makes a deliberate decision" and "turns to modern experiments in the laboratory" to achieve fantastic results.

Incidentally, my first introduction to science fiction was Aldiss's *Barefoot in the Head*, a book published in 1969, which I read when I was ten after finding it at the local library. The novel proposed the idea of people sitting alone in their rooms staring at screens to interact with other humans in a most prescient way. Although it is a psychedelic Gothic novel, it has more philosophical thought amongst the obvious science fiction traits.

Frankenstein's monster is partially a criticism of society: "I am malicious because I am miserable," Shelley writes. The monster is anti-establishment and anti-religious, both of which are very punk and Goth ideas. Shelley herself was an unusual woman for the more straitlaced Victorian times. She was reform-minded and liberal for the era. Although not as radical as her husband, the poet and philosopher Percy Bysshe Shelley, she was a feminist. Beyond her literary works, I see her as an influence for change, albeit gradually, that's taken hold in society.

Shelley wasn't recognized as a distinct literary force until fairly recently. The first scholarly biography of her—Emily Sunstein's *Mary Shelley: Romance and Reality*—was published only in 1989. Despite the enormous popularity of her creation and its influence on pop culture up until then, her gifts were still seen partially as an adjunct to the work of her more famous husband. It seems that a great deal of attitudes changed in the eighties, some that had taken more than a hundred years.

Mary Shelley, Bram Stoker, and Edgar Allan Poe all set their works in ruined castles and haunted graveyards with supernatural figures like vampires, ghosts, and witches to create an atmosphere of terror and suspense. Poe's work, however, with his darkly macabre tales and poems such as "The Raven," which was possibly his most well-known work during his lifetime, always struck me as being rather explicit. It has some of the hallmarks of what we might think of as Gothic, with references to late-night hours reading the "forgotten lore," that is, occult works.

On a dark night in December, the narrator of the poem is visited by a raven tapping on his window. He lets him in and asks him his name as the bird is perched in front of him. The raven replies, "Nevermore," which is all he ever says.

It seems that other poets and writers did not care too much for Poe. W. B. Yeats called "The Raven" "insincere and vulgar . . . its execution a rhythmical trick." And Ralph Waldo Emerson declared, "I see nothing in it." It reminds me of a more theatrical version of Goth, a little like the Haunted Mansion at Disneyland, in that it looks like Goth but doesn't feel like the version to which I respond. There are the ghostly and occult connotations in "The Raven," but I think on the whole they are for window dressing. I am generally drawn to the more serious endeavors.

I eventually became enamored with writers like Charles Baudelaire and H. P. Lovecraft, for their work that was emblematic of the darker side of literature. In Baudelaire's masterpiece, *The Flowers of Evil*, Goth is outlined as a sort of shadow genre:

> It is Boredom!—an eye brimming with an involuntary tear,
> He dreams of the gallows while smoking his water-pipe.
> You know him, reader, this delicate monster,
> —Hypocrite reader,—my twin,—my brother!

There is also the romantic Gothic strand to consider, which is best illustrated by unrequited love and longing in *Wuthering Heights* by Emily Brontë, a masterpiece of Romantic Gothic literature. Although, I view it as a brutal love story with revenge thrown in for extra sparks. I also agree with Derek Traversi in the *Dublin Review*, who sees it as "a thirst for religious experience which is not Christian." In the modern era, Kate Bush made her own version, and although not strictly Goth, there is undeniably a sinister and malevolently spooky streak running through the work.

For Fahey, Brontë's *Wuthering Heights* is the quintessential work of Gothic literature that speaks directly to the mood of Gothic music.

> It's difficult to pick just one (and there are definitely strong cases to be made for Bram Stoker's *Dracula* or Joseph Sheridan Le Fanu's *Carmilla*), but one that continues to resonate for its central theme of a wild, doomed love is Emily

Highgate Cemetery, London
Credit: Tracy Fahey

Bronte's *Wuthering Heights*. Yes, there's the Kate Bush single of the same name—an eerie howl of a song penned when she was only eighteen. But echoes of Emily Bronte's novel, and the all-consuming, wild love between ill-fated characters Cathy and Heathcliff, haunts so many lovelorn, anguished songs like The Cure's *A Forest*, Joy Division's *Love Will Tear Us Apart*, The Smiths' *I Know It's Over*—and all the many, many Goth anthems that sing of obsessive, destructive, forbidden love.

I can think of one band that wrote a few. Many of The Cure's lyrics explore those themes of otherness and discomfort. A feeling of unease with oneself or the world. There is, of course, the idea of escaping from this world either through love or other psychic experiences. But don't just take my word for it.

"Death," Fahey said, "is a notion consistently re-examined in Gothic music from the 1970's onwards. The Cure draw a direct comparison between love and death in *The Funeral Party*. In both *Frankenstein* and later Gothic music we find the same defining aesthetic, as Gilda Williams puts it: 'The Gothic vision presents a dark picture of haunted, insalubrious and unresolved circumstances, situations that remain thoroughly at odds with optimistic or forward-looking cultural frameworks.'"

This brings me to my long-held belief about modern pop songs. My rule of thumb, based on what I've observed over my long career, is that they are either about death or love. The difference with Goth music?

They're usually about death *and* love in the same song.

T. S. ELIOT: MODERNIST GOTH

THE ROOTS OF MODERN GOTH CAN ALSO BE SEEN IN THE LITERATURE of the early twentieth century in writers like T. S. Eliot and Franz Kafka.

"In my beginning is my end." In this first line from "East Coker," in the second quartet by T. S. Eliot, the whole idea of Goth is spelled out. If ever there was a more Goth line in literature for me, I don't know it.

In the poem there is much about how we have put aside looking at the universe in an environmental way and have disregarded the divine, which brings chaos and disorder. It's a naturalistic way of looking at the world that I believe is at the heart of the true Gothic sense. Utopian but in a dark way.

The poem paints leaders as only interested in material things and not aware of the reality of the world, which is supernatural in nature. Written in 1940, "East Coker" comes from his *Four Quartets* and was published at a time of deep world turmoil on the eve of World War II, something we can certainly relate to today. It underscores the interconnected relationship of all people and presents an alternative way of understanding the universe. We are all here together, but there is an end to this and we should acknowledge that. The journey that we are on is to understand that in relation to the here and now.

However, the poem gets this theme across with bleak images of empty streets and underground shelters. T. S. Eliot was Catholic, and the poem encompasses his beliefs, although it feels more mystical and philosophical to me. It is spiritual in nature.

The poet suggests that in order to comprehend the essential meaning of life "You must go by a way which is the way of ignorance." This acknowledges that the only way to understand is to unlearn your "knowledge" and become a seeker. There's Gothic truth at its heart and mystical understanding in its nature.

There are many poets and writers that illustrate Gothic emotion, but I chose T. S. Eliot as he has connections for me—both with The Cure and my own life. Like most people, I didn't learn about Eliot's racism and political propaganda until later in life. We had the Catholic connection, of course, but there was also the search for truth and authenticity underpinning Eliot's works. Eliot was an admirer of William Blake, whose "peculiar honesty" was "peculiarly terrifying" to Eliot, which I feel underpins many of the emotions behind *Seventeen Seconds*, *Faith*, and *Pornography*.

Dr. Oliver Tearle, a literary critic and lecturer in English at Loughborough University, sums up a section of "East Coker" that, for me, illustrates how The Cure's lyrical approach evolved:

> The dark night of the soul, which is again depicted by way of modern experience—specifically, a theatre when the lights go out, the pause between stations on the London Underground when people run out of things to say to each other and silence descends, and the experience of the mind under ether or anesthetic, when we are conscious, but only "of nothing." This is the kind of darkness—what has been called "the way of negation"—that Eliot believes we should embrace, as a way of reaching God. To possess what we do not possess, we must first learn what it means to experience "dispossession"; to learn what we do not know, we must first learn what it is we are ignorant of.

It is precisely this embrace of nothingness that I believe is at the heart of the three Gothic albums by The Cure. This theme is explored for sure in later works, but in these three albums it feels like the central motif of our art, our organizing principle. This is where it came from, this is who we were back then. This speaks to the ambiguity we felt about being labeled a Goth band. The secret to The Cure's enduring popularity and relevance is a product of both artistic evolution and continuity of themes. Standing still while moving ever forward.

Kafka's surreal stories fused realism and the fantastic in ways that echoed the logic of dreams. His works have been interpreted as dealing with existential anxiety, alienation, and guilt—all themes later explored in Goth music. Kafka, though reclusive and mostly unpublished during his life, exerts a wide-ranging influence over other twentieth-century writers including Jorge Luis Borges, Jean-Paul Sartre, and Albert Camus. The latter two directly inspired the interior explorations of Goth bands like Joy Division and The Cure.

For Jim Morrison and Patti Smith, who is sometimes referred to as the "godmother of punk," the French poet Arthur Rimbaud was an early touchstone. Rimbaud's work drew on dreams and drug-induced states in order to reach a deeper emotional nerve center within. This approach inspired Patti Smith's free-form rock and roll. This dream logic also plays into the Goth aesthetic, drawing up images from the depths of the subconscious, images that are often of a dark and surreal nature.

CAMUS & SARTRE: THE BROTHERS ABSURD

"I do hope you're not one of those angry young men." John Le Mesurier's deadpan line in *The Rebel*, a satirical comedy featuring the late British comic Tony Hancock, is meant as a sardonic jibe, but the whole film is a dig at intellectual pretense. However, I do think that in the late sixties and early seventies, there was more than an unspoken admiration of the French existentialist writers Albert Camus and John-Paul Sartre in the changing landscape of modern thought, despite *The Rebel*'s mocking tone.

It was felt especially among creative artists in the changing tide of English art after World War II. The English never want to give too much credit to their close neighbors across the channel—that's another book right there—but the bohemian Beats and the psychedelic sixties moved the world's young people closer together in terms of ideas and ideals. Remember, teenagers only became a "thing" after the Second World War. Now they had real power. I saw *The Rebel* when I was a teenager and it made me curious enough to search out these French thinkers.

I had seen the books of Sartre and Camus on my French girlfriend's mother's bookshelves, and after reading Camus's *The Stranger*, I searched for them in the local library. Meanwhile, Robert and Michael had found their books too: Robert while studying French literature at college, and Michael has always been an avid reader. In fact, even now, his house is full of books.

The three imaginary boys always venerated the written word. I can trace that back to our high school days with our beloved English teacher Mr. Ansell, who showed us that with words the world was reachable and understandable. We studied Shakespeare and the poets of the sixties with him, and he showed us that the pen was indeed mightier than the sword and that you could change the world with words.

Camus's *The Rebel* is a revolutionary essay, something we yearned for in our suburban desert. For Camus, the urge to revolt was one of the "essential dimensions" of human nature, a struggle of Promethean dimensions against the conditions of existence and established orders throughout history. This was something we instinctively knew, helped along by Mr. Ansell and our French teacher Dr. Weaver.

Camus also demonstrated how well-intentioned revolution inevitably leads to tyranny as the old order is destroyed. Camus's essay, it seems, is as relevant for our times as it was then. We live in a world ripe for revolution with a surplus of tyrants and wannabe tyrants.

As a teen, I felt as though I was looking for meaning in a meaningless world. Being brought up Catholic, I chafed against religious reasoning—the promise of heaven, the threat of hell—but needed something that had at least a sense of morality. Ultimately, I found it not in the Bible but in Camus's belief as laid out in *The Myth of Sisyphus* that the absurd results from the "confrontation between human need and the unreasonable silence of the world."

As young men unsure of where or what we were supposed to be in the new order of the postwar world, we gravitated toward the existentialists to find or deny meaning. To be honest, we weren't quite sure of most things yet. We had only recently become cognizant of the structure society had imposed upon us in our teens. We were still trying out our developing intellectual muscles, which was exciting and a little confusing, as I'm sure it is for many teenagers.

It was hard to see the reason for belief in much around us because most situations seemed devised by the powers that be to keep us firmly in our place. To escape a life of moving from school to a dead-end job, it seemed evident that the status quo must be destroyed first.

Sartre's *Nausea* is somewhere between a novel and philosophical tract. Set in the town of "Bouville" (which sounds like "Mud-town" in French), Sartre's masterpiece of absurdist literature opened my mind to the idea that there was no intrinsic path to follow in life. Something might be wrong or right, but there are no rules. Nevertheless, you had to do something. You had to make a choice.

The only reality is what we perceive here and now, and we don't have the power to determine the outcome. We are only in charge of our own activities, and to that end, we have to take action to make life authentic.

That's how punk poked its spiky head up over the guardrails and gave us wings. Some of us were trying to use the thought process and examples we found in books by Camus and Sartre to understand what we could do to use the philosophy contained within their works.

As The Cure, our first-ever record was based somewhat on Camus's *The Stranger*. Robert took inspiration from the book for both the words and guitar motif for our single "Killing an Arab," backed with "10:15 Saturday Night."

I found the protagonist Meursault intriguing, a cipher for our situation growing up in postwar England. We had been expected to behave in a certain way and react to things the way our elders and "betters" had told us. We didn't think we should conform. Of course, the inevitable clash came during our teen years.

Robert with The Cure in Bourges, France, 1982
Credit: Richard Bellia

These new thoughts and ways of seeing the world freed me from the straitjacket of the conventional life I had been leading. They helped lift that veil from my eyes.

Further assistance came to me in my teens in the form of my older brother John who, on a trip through Europe, had been to Denmark and had obtained a copy of *The Little Red Schoolbook*, which had been recently published by a pair of Danish schoolteachers. This book was an instruction manual on how to question the norms of society. It took a critical view of Victorian morality and the rules that we had been bought up with. More importantly, it tasked us to question this and find our own ways.

The Little Red Schoolbook was hazardous to the powers that be because it encouraged us to think for ourselves. Every aspect of life was discussed and it had sex in it, which was pretty much all that was required to ban it in hypocritically puritanical places like England. Thanks to my brother John, I had a copy! Of course, its real objective was a personal revolution, which is why it was banned. It was dangerous.

It was also very successful and was translated into many languages. I found it opened up my already yearning mind to other modes of thought and different ways of being. It also sowed some of those dangerous seeds. I realized the best way to get things going that you felt were important was to start doing it yourself and not let fear control you. It taught me autonomy.

Then punk came along. It set my world on fire. Add to it the philosophy of existentialism and absurdism from Camus and Sartre and that was all the inspiration I needed to get out there and *do* something. Exactly *what* mattered less than actually going through with it. The die was set, and there was no going back. I felt as long as our actions were authentic, we were going in the right direction.

Mark E. Smith of The Fall said, "Eat yourself fitter." With the brothers absurd, I found I could read myself better.

SYLVIA PLATH: THROUGH A *BELL JAR* DARKLY

I consider Sylvia Plath to be the patron saint of postmodern feminist Goths. I made this dramatic discovery in my teens.

It's strange that an English teenage boy would find the symbols that she laid before us so clearly in her words and that they would resonate so perfectly in his own existence. Her most famous collection of poems, *Ariel*, published posthumously, was my introduction, and I soon hungrily sought out more.

Sylvia Plath was my first poetic love and remains so. She spoke to me, as an angst-filled teen growing up on the periphery of the English capital, and to my longing for a new and unique experience of life. One not sullied by the beige normality that passed for existence in the English postwar years.

She was to become the beautiful curator of my dreams of escape. The first time I read her poems it was all over for me. I was smitten with her art. The precise scalpel of her thoughts ignited a fire that's never gone out, dimmed perhaps sometimes, but never gone. I felt the exquisite shock of her writing combined with this unnamed longing in my very bones.

Admittedly, it was a strange connection: the America of her youth was not what I experienced growing up in seventies Britain. I discovered that she had been to the "perfidious Albion," as some would have it, at least twice, including at her untimely end, when at the peak of her powers she wrote the poems that became *Ariel*. The twin longing to escape society's straitjacket of crushing normality and personal pain joined us at our souls—at least in my mind. I also felt that I should make amends for what I perceived as my homeland's grave mistakes with her. As far as I was concerned, she was that perfect teenage dream of unrequited love and angst combined.

Her poetry explored the themes of unequal power and oppression that we too felt growing up in seventies England, and although a great deal of that was gender-based in Plath's poetry, it still resonated with me. It was this oppressive atmosphere that produced punk.

I felt a connection with her startling imagery of men as vampiric fascists in "Daddy," arguably her most famous poem. Her alienation helped me feel aligned as a sort of soul mate. In her pain she had given me permission to look on the other side of society's equation and be vulnerable too.

Plath grew up in suburban Boston, Massachusetts, one of the oldest cities in America, founded by Puritan settlers from England. Being Puritans, they of course didn't waste anything, not even words, so their settlement became

Boston, after the small town in England they arrived from. An academic and cultural center of excellence, to this day.

Plath was born to a second-generation American mother of Austrian descent, Aurelia Schober Plath, and a German father, Otto Plath, a professor of biology at Boston University. Otto Plath was to pass away shortly after Sylvia's eighth birthday. For Sylvia, raised as Unitarian, the death of her father caused a rent in the fabric of her faith from which she did not recover.

As a young woman she went to Smith College, a liberal arts college in Northampton, Massachusetts. In a curious confluence of lives, I was to perform at Smith in October 1985 with The Cure, an occurrence of vital import that was not lost on me. I spent much of my day there, before and after the concert, in a melancholy meditation, soaking up the atmosphere of what I imagined to be Plath's ghost circulating around the corridors and rooms of the venerable school.

For me it all coalesced in the words "confessional poetry." This was the term that had been given to Plath's work and to that of her peers like Anne Sexton, Robert Lowell, and Allen Ginsberg. The personal exploration of feelings and experiences of trauma, despair, and angst was far closer to what I wanted to express than what was delivered in the old rock model.

The tired templates fell away as I realized I had far more in common with her poems than the misogynistic lyrics of most seventies rock music. Certainly, I still felt sympathy for those that came before like the Beats and their route of psychedelic discovery, but the harsher realities of growing up in the socially challenging changes of England were more closely served by the confessional approach of poets like Plath. Like the existentialists of the fifties and sixties before, they encouraged the deep introspective, personal analysis of what it means to be here in this world as a feeling, vulnerable soul and gave me clues of how to deal with the absurd vagaries of life. Those slings and arrows of outrageous fortune we all meet, but their sting is especially sharp during the raging uncertainty and challenges of adolescence and early adulthood.

As our band The Cure became a reality and we could analyze and distill our true feelings in our songs, it became obvious we were not going to write "Moon in June"–type material, although occasionally hope surfaced as well as doom.

Messages from the dark night of the soul became our stock in trade fueled by the directions given to us by Plath and Co.

I had grown up a Roman Catholic in a decidedly un-Catholic country. My mother had converted from the standard Church of England, and so I was marked as an outsider from birth. English, but not C of E. Not "one of us." This established the blueprint for feeling adrift and unmoored from the fabric of local life. Hell, there wasn't even a Catholic school in my hometown. I had to get on a bus and travel to the next town to find such a place.

No surprise then that I and my friends that formed The Cure in our teens identified with all these misfits and postmodernists. We only had our experiences to refer to and our own nascent values. In our rebellion we rejected that which we had been taught growing up in the strange, guilt-ridden, and darkly theatrical religion of our youth. Punk was the starting point and ever outward was our direction. We hungrily scouted about in the library and local book and record stores for further clues.

I found further connections in the posthumous Plath poetry collection, *Crossing the Water*, curated by her husband, Ted Hughes. The bleakness of the words still has a spark of light inside. They mirrored the sadness of the lyrics I was to write with a searching for some hopeful end.

It didn't matter to me that the focus was clearly not aimed at making men comfortable in their own skins. It was a cry from her soul to be liberated at a time and place that was more accustomed to madmen than sexual equality. A time that didn't acknowledge her femininity except in a societal straitjacket designed to keep the status quo of the patriarchal veil of womanhood intact and unmoved by changing postwar realities.

What I related to mostly was a yearning for a different experience from the one I had come to be aware of in my childhood. The confessional nature of our longings, sexual or otherwise, and the exploration of our personal needs and desires that we were heavily instructed to feel shame about from our Catholic life. Remember, in Catholicism confession is a sacrament.

In her East Coast, middle-class upbringing, Plath uncannily mirrored that stifling conformity of our English class-ridden society, which I felt all but suffocated by until we formed The Cure. I realized that there was true liberation to be had, and Plath wrote several of the reference books for that. I soaked up everything I could find of her writing. However, even more than the poetry that beguiled and bruised me, I found her novel *The Bell Jar* a startling expressive source of inspiration.

The novel is a thinly veiled autobiography of Plath's life. In it, the protagonist Esther Greenwood has a summer internship at the fictional *Ladies' Day* magazine in New York. She is not impressed by the big-city life, her work, and the fashion world that seems to engage and enthrall her peers at the magazine. She in fact becomes depressed and beset by anxiety as the novel proceeds. Gradually through several episodes and misadventures, including a sexual assault, we start to realize that Esther has some serious mental health problems. These problems cause her to leave New York and her internship prematurely, and she returns home to Massachusetts.

Her mother suggests she should see a psychiatrist for her worsening condition as she is not sleeping or doing well health-wise by this point. She undergoes ECT (electroconvulsive therapy), which does not improve matters initially, but eventually, after a few suicide attempts, she comes to a sort of impasse and the novel ends with her talking to her doctors to decide if she can leave the hospital as her depression has lifted somewhat. Her psychiatrist's inconclusive diagnosis is that her illness was "a bad dream." One she cannot escape, it seems.

At the time, I was also reading the writing of R. D. Laing, the Scottish analyst, who helped me traverse some of the themes in Plath's book. On one hand it's an almost naive first novel, but it's threaded through with the startlingly observational and descriptive skill of her more intense poetry. This struck me as a female *Catcher in the Rye*, another work I venerate. In its portrayal of her own zeitgeist, I felt a sympathetic understanding of my own journey. As I connected closer and deeper into her world and work over time, I had discovered her only novel, the autobiographical apprentice work *The Bell Jar*, of which she said, "I had to write to free myself from the past." Bingo! And, ergo, the very reason for my veneration of words and their power.

The Bell Jar was published in January 1963, originally under the pseudonym Victoria Lucas, which apparently was to spare her mother's feelings and various other people characterized in the book. At the time, Sylvia Plath was living in London, recently separated from her husband, Ted Hughes. Alone with her two children, she had just written the poems of *Ariel* in quick dark nights. The end was racing up from the depths of despair. Life was to mirror art. Less than a month after publication of *The Bell Jar* she committed suicide at her flat at 23 Fitzroy Road in London.

Truth, it is said, is stranger than fiction. Plath considered it a good omen, when she moved into the flat some months earlier, that the writer W. B. Yeats previously inhabited the house but of course that didn't save her. It was also coincidentally on the same street that many years later one of the members of The Cure briefly resided, but they lived to tell the tale.

ANNE SEXTON: SUICIDE AND TRANSFORMATIONS

ANNE SEXTON WAS A POET WHOSE WORK EXPLORED HER LONG STRUGgle with depression and suicidal ideation, and her personal relationships with her family. She was born Anne Gray Harvey in Newton, Massachusetts, in 1928 and spent most of her childhood in Boston. She married Alfred Sexton in 1948, and in 1953 the couple had their first child, Linda Gray Sexton. Their second child, Joyce Ladd Sexton, was born two years later, in 1955.

Sexton struggled with bipolar disorder for most of her life. She had her first manic episode in 1954, and after her second episode, the following year, she met Dr. Martin Orme, who became her therapist for the rest of her life. It was Dr. Orme who encouraged her to write poetry. Despite being terrified of signing up, Sexton attended a poetry workshop led by John Holmes. She found success and many of her early poems were published in the *New Yorker* and *Harper's*, among others. Sexton continued her study of poetry with Robert Lowell, who also suffered from bipolar disorder, and her fellow students included Sylvia Plath.

Her first volume of poetry, *To Bedlam and Part Way Back*, was published in 1960. While in John Holmes's workshop, Sexton met the poet Maxine Kumin and they became close friends for the rest of her life, critiquing one another's work and writing four children's books together. After twelve years of writing poetry, Sexton won a Pulitzer Prize, became a member of the Royal Society of Literature, and was the first female member of Harvard's Phi Beta Kappa society.

By the late sixties Sexton's manic episodes had begun to affect her work but she continued to write, publish, and give readings. On October 4, 1974, Sexton met with Kumin to discuss galleys for her forthcoming book of poems *The Awful Rowing Toward God*. After the meeting, Sexton returned home, put on her mother's old fur coat, poured herself a glass of vodka, locked herself in her garage, and started the car, killing herself via carbon monoxide poisoning. A year before her death, she had stated in an interview that she would never allow the poems to be published before her death.

Sexton's work is seen as the model for the confessional poet in modern literature. She disclosed and examined her own struggles with mental illness throughout her work—often in candid detail. Her poems dealt with topics such as abortion, drug abuse, adultery, and masturbation at a time when none of these were considered suitable for poetry. Much has been made about the connection between her mental illness, drug abuse, and creativity, inspiring musicians such as Morrissey of The Smiths, among countless others who are interested in the internal machinations of the ill.

In fact, this is one of the main differences between earlier rock music and Goth. The lyrical content of rock before Goth is externalized without much in the way of analysis. Emotions are simplified, hence statements like Bad Company's "Feel like making love" (Rodgers/Ralphs) and Queen's "We are the champions" (Mercury). In Goth, lyrics form *out* of emotional vulnerability as opposed to bravado and certainty. The process is one of internal analysis and confession, revealing to the world frailty and humanity. It's all-inclusive, therefore attractive to the maligned and sidelined of the world. The connection is the reason.

CHAPTER THREE

PROTOTYPES

THE DOORS OF PERCEPTION

In the realm of darker music, the term "Goth" was first used by rock critic John Stickney to define a Doors gig when he described the cavernous venue as the perfect location for the "gothic rock" of the band. Later, the darker-edged psychedelia of The Doors would influence scores of bands, including Echo and the Bunnymen, Siouxsie and the Banshees, The Sound, and Joy Division.

An American psychedelic rock band, The Doors consisted of vocalist Jim Morrison, keyboardist Ray Manzarek, guitarist Robby Krieger, and drummer John Densmore. The band released six albums in four years between 1967 and 1971. The Doors began with a chance encounter between Manzarek and Morrison on Venice Beach in July 1965. The two recognized one another from UCLA, and Morrison told Manzarek that he had been writing songs. Morrison sang Manzarek the opening lines to "Moonlight Drive," and the evocative lyrics inspired Manzarek to come up with music for the "spooky"-sounding words.

I've lived in Los Angeles for over a quarter of a century now, mostly by the ocean. After a while you begin to realize the bohemian ghost of The Doors is still with us down by the beach. It's called Silicon Beach now by Realtors and the like because of all the tech companies that have moved in, but it doesn't

Siouxsie Sioux and John McKay of Siouxsie and the Banshees
Credit: Mick Mercer

need the new moniker. It's always been a vital place and the essence hasn't changed much since the seventies. The boardwalk is there still, the faint smell of patchouli oil wafting among the Venice Beach T-shirt vendors and sidewalk entertainers, waiting for the return of the Lizard King.

On the westward plaza by the beach, the police station is enveloped by a wall. A special wall of poetry. Morrison's lines decorate this wall. He might be dead now, but his message isn't going anywhere.

This is where Jim Morrison and Ray Manzarek started playing together in May of 1965 as Rick and the Ravens in a little bar just off the beach called Turkey Joint West on the corner of Second and Santa Monica Boulevard.

John Densmore, from another local band called The Psychedelic Rangers, joined up with Ray and Jim. John recommended they take on his former bandmate Robby Krieger also from The Psychedelic Rangers. As The Doors they recorded their first demo in September, and within a year, on August 18, 1966, they were signed to Elektra Records.

The Turkey Joint West, the venue The Doors first played in, is still there. Now it's called Ye Olde King's Head, a British pub, and on most nights it's full of expats. The English like Santa Monica. I suppose it reminds them of Brighton with better weather.

Almost thirty years later to the day that The Doors was signed to Elektra, The Cure played an impromptu set at Ye Olde King's Head. Coincidentally, The Cure was also signed to Elektra. I'm not sure what inferences can be drawn from those weird facts, except that Elektra always had the most interesting artists—that was kind of their thing—and that the British still love going to pubs and listening to music.

Jim and The Doors continued their upward trajectory after signing with Elektra. The Doors recorded its self-titled debut album in August 1966 at Sunset Sound studio. This album included "The End," a twelve-minute song that many view as the start of Gothic rock as a genre. With its echoing drums and Indian tuning, it feels malevolent and spooky—especially when you consider the way the lyrics include an Oedipal freak-out right out of one of Dr. Freud's psychology tracts.

It can also be seen as a template of sorts for Bauhaus's epic "Bela Lugosi's Dead." Both songs are exceptionally long and death-haunted. Bauhaus brought it into the Goth era with dub effects and the spooky baritone intonation of singer Peter Murphy. Also, both songs were recorded live with no overdubs.

A year after its debut, The Doors' second album, *Strange Days*, was released but failed to garner the same critical reception as its predecessor despite the successful singles "People Are Strange" and "Love Me Two Times." "People Are Strange" was always my favorite song by The Doors. It's a tale of alienation and being an outsider—central tenets for the punk and Goth movements. A manifesto of vulnerability.

Jim Morrison's late career was marked by notoriety brought on by his out-of-control drinking. The Doors' last show with Morrison was December 12, 1970, during which he had a meltdown and the group agreed it was time for him to retire from performing. The Doors recorded its final album with Morrison, *L.A. Woman*, in early 1971. The title track as well as "Love Her Madly" and "Riders on the Storm" still continue to receive airplay on rock radio to this day.

Following the recording of *L.A. Woman*, Morrison moved to Paris in March 1971 to live with his girlfriend Pamela Courson. Three months later, on July 3, he was found dead in his bathtub in Le Marais by Courson. He was just twenty-seven years old. There is, it has been noted, a statistical propensity for musicians to die at the age of twenty-seven for a host of reasons, with alcohol and drugs usually being a factor. A sort of ad hoc alcoholic association— Club 27.

I admit I didn't really give it much credence until I found myself walking along that same path of destruction. The Cure's Pornography Tour ended in the summer of 1982. Everything was falling apart. Simon and Robert had a big bust-up in Strasbourg at the end of the tour and effectively split up the band for a while. I decamped to Paris, and by way of licking my wounds I was producing an album by the French post-punk band The Bonaparte's. I lived with one of the band members while recording the album with them.

After the Sturm und Drang of the tour, it was an inspired and peaceful recording session. Although my heart was heavy with the thought that The Cure might be no more, I was buoyed by the creative music I was helping to

Simon Gallup in 1982
Credit: Richard Bellia

bring into the world. Every day we went to the studio and gradually I felt my soul lighten. I played some keyboards for them as well as producing the record and felt the infectious joy of this ragtag group of French post-punkers. We got along well, and I experienced the simple beauty of making music just for the pleasure of it. I also stopped drinking so much.

I don't recall how long the whole session was, but it must have been a few weeks and we had one day off in the middle. I remember waking up in the sparsely furnished apartment on our designated day off, looking forward to a day of leisure. The night before I had recorded some vocals for The Bonaparte's. I made the singer stand on the roof of the studio in the misty moonlit Parisian night, and we recorded outside in the elements, open to the night air. I hoped this strange experiment inspired them a little. I felt a freedom to experiment that had been missing during the long slog of the tour. Anyone who's been in a band for a long time will tell you the band gets to develop its own methods for things, and ours had become a little stifling. It felt good to step outside the boundaries.

That morning we all went for a walk to a nearby café and got some coffee and croissants. I felt at home in Paris. The history of existentialists like Sartre and Simone de Beauvoir permeated the café-lined streets around me. Having finished breakfast, we carried on strolling the boulevards, and as we rounded a corner I noticed we were in front of the largest cemetery I had ever seen in my life. My hosts told me this was Père Lachaise: the biggest cemetery in Paris and rumored to be the most visited in the world. Oscar Wilde is buried here along with Marcel Proust and Edith Piaf. The most famous resident of our era, however, is none other than Jim Morrison.

When we walked through the gates, the first thing I saw among the Gothic-looking temples and columned crypts was graffiti plastered on the walls: "Jim—this way," with arrows pointing farther into the interior of the cemetery like a kind of spray-painted guide rope among the maze of mausoleums.

We followed these for a short while, nervously anticipating what might be at the end of the line until we came upon a strange and unsettling sight. Fifteen or twenty mods in parkas and cashmere suits were sitting around what, to all intents and purposes, looked like a sort of homeless hippie encampment in the middle of the cemetery. Lots of handwritten messages and graffiti were scrawled over what appeared to be a rather modest marker, and a chipped and garishly colored bust of Jim presided over this dismal scene, surrounded by half-empty bottles of alcohol and wilted flowers.

Two of the mods started pushing and swearing at each other in Italian, smashing the quietness of the graveyard while drunkenly swigging cheap vin du pays from green plastic bottles. Italian mods in Paris.

Suddenly the tawdry scene in front of me saddened me beyond belief, and whether he knew it or not, Jim Morrison had kept me from my own devastations and helped me surrender my possible membership in Club 27.

Wherever his ghost resides—in California or Paris—forever on the astral plane.

Thank you, Jim.

SUICIDE: SUICIDE TIMES

SUICIDE. YOU MUST BE COMMITTED, IN BOTH SENSES OF THE WORD, TO call your band Suicide. Right there with the name, the band provokes controversy.

Alan Vega of Suicide at The Venue in London in 1983
Credit: Mick Mercer

Add to this their music, an unholy mix of noisy synth and organ drones over a backdrop of primitive rhythm boxes punctuated by Alan Vega's nervy yelps and screams, and you can begin to understand why Suicide both fascinated and repulsed audiences in 1970s New York.

Formed in 1970 by Martin Rev (Martin Reverby) and Alan Vega (Alan Bernowitz), who met after the demise of Rev's avant-garde jazz group, the initial lineup also included Paul Liebegott on guitar. They played their first gig at the Project of Living Artists in Manhattan on June 19, 1970. Alan Vega began his career as a painter in Lower Manhattan's vibrant avant-garde art scene. He was involved in the Art Workers' Coalition, a radical artists' group, and the Project of Living Artists, an artist-run multimedia space. He graduated from painting to light sculptures made of electronic debris and, eventually, after seeing a 1969 performance of Iggy and the Stooges, to electronic music.

Liebegott left at the end of 1971 and Suicide continued as a duo, with Rev focusing on synths, organs, and rhythm boxes and Vega singing. The band was the first to use the term "punk music" on flyers as early as 1970, a phrase Vega appropriated from Lester Bang's "punk music mass," and their look, a sort of artsy street-thug attire, complemented this description. The sound was informed by experimental music, performance art, pop music from the fifties and sixties. The band also drew from lowbrow pop culture: the name Suicide is from the title of an issue of the *Ghost Rider* comic, "Satan Suicide." Suicide was not always well received, even in the open-minded art circles of Manhattan, where several of the group's performances descended into mini riots, which is saying something as the group's early shows were held at the Mercer Arts Center, where they shared bills with groups like the New York Dolls. Suicide then performed at venues like CBGB and Max's Kansas City with emerging punk bands before they were banned. It must be said their shows were often violent and confrontational, which kind of went with the territory back in 1970.

New York City in the seventies was a despairing and dismal place. The middle class could see the writing on the wall—literally, in many cases—as graffiti took over as communication in the mean streets. Many fled from the harsh and violent city to live in the boring but predictable suburbs. The city had suffered in a terrible way from a nationwide recession. With the flight to the suburbs, the city lacked the tax revenue to maintain basic services and it spiraled ever downward. NYC, like London, was a fairly bleak place in dire straits in the late seventies.

It is against this backdrop of chaos and desperate deprivation that Suicide was formed.

Suicide's first release was the track "Rocket U.S.A." on a 1976 Max's Kansas City compilation, which was followed in 1977 by their eponymous debut album on independent label Red Star, which was founded by Marty Thau. The record was produced by Craig Leon, who had previously worked with Lee "Scratch" Perry and Bob Marley and helped the group use dub effects such as reverb and delay to augment Vega's vocal tracks and Rev's sparse organ work. "Frankie Teardrop" was a standout track. It tells the story of a factory worker driven to insanity by poverty—a proto-Goth theme for sure. The record received positive critical assessments in the UK but failed to chart in either the US or the UK due to being an independent release. Despite this, Suicide toured the UK and Europe with Elvis Costello and The Clash in 1978.

The group's follow-up album *Suicide: Alan Vega and Martin Rev* was produced by Ric Ocasek, whom the group met while on tour with The Cars. Vega distanced himself from the production of the music to focus more on the vocals for this album, with the bulk of the tracks being written and composed by Rev and Ocasek. Vega later stated that "nothing big happened" after the release of the album and the group wouldn't release another record until 1988. Vega and Ocasek were strange bedfellows, but it was a strange era too.

I first heard Suicide on John Peel's radio show on the BBC, which prompted me and Robert to go see them on July 8, 1978, at the Crawley Leisure Center, one of the band's first shows outside America when they opened for The Clash during its Out on Parole Tour. We witnessed a unique spectacle, a crucial cultural flash point. Not because of the malevolence of the skinheads that crashed the gig that night and the fight that ensued when one of them got onstage and assaulted Vega. No, it wasn't just the predictable chaos that followed the wild tour that night; rather it was the strands of the past, present, and future of outsider music inhabiting the same molecular space for one special moment.

There was the old guard in Vega and Rev, the new wave represented by The Clash, and us, in the post-punk movement, which was starting to emerge into the big wide world. Sometimes the stars align, and the seeds of the future culture were germinating in the heady mix congregated in the nondescript hall. For a single night, we met at the crossroads of a new alternative culture in a dark, chaotic space south of London.

The Specials were also on the bill that night, and they had their own way too with their vibrant version of ska. Horace Panter recalls that night in his memoir *Ska'd for Life: A Personal Journey with The Specials*. "We went down reasonably well—the hall was only half full, and we played 'Liquidator' in our set. 'Hey Skinhead, you're supposed to like this!' Suicide bombed big time. A skinhead jumped up on stage and socked Alan Vega in the face. He came off-stage madder than usual and hurled a chair into the plate glass mirror in the dressing room, shattering it. His nose was bleeding, and he was on 'the next fuckin' plane home.'"

Fast-forward a decade and by 1988 Suicide's position as progenitors of not only punk but synthpop, industrial, and new wave was well established. The form of the duo, with one member behind the mysterious machinery of synthesizers and one up front singing, became a blueprint for legions of 1980s synthpop groups. Suicide was proto-*everything* and their influence continues to resonate today in bands like Boy Harsher, Spike Hellis, HTRK, et cetera. In a way, we can see the roots of techno, acid house, and industrial in the music of Suicide as well, though what they were doing was more rooted in a primal version of rock and roll transmuted through the frazzled circuits of early electronic instruments. To us, it was very exciting.

Their lyrical content, which deals with the breakdown of American postwar society and the struggles of the working class, had familiar themes for bands in the UK, but the interweaving of sex and violence also influenced the darker bent of Goth and post-punk bands to come. As Vega said to Simon Reynolds in *Pitchfork*, "We were talking about society's suicide, especially American society. New York City was collapsing. The Vietnam War was going on. The name Suicide said it all to us."

In the end, Suicide survived as the antithesis to their name. They were Suicide survivors.

I feel Suicide is summed up best by looking underneath the pose and the posturing with Vega's observant quote from a French TV interview some years back. His raison d'être perhaps?

Alan Vega at The Venue
Credit: Mick Mercer

"Lonely man, in a lonely street, in the middle of lonely nowhere . . . it's a loner thing," said Vega of his work.

L'Homme existential. It's a startling image of the outsider, the misfit, who was and is always attractive to me. An image of pure truth for rock and roll.

We are always on the edge of town.

NICO: NOTHING
MAY 17, 1983, BRIXTON

It was a dreary damp night when I finally saw Nico play. The sort of dismal drizzle that England specializes in, bone-chilling fans of the German chanteuse out in the frigid night, doggedly lined up in front of the Ace in Brixton to come hear their "femme fatale."

I knew her songs because I'd found her and The Velvet Underground in my teens but precious little else about her. She was an enigma, which obviously intrigued me, but it wasn't until years later when I read James Edward Young's *Nico: Songs They Never Play on the Radio* that I understood more about what was going on from 1982 to 1988.

Told from his very personal perspective—he was her musical director throughout those last years—it's the story of her final dance before she shuffled off the mortal coil. By the time I got to see her she had begun her sad, slow descent into terminal drug addiction. However, none of this was really my "knowledge" yet. I mean who ever really knows another, as Baudelaire mused?

Nico was born Christa Päffgen on October 16, 1938, in Cologne, Germany. She was born to the wealthy Päffgen brewing family. A tumultuous childhood saw her moving with her family during World War II into the Spree Forest to escape the bombing of Cologne. Her father was conscripted into the Wehrmacht and later died in mysterious circumstances. Now fatherless, Nico and her mother moved to Berlin after the war in 1946.

Nico became a seamstress selling lingerie in the department store KaDeWe. She was "discovered" as a model by Herbert Tobias when they both worked at the store. Tobias gave her the name Nico, after the filmmaker Nikos Papadakis, with whom he was in love. She moved to Paris, and by changing her hair color her stark features, now framed by a blonde hairdo, got her a minor role in the Federico Fellini film *La Dolce Vita*, playing herself. She then moved to New York and started taking acting classes from Lee Strasberg.

The swinging sixties brought her into contact with Brian Jones of the Rolling Stones in 1965, and she recorded her first single, "I'm Not Saying," which was produced by Jimmy Page. Moving into the art circle led her to work with Andy Warhol and Paul Morrissey on experimental films. Warhol began managing local rock group The Velvet Underground and suggested that they take on Nico as a "chanteuse." Nico sang lead vocals on three tracks on The Velvet Underground's debut album, *The Velvet Underground & Nico*: "All Tomorrow's Parties," "I'll Be Your Mirror," and "Femme Fatale."

The relationship between The Velvet Underground and Nico was strained from the beginning, and after the record's release, Nico began pursuing a solo career. Her debut solo album *Chelsea Girl* in 1967 featured songs by Bob Dylan and Jackson Browne and musical contributions from Lou Reed, John Cale, and Sterling Morrison. The album is chamber-folk in a typical late sixties style with string and flute arrangements. Nico was not given much control over her work on this album and confessed afterward that she hated it.

However, her follow-up album in 1968, *The Marble Index*, was much different, using the harmonium as its sonic center around which swirl dark washes of strings, bells, and psychedelic effects in a disorientating and dark, cultlike atmosphere. John Cale's production and arrangements give the album a medieval-meets-psychedelic mix that eludes comparison. This was the period that influenced Goth and post-punk music many years later. She was so venerated by Siouxsie and the Banshees that the band invited Nico to tour with them in 1978.

Her next album, *Desert Shore*, was also produced by John Cale and expanded on the dark atmospheres of her previous album, but with more pop sensibility. My personal favorite track on the album is "Janitor of Lunacy," which was written as a tribute to her friend Brian Jones, who died in 1969. These two albums are really Nico writ large for me. The essence of her very different and nonstandard musicality and genius.

On this damp, cold London night I was going to see a strange enigma, someone I felt could help illustrate to me just where I had travelled to and come from. Of course, I was intrigued. I brought my friend Gary with me. Gary was from our hometown and worked for The Cure. In an echo of the sad path that surrounded Nico, Gary was to pass away in a lonely small bedroom off Hollywood Boulevard, bathed in the chaotic nihilism of addiction. I still miss him terribly.

We left my flat in North London, taking the subway south under the dark, deep snake that runs through the heart of the capital, the River Thames, the tunnel piercing the clay and gravel under the ancient waterway. It used to be said there are few tube stops in South London because of seventeenth-century plague pits. Apparently, the mass graves where diseased bodies were interred made tunneling hazardous. A Gothic horror story to be sure, but the truth is far more prosaic. South London had plenty of rail connections before the tube started in the mid-nineteenth century, but the commercial prospects in North London were much better for investors where the tube network started to proliferate in the 1860s.

In the early 1980s, Brixton was not the gentrified hipster area it is today. The Brixton riots of April 1981 were still fresh in the capital's psyche. In fact, they were embedded in my memory personally as I had moved out of my parents' house farther south in the suburbs the very weekend the riots sparked a terrible firestorm of anger and destruction that continued furiously for several days. The usual suspects of inner-city pain existed then as now—economic deprivation and overzealous policing—being unfair and discriminatory to the local inhabitants who were mostly of African and Caribbean origin. All you really need to know about it is in The Clash's song "The Guns of Brixton."

Gary and I stepped out of the tube station and started to walk toward the Ace. It was early yet, so we decided to drop into the nearest pub, whose name I now forget. Let's call it The Slaughtered Lamb. Having ordered our drinks, we stood in a corner to chat and imbibe together. The pub was full, and you could surmise from the demeanor and furtive stance of a few of the clientele that we had walked into the local dealer's hangout. This wasn't a big deal to us. We started playing in the same kind of place back at the beginning of The Cure, so it was easy for us to recognize. In short order several figures appeared to try and sell us something. Not a surprise, but that was not on our minds that night. Instead, we drank up and headed out to the street again and arrived in a few minutes at the Ace, our destination for the evening.

Originally an Edwardian cinema called the Palladium, it closed in 1981. Eventually it became The Fridge in 1985, but in the intervening years it was the Brixton Ace. It's where The Clash and The Smiths, among others, played in the early days. In 1983 the club was beginning to look a little woebegone. The seats on the main floor had been removed long ago, like all London venues of the time, a little downtrodden, a bit forgotten.

Only a couple of years before the recession was in full swing, so there wasn't much joy to go around. Not that Nico promoted joy necessarily, although quite a few present seemed lovingly devoted to her. We got ourselves into a good vantage point to see the stage, which was conveniently by the bar, and waited for her to come on.

In a few years she would take a vacation in Ibiza with her son, Ari, exhausted from her endless touring during much of the eighties. She was trying to get clean, bicycling and eating healthy foods on the Balearic Islands in the middle of the Mediterranean. A fall from her bicycle gave her a cerebral hemorrhage and she died. She was not even fifty.

That night at the Ace I recall Nico looking over the top of her harmonium like a decadently hip church organist, playing and singing "Janitor of Lunacy" with her distinctive style, a song that Robert liked to sing during sound check with The Cure. For someone like Nico, for whom English was a second language, the song still has a remarkable and terrifying power. That night was no exception. To Gary and me, it was sublime.

With this one song, and its haunting evocation of "living dream" and "begging scream," Nico had foretold Goth. It touched us both that night, and out of the heart of Brixton we carried a small eternal flame, her sad life and her gift transmitted to us both. For Gary it would end the same way as it would for Nico, and for me she's been a small beacon in a life of lunacy.

ALICE COOPER: SNAKES ALIVE!

Alice Cooper figured in my thirteen-year-old psyche more than any other musical act. I had seen him on the cover of *Melody Maker* and straightaway there were several things that fascinated me about him.

The first, although seemingly obvious but unexplainable to me as a teenager from suburbia, was why did a man have a woman's name? "How was that even possible?" ran the script in my head. Didn't his parents know they'd given their son a woman's name?

Gradually, with a little more research, I realized that this was on purpose, and he had originally been christened with the more straightforward moniker of Vincent Damon Furnier, which I have to say was partially a relief but also a disappointment.

Vincent/Alice started a garage rock group in Phoenix, Arizona, in 1964 called The Earwigs. They eventually ended up being called Alice Cooper after a few other name changes because it sounded innocuous and wholesome in contrast to the music they were playing: a theatrical mix of garage rock and horror aesthetics. Cooper was inspired by films, especially the movies *What Ever Happened to Baby Jane?* and *Barbarella*, and decided that the Alice Cooper look would derive from these movies.

Which brings me to the other aspects of what I found interesting about Alice. The stage show. It looked wild with guillotines and other horror stuff. I associated excitement at that age with the funfair and especially the ghost train. This reminded me of that. For me, the funfair that came to our small town every year was the most thrilling thing to happen in my sheltered life. It was both outrageous and scary. It was a sort of prelude to seeing music shows. Larger-than-life characters worked there and showed me not everyone had to look like my neighbors.

The ghost train ride was the apex of thrills mixed with fear for a few years (apart from the time that kid fell out of the dive-bomber at the fair and mangled his toes in the machinery on the way down). But the thing that really scared the bejesus out of me with Alice was the snake. A snake, my god!

I wasn't quite sure what it had to do with music, but I was pretty much in awe of anyone who could handle a snake like Alice. Me? I was terrified of them. I have a theory: people are afraid of either snakes or spiders; they're either ophidiophobes or arachnophobes. I am not afraid of spiders, but snakes give me the heebie-jeebies. Robert's apparently the other way around. (See The Cure's song "Lullaby.") I wonder what Freud would make of that?

That year when I was thirteen a new teacher came to our school. He was an American man in his early thirties with a beard. Let's call him Mr. Jones. He had stood up at the back of the school hall when he was introduced to us at the morning assembly and in a strange accent told us his name and that we might find him "somewhat dyspeptic," which we later learned meant he could be a little touchy. Well, that was nothing new. Most teachers and adults appeared that way to us.

We gradually got to know this new teacher, and it turned out he quite liked "modern music." Not quite as modern as us, but he tolerated The Beatles, which was something.

We were in the last year of middle school and starting to be treated less like little kids, and we had a shared lingua franca in music. One of the other things that changed was our involvement with school activities, like the end-of-year assembly, which was supposed to be a celebration of sorts and a farewell to the outgoing students headed to high school. When we talked about this with Mr. Jones, he said to us, "Maybe you want to pick some music for the final assembly to play as you leave school?"

Yes, maybe we did. Alice Cooper and his band had been making inroads into our consciousness the whole of that year.

They had originally been signed to Frank Zappa's label Straight, and the band's first album *Pretties for You* was a mishmash of avant-garde and psychedelia. Released in 1969, it didn't do much, and after their second album did worse Alice Cooper had to rethink the band's strategy.

The group increasingly found themselves at odds with psychedelic hippie bands of the day. Their hard-rocking sound and interest in sex, death, and violence feels more in consonance with the forthcoming punk, metal, and Goth movements of a decade later than with the bearded, peace-loving bands of the time. Their big break came with their third album, *Love It to Death*, which was their last release on Straight. The record produced a hit with "I'm Eighteen." The record turned out to be the breakthrough for the group, leading to increased exposure and chart placement.

The stage set for the group's 1971 tour included Gothic torture like gallows and electric chairs. The band dressed in tightly fitting glam outfits with Cooper himself taking on the look of a villain. Overall, they seemed strange and very exciting to us. The dark bent of Cooper's show prefigured the gloomy and macabre acts of Goth bands later on.

Their most famous single, "School's Out," was released in the summer of 1972. It was also the year we were leaving middle school, and that gave us an idea for the end-of-year assembly. In the same way that the name Alice Cooper gave the band cover for their more outré music and presentation, we figured that maybe Mr. Jones didn't really know very much about it. Turns out that was a correct assumption.

We casually suggested to him when discussing the end-of-year show that we could play a record by an American musician named Alice Cooper at the final assembly.

"Cooper?" he said in his dyspeptic tones. "I don't think I know her."

The die was cast. "Yes, sir," we said. "It's called *School's Out* and as you're American, isn't that what they say in America when the school year's ended, sir?"

Jones fell hook, line, and sinker for the trap. "Hmm, well, yes, that sounds like a great idea, boys!"

We set it up like a military op. We would all chip in some money and go buy the single in Horley so nobody would see us buying it in Crawley, where the school was, and give the game away.

Finally, the day came for the end-of-year assembly. Crowded together in the hall was the whole school: teachers, students, everybody.

The assembly got underway with the usual platitudes to "Do your best wherever you're going next" and some awards for the more academic- or community-minded students. So far, so boring. But we had a plan to change that.

We watched from the side of the hall just inside the audio booth, which was really a glorified cupboard that was off to one side, and there was the amp for the stage mics and a turntable to play music. I don't recall which of my friends accompanied me to the little audio cupboard to get the track ready to play and helped me to cue up our "special" end-of-year song vouched for by Mr. Jones. We placed the record on the turntable mat and it was ready to go.

The headmistress stood up and announced at the microphone, "Grus and Indus students are leaving this term, so they have a song by an American woman singer Alice Cooper about the end of school year for you all to hear." (Our middle school was a little experimental, so all the classes were named after star constellations. I was in Grus and had some friends in Indus. Bloody hippies.) The few titters in the audience should have been the clue to the teachers and the head, but nobody seemed concerned, least of all Mr. Jones, who smiled wanly. He obviously hadn't done his research.

The needle slowly lowered onto the black single going round on the mat and the instantly recognizable first notes of the guitar for "School's Out" started, followed by Neal Smith's pounding drums tumbling in.

We looked anxiously around the hall. The kids were transfixed with a kind of joyous fear. Expecting the worst, everyone's gaze fixed on the teachers onstage. Initially a little foot-tapping here and a semi-jocular swaying from side to side to indicate the faculty were taking this all in their stride, young people's music, et cetera. Then, as Alice's gruff vocal appeared and the lyrics started to be deciphered by the staff, the scowling face of the headmistress turned first to Mr. Jones's now-exasperated frown, then firmly toward us in the audio booth, glowering at yours truly.

Not five minutes before I had been given and accepted an award for having "esprit de corps" by the school, which I feel was probably justified. It just wasn't their particular group I was becoming devoted to.

SCOTT WALKER: DRIFTING

IF EVER THERE WAS A MAN DESTINED TO EXPLORE THE POLAR OPPOSITE of his beginnings it was Scott Walker. Walker (born Noel Scott Engel) was an American singer-songwriter, composer, and record producer who lived most of his professional life in England. In 1961, while playing with the group The Routers, Walker met John Maus, who was using the name John Walker on a fake ID to play gigs. The two formed The Walker Brothers in 1964, roping in Gary Leeds as drummer.

Maus convinced the group to all take the surname Walker and the band cultivated a family-friendly image. Originally, Scott was not the lead vocalist, but his baritone became the distinctive lead. The Walker Brothers' various pop ballads were big hits in England in the mid-sixties and reached number one with "Make It Easy on Yourself" in 1965 and "The Sun Ain't Gonna Shine Anymore" in 1966. Their popularity in the UK, among teenage girls especially, was only matched by the demigods of teen bands, The Beatles. Their flame burned bright and burnt out fast, and by 1968 The Walker Brothers had disbanded. Their once-wholesome sound now seemed old-fashioned in the fast-moving currency of the British pop music scene.

Fast-forward to 1981 and Julian Cope's compilation *Fire Escape in the Sky: The Godlike Genius of Scott Walker* renewed interest in Walker's work. The success of the compilation allowed Walker to secure a recording contract with Virgin, and in 1984 he released his first solo album in a decade, *Climate of Hunter*. While loosely based on the aesthetics of eighties rock compositions, *Climate of Hunter* embraces a fragmented and drone-like approach to pop, which was what made Walker intriguing to me. Something had shifted a little to the left and I became interested. Thank you, Julian!

Despite that early introduction to his genius, Scott Walker wasn't completely on my radar until 2006 and it came to me by another art form. I had just seen an amazing film, *30 Century Man*: a documentary by filmmaker Stephen Kijak about the musical career of Scott Walker. Kijak filmed Walker recording the second of his experimental and outré trilogy of albums, *The Drift*. One memorable scene has Scott directing the recording of a slab of meat as a percussion instrument. That's all it took for me; I was hooked. I went out and bought *The Drift* immediately after it came out and it gave me a totally different view of Walker's work. No longer an inconsequential pop star. He had changed, and dramatically so. "Imagine Andy Williams reinventing himself as Stockhausen," said the *Guardian*. They weren't far wrong.

The only connection I could make with the old Walker Brothers was Scott's voice, or maybe it was only the fact that I was aware it was Scott Walker singing. The music was dark, disconcerting, and experimental in nature. It took concentration to listen to the album as the songs unexpectedly went from loud to quiet. The subject matter was not the normal pop fare. Gone were the plaintive songs about crying and needing your girl, and in their place were songs about 9/11, torture, disease, and the Srebrenica massacre. The music itself was terrifying: dull drones with stark staccato drums and all the time that unforgettable voice. It's as if Scott walked through Dr. Caligari's cabinet and found himself in the lower portion of hell's landscape. It's unsettling, cerebral, and bleak. Music from dreams and nightmares—or both together at the same time. I fell in love with it immediately.

The Drift demanded that you listen and experience its depth. It begged you to be attentive and understanding, because if you weren't prepared it was going to hurt you until you succumbed. Its reward was a new framework to hang your thoughts on. You and me against the world. That I understood.

Then I met Stephen Kijak. I had been so intrigued by the documentary that I searched on the website and bought some paraphernalia connected with the film. With the confirmation of my purchase came an email: *Hi thanks for your order. BTW I think I know who you are . . .*

Such was my interest in Walker that I did something I never do; I acknowledged his assumption was correct. We met and talked and we are still talking to this day. One artist connecting us by the power of his work. At Stephen's behest I made a version of the Walker track "The Old Man's Back Again" for the soundtrack album of the film.

Walker followed up with a final album, *Bish Bosch*, in 2012. It was his fourteenth solo album and would finish the trilogy that started with *Tilt* and continued with *The Drift*.

Ultimately, Walker's transition from sixties pop star to a dark and brooding experimental composer is one that took his whole life to complete and presents the arc of late twentieth-century music in the space of one man—from the optimism of the sixties to the frivolity of the seventies into the darkness and nihilism of the eighties and beyond.

MARC BOLAN: LIFE'S A GAS

THEY SAY A PICTURE IS WORTH A THOUSAND WORDS. WHEN I FIRST SAW the cover of *Electric Warrior* by T. Rex, I understood that truth. It spoke in an eloquent outpouring of emotional poetry to my barely teenage self. The cover is mostly black with a gold aura framing Marc Bolan, the elfin singer and guitarist of T. Rex, who was pictured purposefully striding, guitar in hand, in front of an impressively large amplifier. This album cover was succinct in its message to me. The shimmering halo around Bolan gave him a powerful otherworldly sense of being someone more than mortal but also accentuated the mystical title. Looking at it, I had the strange feeling of entering another world. It seemed to me to be the gateway to another place, a faraway dimension. I didn't question it. I just knew it was where I wanted—no, needed—to be. The image was so powerful, I was won over before I had even heard the music.

I was in middle school when it came out in the autumn of 1971, just twelve years old and yet I could sense that everything I wanted to know was inside the sleeve of that second album by T. Rex. Even though I couldn't yet quite afford it on my teenage income of about next to nothing from my paper route, I diligently saved up over the weeks and eventually a copy was mine.

The first time I put it on and heard the first line of the second track "Cosmic Dancer" about dancing "when I was twelve," I hugged the cover to my chest. I was home.

I could spot another zealot carrying a copy under their arm from a thousand yards. If you had a copy, I understood we were going to be friends. Both Robert and Michael, my future bandmates, had it. In fact, I recall one of Robert's first attempts at lyrical poetry in our school English class was an ode to footballer Rodney Marsh to be sung to the tune of "Jeepster," a track from *Electric Warrior*.

Bolan emerged in the late sixties as a psychedelic folk musician in the group Tyrannosaurus Rex, with whom he recorded four critically acclaimed records, having a minor hit with that song. *Electric Warrior* was the turning point for

Bolan's transition from the first gentler incarnation as Tyrannosaurus Rex into the poppier and sexier T. Rex. In 1970, Bolan wrote and recorded what would become his first big hit, "Ride a White Swan," produced by Tony Visconti. The song definitively marked Bolan's transition to an electric sound.

Bolan only graced this earth for twenty-nine years, but in his short life he managed to pioneer glam rock, a genre of music and fashion that mixed outrageous costumes and hairstyles with art-rock, cabaret, and fifties bubblegum pop. Glam rock satirized the "throwaway" culture of postwar UK and America as well as the revolutionary and idealistic bent of sixties culture in favor of decadence and dandyism.

It wasn't just Bolan that took my fancy with his corkscrew hair, which was rather like my own at that point. No, I loved the setup with him and Mickey Finn on percussion. Perhaps that's where my urge to be a performer came from. He was just so cool playing the congas at the front of the stage with Marc, a yin to his yang. A perfect foil to Bolan's pixie rocker. I loved it all. Especially when, one night, on *Top of the Pops* Mickey wore an old grey children's plastic breastplate costume piece. Perhaps it was a toy? It was seriously cool and goofy at the same time. Clever and silly all at once. A quality I'd come to value in my late youth as punk had that irreverent attitude in spades.

Bolan had begun to show more electric influences on his last album as Tyrannosaurus Rex, *A Beard of Stars*. Bolan played "Hot Love" on BBC's *Top of the Pops* wearing glitter on his face, and the moment would come to define the advent of the sexy sparkle of glam rock. There are different stories about how Bolan came to wear glitter on his face: one theory is that it was inspired by his personal assistant, and another is that he saw it on his then wife June Child's dressing table and casually tried it on before an interview. What I feel is certain is that the application of glitter and the choice of feminine clothing cultivated a sexually ambiguous and androgynous image, an image that David Bowie would continue to expand on. Bolan had another connection with Bowie—the producer Tony Visconti.

"Hot Love" was a number one single in the UK, and later that year *Electric Warrior* came out and we were forever smitten with the black-and-gold image from the front cover. It showed us the way to be both long-haired and cool, not just hippies. In many ways, Marc Bolan and T. Rex were the bridge we used to understand who we were or might be. Up until that point we were sidelined as outsiders and neither one thing nor the other. Bolan was different in that he was at once erogenous and sexy and believable as a pre-punk poet. He possessed the duality of intellect and sexuality. He was a stepping stone for combining a visual aesthetic with the power of rock. Coming from the hippie folk era, he had old-school credentials, but he had evolved into a figure we felt we might emulate and admire. For a couple of years in the beginning of the seventies, Marc Bolan was the "Mambo Sun" of *Electric Warrior*.

After several successful singles, including "Jeepster," "Get It On," and "Metal Guru," the classic T. Rex lineup disintegrated along with Bolan's marriage to June Child, due to his affair with his backup singer Gloria Jones. In the period between 1973 and 1976 Bolan spent much of his time in the US recording R&B-influenced music. Bolan returned to the UK in 1976 and released two more albums. On tour for his twelfth and final album, *Dandy in the Underworld*, punk band The Damned opened, linking the glam and punk eras and attracting a new audience of younger listeners.

Unfortunately, Bolan's return would be short-lived as he died in a fatal car crash with his partner Gloria Jones. Bolan's ambiguous, gender-fluid aesthetic and his focus on simple rock and roll structures became a model for not only further glam musicians but also new wave and new romantic artists who would emerge in the decade after his death. His inclusion of The Damned for his final tour represented a passing of the torch to punk, which would spawn post-punk, Goth, and new wave. Bolan is an essential link in the chain from glam to Goth.

With hindsight, I feel I can trace the androgynous appeal of Bolan. He was the first white guy we knew that had that appeal. For as long as I could remember, rock had been the purview of hairy mustachioed guys with a misogynistic swagger. Now there was someone who looked more like us and expressed himself like us. In that way, there was a broader gender appeal and inclusivity in Bolan way before it became a thing in music. But despite that style, or perhaps because of it, my favorite track from *Electric Warrior* is one that sums up his tortured path.

"Life's a Gas" still sings to me of his laissez-faire attitude to life taken from the counterculture of the late sixties and almost forgotten now in the mists of

Dave Vanian of The Dammed at Hammersmith Palais, London
Credit: Mick Mercer

time past, but more than that the song is uncannily prescient about his own existence.

It's almost as if he knew he wasn't destined to be with us for long.

DAVID BOWIE: LOW LEVEL

IN THE LATE SEVENTIES, IT FELT LIKE WE HAD ALWAYS KNOWN DAVID Bowie. He came from around where we grew up near the suburbs of South London. When we saw him on TV, his cadence and expressions were familiar to us. He was one of us—sort of. Everything else about him was completely alien to us.

He was our guide to the demimonde, the sacred underground of our youth. He held the signposts up and said, "Follow me! It's interesting down here . . ." His famous quote, "I don't know where I'm going from here, but I promise it won't be boring," resonated with us a great deal. For the most part, he was true to his word. A few of his more outré excursions didn't connect with me as some of them were before my time. The floppy hat, dress-wearing incarnation of Bowie wasn't really in my purview. I was too young when that one sailed into sight and didn't really understand until much later the androgynous leanings that he was trying on, which he was alluding to. When people say he was ahead of his time, they mean light-years ahead of *our* time.

For whatever reason, I wasn't super aware of Bowie until the second of two events. The first was his July 1972 appearance on the BBC program *Top of the Pops*. His Starman performance was transformative in many ways. It was so glam, and it was very, very unusual. For a thirteen-year-old boy from the sticks, orange hennaed hair was mind-blowing in the extreme! His clothes were also different from what we were used to seeing on the streets of our boring town. It lit a small fuse of wonder and rebellion.

The second event that struck a chord in me came from his album *Low*, which was part of his Berlin trilogy, the three albums he recorded between 1977 and 1979, when he relocated from Los Angeles to Europe in an attempt to free himself from an increasingly severe drug addiction. These records—*Low*, *Heroes*, and *Lodger*—saw Bowie experimenting with krautrock and ambient music, inspired by Brian Eno. The trilogy, referred to by *Consequence of Sound* as his "art rock trifecta," was in collaboration with American producer Tony Visconti, who got his start working with Marc Bolan, and featured guitarists Robert Fripp and Adrian Belew.

Low was life-changing for me because of its ambient sounds and strange atmosphere that combined to create a mood that was different from anything else I had heard at that point in my young life. It was also the first set of lyrical songs that I connected with my own alienation and deeper thoughts. *Low* was a different kind of record from the start. Side One of the vinyl album was composed of five songs with lyrics, and Side Two was composed of instrumental tracks. I instantly identified with the "song" side of the album. "Songs" is a little disingenuous. "Speed of Life" comes flying in from another universe, the plunking bass line and those collapsing drum fills laying down the weirdness that permeates the whole album.

It would be a strange and startling opener to any album full of unknown angst and light moments that suddenly drops down a hole into the middle of serious art anguish played on an ARP synth by Bowie matched with the almost-new-wave chopping of Carlos Alomar's guitar.

The bombast of Dennis Davis's staccato drumming pushes into "Breaking Glass," the second track, and those wonderful lyrics that said so much with so little. I felt I understood what he was talking about. It was a strange feeling that completely took me out of the normality of being eighteen and living in nowheresville at the end of the seventies.

"What in the World" followed with Eno's bubbling synths sequenced by whatever strange device they had hooked up as the basis for a signal. For the best part of a decade, Dennis Davis, Carlos Alomar, and George Murray formed the D.A.M. trio on some of Bowie's finest work.

Like every punk and new wave drummer in the UK, I was completely entranced by Davis's sound on his kit. It was unlike anything we had ever heard. The snare was mechanical and the brute force of the overall sound was liberating to me. It sounded, well, Neu! Producer Tony Visconti used an Eventide H910 Harmonizer to process Davis's drum sound. When asked what it did, Visconti reportedly replied, "It fucks with the fabric of time." It certainly messed with my idea of what drums could sound like, and with it a whole new type of percussion was introduced into the milieu of rock.

It was indeed a revolution in sound. Some years later, when The Cure was recording *Pornography*, I tried to channel that kind of explosive power into my own playing. Of course, I had been attempting that with different results for *Seventeen Seconds* and *Faith*.

The other revolution was hearing the single (as it was released in the UK) of "Sound and Vision." I still recall the party I went to shortly after my nineteenth birthday and hearing it shimmering along with Mary Hopkin's (of Eurovision song contest fame) wordless backing vocals. To say it entranced me was to miss the point here entirely. It was a consummate pop song. It reached number three in the British charts, but it did so entirely on its own terms.

Yes, it was pop, but it was the weirdest pop you ever heard. That was the revelation to me: that you could be something perfectly true to yourself and still have a successful pop song.

Bowie's vocals on "Always Crashing in the Same Car" are simultaneously sexy and plaintive, and then at precisely thirty-six seconds Dennis Davis comes crashing in with the most beautiful snare fill I have ever heard in my life. It also confirmed to me that the drums were a real musical instrument—not just a metronome. This discovery influenced my own playing. Sound and vision became sound and rhythm in my mind.

"Be My Wife" is another slice of modern sound with a shimmering piano as counterpoint to the searing guitar. Bowie's vocals beautifully articulate the sadness of the artist moving everywhere and nowhere, an expression of his loneliness in this world. Finally, the dark grey, muted tones of "A New Career in a New Town" spoke so eloquently to my teenage longing for a change in my life and circumstances, and curiously enough there is Dennis Davis at exactly thirty-six seconds again, bursting into the track. Coincidence or not?

If Side One is more avant-pop laced with fragments of art-rock inspired by Eno's *Taking Tiger Mountain (By Strategy)*, Side Two seemingly featured no real songs at all. It is made up almost entirely of instrumental mood pieces, incorporating the sounds of *kosmische musik* inspired by groups like Harmonia and Can.

All the pieces on Side Two contain references to the Eastern Bloc. Berlin was still a city divided by the Berlin Wall. It was as if we caught Bowie straddling the border between the past and future at the same time. This was reflected in his life at the time, having come from the hedonistic and decadent scene in Los Angeles to the endless winter of the Eastern Bloc.

In Berlin Bowie was confronted by the aftermath of war. It was all around him. He had visited Warsaw in April 1976, which had been in ruins after World War II. Although there had been some rebuilding, it still felt like an empty, desolate place. This is described perfectly in the opening piece "Warszawa."

I visited Warsaw in the early aughts and found it much the same. The vast Plattenbau housing tracts, with their massive prefabricated slabs, are still visible in the countryside around Warsaw. The only nod to modern life since the Communist era are the ubiquitous satellite dishes sprouting like mushrooms across the grey concrete blocks. The next piece, "Art Decade," a pun on art decayed, evokes the melancholy mood.

The vibraphone and xylophone feature heavily on "Weeping Wall" in an almost Steve Reich style, which was intended as the minimalist composer was an influence. The last piece, "Subterraneans," has strange vocal phrases mashed together with Bowie's beautiful jazzy sax over the top.

In many ways the second side foresaw the ambient revolution in modern music. To us, in the late seventies, it was otherworldly and unlike anything that we had heard before. I was completely in love with *Low*.

The mark of a truly great piece of art is one that stands the test of time. Playing *Low* over forty years later, it still has surprises and charms to uncover. *Low* came at the intersections of extremes for Bowie, which is often where we find an artist's greatest work.

Bowie had moved to Los Angeles in early 1975 to record *Young Americans* and *Station to Station* as well as taking an acting role in the film *The Man Who Fell to Earth*. He abandoned a soundtrack idea for *The Man Who Fell to Earth* and began rehearsing for his Isolar Tour supporting *Station to Station*, which kicked off in February 1976. Following the end of the tour in May, Bowie and his wife Angela moved to Switzerland, getting ever closer to the eventual lodestar of Berlin, where he would produce *Low* and free himself from the deadly cocaine addiction he had cultivated in Los Angeles.

This aborted soundtrack became the basis for *Low*, a haunting and beautiful record that heavily features reliance on synthesizer textures and lush arrangements. Some influences on this record came from Brian Eno, whom Bowie met backstage on his Isolar Tour in May 1976. Eno had released two ambient records in 1975, *Another Green World* and *Discreet Music*, the latter a favorite for Bowie during this period. Both Eno and Bowie were obsessed with the German music genre krautrock and its associated acts Harmonia, Neu!, and Tangerine Dream. Eno had worked directly with members of Harmonia, while Bowie had already shown a heavy krautrock influence on *Station to Station*.

Bowie booked studio time in the Château d'Hérouville, a residential studio in France, in late summer 1976, to write and record with his friend Iggy Pop, who was also trying to get sober. Bowie composed much of the music on *The Idiot*, with Iggy writing the lyrics. He developed what he called a "three-phase process" for this album, where the backing tracks were recorded first, then overdubs, and finally the lyrics would be written and recorded last. He used this process for the remainder of his career. Since *The Idiot* predates *Low*, the album is seen as the unofficial first album of his Berlin period. Tony Visconti and Bowie mixed this record at Hansa Studios in West Berlin, and Bowie fell in love with the city and decided to move there.

It was a seismic change for him. Naturally, his record label was shocked by the album; RCA initially delayed the release of *Low* and did very little promotion when it was finally put out January 14, 1977, less than three weeks before my eighteenth birthday.

Often eighteen is seen as the "age of majority," the phase of a person's life when they pass through childhood to become a legal person, when the law grants you the rights and responsibilities of an adult in most societies in the West.

For me, *Low* brought with it an extra set of occurrences. I had finally started on the long road out of others' expectations of what my life might be and was now tempered by my own burgeoning sense of existence in the world.

Although Bowie has been a touchstone through all my musical career right up until he passed away, *Low* had the most profound effect on me. It taught me that being myself—with all the strange feelings and questions starting to manifest in me as a young adult—was enough and I didn't have to conform to society's straitjacket. Armed with Bowie's *Low* and the first album by The Clash, I felt free to do anything at all.

The author in Bourges, 1982
Credit: Richard Bellia

PART TWO

ETERNALS

CHAPTER FOUR

ARCHITECTS OF DARKNESS

JOY DIVISION: THIS IS THE WAY, STEP INSIDE
JUNE 4, 1976

Bernard Sumner and Peter Hook separately attended a concert by the Sex Pistols at the Manchester Lesser Free Trade Hall. The experience inspired them both to start a band. Sumner felt that the Pistols destroyed the image of the pop star, that the experience opened the role up to people like him, which was quite a psychological barrier back in those times.

The next day, Hook borrowed money from his mother to purchase a bass guitar, Sumner bought a guitar, and their schoolfriend Terry Mason, who was also at the Sex Pistols show, obtained a drum kit. Their friend Martin Gresty was tapped for vocals but backed out when he got a job working at a factory, such were the grim realities of the late seventies in postwar Britain, dropping your dreams just to survive.

The trio then placed an ad for a singer at the local Virgin Records store and Ian Curtis responded. They hired him without an audition. The band settled on the name Warsaw shortly before their first gig, inspired by the David Bowie song "Warszawa." With new drummer Tony Tabac, who had joined the band two days prior when Mason vacated the drum stool to become the manager, Warsaw played its debut show opening for Buzzcocks on May 29,

1977, at the Electric Circus. Reviews in the *NME* and *Sounds* helped attract national attention to the band, which is about the time I started to take notice of them.

Tabac was replaced by Steve Brotherdale in June 1977. Brotherdale attempted to pressure Curtis to join his band the Panik, but he soon alienated Curtis and the other band members. Returning from a recording session at Pennine Sound Studios in Oldham, they asked Brotherdale to check on a potential flat tire and when he got out of the car, they drove off. He got the message.

The band placed an ad in a music shop window for a new drummer to which only Stephen Morris replied. Morris fit perfectly, and according to Deborah Curtis, Warsaw became a "complete family." The band changed its name to Joy Division (after a wartime brothel mentioned in the novel *House of Dolls*) to avoid confusion with the London group Warsaw Pakt.

On December 14, 1977, the band returned to Pennine Sound to track their debut EP *An Ideal for Living*. The EP featured a blond Hitler Youth on the cover, coupled with the name Joy Division, and led some listeners to believe the band had neo-Nazi sympathies. The record was self-financed and released on the band's own Enigma label in 1978. When the record was rereleased as a twelve-inch later in the year, the cover was replaced by one of scaffolding to distance themselves from further controversy.

The record's sparse sound and songwriting show the group's early punk influences rather than the gloomy and Gothic post-punk sound they would later be known for. They sounded more like Iggy and the Stooges than Joy Division at this point, but it is still an interesting prelude to their short career. They played their last gig as Warsaw New Year's Eve of 1977 and their first gig as Joy Division on January 25, 1978.

The band caught the attention of music producer and television personality Tony Wilson and manager Rob Gretton at the Stiff/Chiswick Challenge concert on April 14, 1978. Curtis berated Wilson for not showcasing the group on his Granada Television program *So It Goes*, and Wilson responded that they would be the next group featured. Gretton, who was the club DJ, was so impressed that he pushed the band to take him on as their manager. It was Gretton's business savvy that allowed Joy Division to concentrate on musical creativity. On September 20, Joy Division performed "Shadowplay" on *So It Goes*, introduced by Tony Wilson. The band contributed two songs to a release on Wilson's Factory label, a split double EP called *A Factory Sample*. Shortly after, Joy Division signed to Factory with Gretton as a label partner.

On December 27, while driving home from a gig, Curtis experienced his first epileptic seizure. The band recorded a session for John Peel in January, and Curtis appeared on the cover of *NME*. The band recorded their debut LP *Unknown Pleasures* in April 1979, and it was released in June of that year. The initial pressing of ten thousand sold out quickly and turned Factory into a viable moneymaking enterprise that operated outside the major label system. Factory was one of the first independent record labels that garnered any success.

Joy Division embarked on a twenty-four-date tour in October with Buzzcocks. In November, the band released the nonalbum single "Transmission," which allowed them to finally quit their day jobs. The band then toured Europe in the beginning of 1980. On their return, they recorded their follow-up album *Closer* with Martin Hannett at Britannia Row Studios in London in March. On April 7, Curtis attempted suicide by overdosing on his anti-seizure medication. By this time his seizures had become almost uncontrollable and he often lapsed into them onstage, which made for an intense and sometimes frightening experience for both the singer and audience.

Joy Division played its last gig at the University of Birmingham on May 2, 1980. This performance included the track "Ceremony," which would later be recorded by New Order. The band was slated to embark on its first North American tour in May, a prospect that Curtis spoke about excitedly. However, his marriage to Deborah was deteriorating due to his relationship with Belgian Annik Honoré, whom he met on tour in 1979. Incidentally, I recall seeing her at several of The Cure's shows in Europe around that time as she co-founded record labels Les Disques du Crépuscule and Factory Benelux.

The night before the band was due to depart, Curtis returned to his home in Macclesfield to speak with Deborah. He implored her to drop a divorce suit and asked her to leave him in the house alone until he caught his train in the morning. She did so, and he spent the night watching the Werner Herzog film *Stroszek* before hanging himself in his kitchen.

Deborah discovered his body in the morning on her return. Curtis's suicide led to the cancellation of the US tour and left the band in shambles. *Closer* would be released in July of that year to critical and commercial acclaim, Curtis's suicide immortalizing the group forever. The remaining members eventually regrouped and formed New Order, which has had wide-ranging commercial success with a more electronic and dance-oriented sound.

FEBRUARY 16, 1979

I HAD HEARD THE JOHN PEEL SESSION OF JOY DIVISION'S FIRST BROADcast on February 14 of that year. I don't know if you agree with Oscar Wilde's saying, "Life imitates art far more than art imitates life," but I've concluded that lots of clues from their environment trace the story of many of the bands and artists mentioned here. It's more that you can't separate the art from life as that's what fuels it. The fact that Joy Division came from the cold hardscrabble north of England, Salford, a city within greater Manchester, seems to bear that out, but closer investigation makes it even more certain.

The Cure's first show in Manchester was February 16, 1979, just after that Peel session and shortly after my twentieth birthday. It is still memorable to me for the first impression I had of the place Joy Division hailed from.

We played at The Factory/Russell Club. I remember driving up from our home base in the south of England in Michael's white transit van. This was how we got around to shows in those days. That long dismal slog, mostly on the M1/M6 motorways intimately known to every British band since time immemorial.

When we arrived in Hulme where the club was located, it was a real and visceral shock to our system as nice middle-class boys from the leafy suburbs of South London. The whole area looked as if it was just five minutes since the World War II armistice. The club was on a scrubby and scruffy parcel of wasteland with broken bottles and detritus everywhere, but our eyes were drawn to the large foreboding buildings in the near distance. This was the Hulme Crescents housing development—the largest public housing project in Europe—an urban experiment in trying to repair the country after the Second World War gone horribly awry. Built in the early seventies while the sting and destruction of the war were still visible some twenty-five years after the end of the conflict.

Hulme Crescents was designed to liberate the local population from the previous lodgings of unsanitary and depressing Victorian slums, which had been razed to provide space for these brutalist blocks of grey doom. As with many housing ideas of the time, it proposed putting as many people together in close proximity with each other as possible. In the end, some thirteen thousand desperate souls were housed here. A hopeless and dehumanizing situation for the inhabitants.

The Hulme Crescents was the urban equivalent of factory farming. It turned its inhabitants against each other with violence to one another and to themselves. It was, by all accounts, a terrible place to live.

Within a couple of years of being built in 1972 the projects had become uninhabitable for families and were designated as adult housing from then on, with students and adult-only families. The place was doomed from the start with bad planning and poor construction. The four large buildings facing south were plagued with vermin infestation as the new buildings were heated underfloor with ducts running from flat to flat, which provided useful paths for the rats that inhabited them and gave them constant access to food waste areas.

This ease of entrance for the rats and other vermin was combined with the dangerous use of asbestos in the ducts, which meant there was very little safe access to the actual systems, so council workers were unable to prevent the cockroaches and rats from thriving in the extensive ductwork.

The initial idea was to have deck-access homes, "streets in the sky" that would encourage neighborly activities and provide a place for children to play unsupervised. A utopian dream that was to turn into a nightmare. Terrible design flaws, such as thick concrete balconies, prevented residents from actually being able to see one another, compounding the sense of isolation the residents felt. This was exacerbated by the routing of the Mancunian Way and Princess Parkway roads, which effectively cut them off from the rest of the city.

The balconies of the flats had a horizontal aperture, a fatal design feature that allowed curious children a foothold to climb onto the balcony ledge. In

1974 this disastrous flaw caused unspeakable tragedy when a five-year-old playing on the balcony died after falling from the floors above.

After the incident, and with pressure from a heavily subscribed petition, Manchester City Council agreed to rehouse families with children, and the flats were offered to students and all-adult households.

Despite the council's management efforts, Hulme Crescents went from bad to worse. Just a few years after we first witnessed the urban decay of it all, the situation got so bad that the council actually stopped charging rent. Many flats were abandoned, but the exodus was stemmed somewhat by the local council still supplying electricity for those that needed it. The next few years saw the Crescents taken over by various artists and bohemians looking for cheap housing and, of course, squatters and criminals.

Strangely, this sea change breathed new life into the place and it became a destination where art and difference flourished. All the prerequisites for creation and creative thought, as in post-wall Berlin, were present within the largely empty buildings, which was attractive to its youthful inhabitants who put in an art house cinema with a club night and a burgeoning fashion sense particular to the place. Though, when we got there, it was just really scary and dismal.

The air outside the club was that peculiar cold dampness that England specializes in, and in the wintery afternoon long shadows were fading into the early darkness and drizzle. We moved our scant gear into the back area of the club and soon discovered that there wasn't the usual courtesy of a "dressing room" for us to use as a band. In fact, the back of the stage was bisected by a thin plywood wall that opened at either end onto the stage. The wall made a small corridor between it and the outer wall of the club building, in which presumably we were going to hide until we were due to play. It had no separate door, so the only way to access it was to walk directly across the stage. It also had no separate light or sink, so nothing we could use to prepare for a show or (as was usually more useful for us) to change out of our sweat-soaked shirts after the show into a dry T-shirt. It was just a dark anteroom to the stage with no couch or chairs to relax on, a cramped space to stand and wait.

Based on what we had seen outside, this was not really a surprise but confirmation that we were in the not-so-good part of town. Or perhaps the really bad side of town. This was where the Joy Division sound came from. It spoke to me of their fraught music as eloquently as any other description.

In nearby Salford, where Sumner and Hook came from, they didn't go for the desperate model of Hulme Crescents but rather the just as depressing high-rise residential tower blocks. We finished what passed for our sound check in the woefully spartan club. We hadn't been "professional" for very long by this time. Our manager, Chris Parry, had started paying us a small wage of twenty-five pounds per week a few months beforehand, but we already could cast a somewhat practiced eye around the venues we had played so far and knew roughly what to expect in terms of facilities.

This place, I realized, was not going to be one of the more salubrious joints, and it would probably be a struggle to find any sustenance or beer, which was of vital importance to us back then. Out of the dimly lit bar popped a middle-aged gentleman with a rather old-fashioned hat and manner. He introduced himself as the photographer for the local Manchester newspaper. He had that well-worn and slightly cynical look I've come to recognize in many of his profession, and I could sense the battered and shabby demeanor of a life lived in the long shadow of the dark behemoth that was Hulme and its Crescent.

He asked that we line up for a photograph or two "for the local paper, you understand, lads," and we pretended that we did. Although we considered ourselves professionals by now, we were also still a little wet behind the ears when it came to promotion and publicity. We hadn't been at this for long. Our new photographer buddy encouraged us to pose for the photos and at the end of each click of the camera would announce mostly to himself, or maybe anyone within hearing distance, "Oh my goodness! That's a Rembrandt!"

The show came and went as many did in those early years with little fanfare or differentiation except for the ominous looming of Hulme Crescents and the strangely friendly photographer.

MARCH 4, 1979

I FINALLY MET IAN CURTIS AND JOY DIVISION QUITE SOON AFTER OUR first show in their hometown. I knew our manager had been in touch with

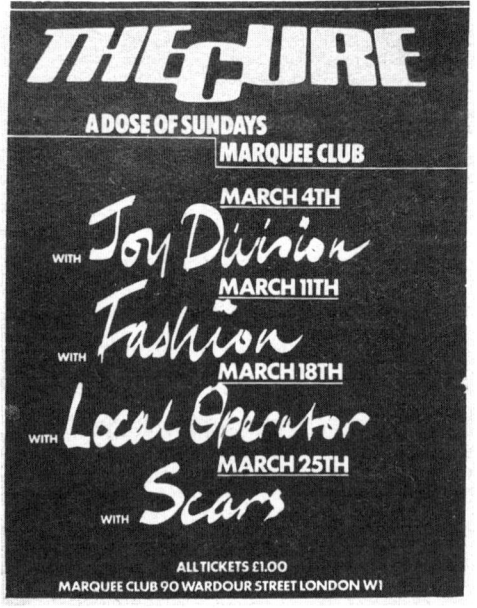

"A dose of Sundays" with The Cure at the Marquee in 1979
Supplied by JC Moglia

their manager, Rob Gretton, to arrange for them to open one night for us in London.

Chris Parry had organized a series of four Sunday-night shows at the Marquee Club. "A dose of Sundays," he called it. I spent the week between shows playing the length and breadth of the UK, returning to London once a week on Sunday to play the Marquee with a different band each week that we personally picked to open for us.

Joy Division was one of those bands because we thought they were great. I remember quite vividly the scene in the Marquee Club dressing room where I would first see Ian Curtis in person. The dressing room resembled nothing more than a badly kept public lavatory with graffiti—and that was on its better nights. With a persistent background of its most unpleasant olfactory gift, a mix of sweat and vomit. I don't think I ever sat on the sparse couch, which may have just been some pillows thrown over a board on bricks, for fear of catching something dreadful from its dirty beer-soaked covering. It was the only place the bands could prepare away from the bar or main hall of the club.

The night Joy Division opened for us, the room was loud with the anticipation of a decent and enthusiastic crowd. As there was only one dressing room, I suppose we sat at opposite ends of the dilapidated space in two different camps.

Our music and presentation were not that dissimilar. Young earnest men playing dark post-punk music, except I probably didn't call it that then or realize quite what it was. It was just what we did. Our music. The Cure's music.

In the corner the gaunt figure of Ian Curtis sat a little hunched over on a chair. All around him the atmosphere of the room was electric, buzzing with the excitement of the show and night to come. He was quiet and motionless amongst all the activity, lost in some faraway thought perhaps. I may have passed a couple of minutes in small talk, but the overall impression I had of him that evening was of a deeply troubled man locked in his own thoughts. Although it is only my own personal feeling, I believe that he sought and got relief from whatever was troubling him while helping to compose the songs Joy Division performed that night.

The best music always comes from a place of authenticity. The human spirit needs to express its deepest meaning to be able to live in peace, even just to exist sometimes. I have known several artists who could not pull themselves out of the spiral of dark moments that leads to the end that befell Curtis. It's true that "music hath charms to calm the savage breast," but unfortunately sometimes it's just not charming enough.

OCTOBER 3, 1979

THE SECOND AND FINAL TIME I SAW CURTIS AND JOY DIVISION WAS later that year. The Cure had been the special guests on the Join Hands Tour with Siouxsie and the Banshees. Of course, that tour initially started in the late summer of 1979 and came to a grinding halt just a few days into it when guitarist John McKay and drummer Kenny Morris abruptly quit in Aberdeen, Scotland. They got on a train and hotfooted it back to London, leaving both the Banshees and The Cure with an angry crowd and only half a band.

The fact that the Banshees had to regroup left us all out in the lurch for a while. We reconvened and started out on the reconfigured Join Hands Tour again in the fall, with Robert doing double duty with both bands and the Banshees with new wunderkind Budgie on drums.

As I recall, Sioux fell ill at one point when we were playing in the north and a couple of shows were cancelled. We were left with a day or two to ourselves, wandering around the north without any gigs to play until Leeds University on October 5. Joy Division was to open for Buzzcocks at the same venue two days before, and that is where I saw Joy Division play for the last time.

By this time Ian Curtis was in the full throes of whatever particular spirit had overtaken his psyche. I don't believe it was malevolent. It was, I think, a combination of his own physical/mental health problems—epilepsy and depression—manifesting itself in ever more extreme movements onstage. I feel that playing the music was maybe the only relief he had from his dark anguish and so he had to go on until the bitter end. Closing the performance, he was helped off the stage. Everything was firing with too much psychic intensity for him to be able to stand upright any longer. He was sporadically jerking around like a marionette controlled by unseen forces whilst singing and emoting the angst and trauma of Joy Division.

Dressed in simple black trousers and a dark-colored shirt, he was the epitome of every man struggling with the deep emotional pain he obviously felt and also an avatar of all our psychic pain and trauma manifest on the stage for us to witness. It was mesmerizing and I could not look away even if I wanted to. The vision and experience of that night resonated deep within my soul for a long time. Of course, the end was quite near. Even if we didn't know it then.

JUNE 6, 1980

THE CURE WAS ON TOUR FOR ITS SECOND ALBUM, *SEVENTEEN SECONDS*. We had been on the road for some months and played about fifty shows and it was still only June. So, it was a somewhat exhausted band that rolled into Rouen, a port town in Normandy in northern France.

Full of Gothic architecture and medieval half-timbered houses, Rouen was the very epitome of France's ancient and brutal religious past. Joan of Arc, the famous saint, was burned at the stake here for heresy. Outside the Eglise Sainte-Jeanne-d'Arc there is a statue at the very spot where the saint's life is said to have ended. In its cobbled streets I could feel the tumult of the town's history and sense the spirit of troubled times. The past was, in a very present sense, available to our reality.

I don't recall what time it was when we arrived, but it was most likely midafternoon the day we were due to play at Studio 44. Rouen is a couple of hours' drive northwest of Paris, where we had played the night before at the Bataclan, a famous Parisian venue that was to be very infamous thirty-five years later for an awful and tragic occasion.

We had been asked to do an in-store appearance at the local record store, which was owned by Jean-Pierre Turmel and Yves Von Bontee, who also owned a small independent label, Sordide Sentimental.

Back in the early eighties record stores really were the center of a music fan's world in that window before MTV and the internet took off. Information about new music was gleaned from two sources: radio and the music weeklies, especially in the UK. These two sources coalesced in the local record store in England, and in America they had a big pile of those free local newspapers at the entrance. In stores like Tower Records on Sunset Boulevard, for instance, the *LA Weekly* had articles about bands and the local places that they might be playing.

In our small suburban outpost, we only really had one record store staffed by Simon Gallup's brother, Ric. He would bring the music to us on frequent visits to the capital, where he would find the harder-to-get items not available generally to us in the sticks. We avidly consumed whatever information he also brought back from London, the epicenter of all things exciting and musical, or so it seemed to us.

It was natural when we were on tour to go into the local record store wherever we were to see what the local scene might be like and interact with other like-minded people. The record labels had been quick to notice the attraction of the stores for fans and made elaborate displays to promote the latest recorded offering for some of the bigger stores like Tower in America and HMV or Virgin in the UK. Unlike now, record stores were not eccentric relics from the past, they were where you went if you were passionate about music. And we were very passionate about music!

It didn't take the labels very long to figure out that putting their artists in the store for a few hours to sign records and take photos with fans was an easy and profitable promotion.

The Cure had done a great many of these appearances all over the US, Europe, and elsewhere. Most record store owners appreciated the fact that they

Flyer on The Cure's first American tour at the Hot Club, Philadelphia
Credit: Bobby Startup

would sell many copies of your album (and merchandise if you brought any with you) and tried to make the process as smooth as possible by supplying comfortable facilities to do this, with tables and chairs to make the event run simply and quickly. If you were a major act, you could expect several hundred people or more to turn up for an in-store signing.

So on this particular day I was prepared for the usual record-signing routine: meet and greet, or shake and sign. Whatever you want to call it. Having imbibed a fair bit of vin du pays the night before, I was looking for a strong coffee and perhaps that great French cure for a hangover: a large, ice-cold *citron pressé*, to rehydrate me.

Inside the store were the usual records in racks, and in a corner the chairs and a table for us to sit at while we signed the records. This was almost by rote now, so I wasn't taking much notice. I sat down at the table and allowed my gaze to idly wander along the shelves at the back of the store and behind the counter.

Then I saw it. A blue record cover with a dark hooded figure on top, longer than a regular single but not as big as an album. Initially I was puzzled because, having scanned the shelves as I sat at the table, I saw the usual suspects of the day, the punk and newly-punked-up albums on sale. Being part of the cognoscenti of that time (or at least I thought I might be), I was momentarily confused because I registered that this cover was of some significance, but I couldn't quite place the item. I turned it over and over in my mind . . .

Then, suddenly I realized what it was. I had heard about a new single Joy Division had put out on a small French label about three months before. Only a small run of 1,578 copies, apparently. I remember that fact piqued my interest. I thought it was strange to pick such a random (it seemed to me anyway) number for the pressing. Usually, records were pressed in multiples of one hundred or one thousand. I don't know why they picked that number. Perhaps it had something to do with the capacity of the record-pressing plant or for packaging the records up in boxes. Somebody told me the number had some historical significance for Rouen; I wasn't sure. But I was sure that this was definitely the single I had read about.

I sat through the rest of the signing session somewhat distracted, musing about getting a copy of the object of my desire.

After the signing, the owner, whom I presume was either Jean or Yves, asked if we would like a couple of items from the store. This was the usual and courteous gesture customarily made by record store owners for dramatically increasing their revenue for an hour or so, and we appreciated it as I'm sure most bands did.

I made a cursory scan of the racks and returned to the counter and pointed to the cover of the single. "I'd like that one, please," I said.

Although they tried to dissuade me for a brief second, they soon acquiesced in a very gentlemanly and generous fashion and gave me the coveted single. It was a gesture I deeply appreciated.

On reflection, France was very good to The Cure and not just because of that incident. I think the French understood us and our music in a way that gave us hope and encouraged us to continue when we were at a point where things could have gone either way. Touring that year was difficult. We were a four-piece band at that point, but after we finished an exhausting tour in Australia in August, Matthieu left the band and we were once again back to a three-piece. We might have stopped then but, of course, we didn't.

I still have the single and I shall never part with it. The record's value lies in what it represents to me more than the money I could get for it. It symbolizes a time in my life when I was just completely in love with the power of the music that we were making. In fact, it was all I had to help me through my life. Seeing that others were on that path too gave me some validation on the lonesome road I would have to tread in the following years. That's what makes it precious to me.

Of course, there is another more poignant and tragic reason the record is meaningful. The troubled singer of Joy Division committed suicide some twenty days before I possessed the record. Another instance of an artist falling into the void of nothingness before he could bear witness to his own success.

SELECTED DISCOGRAPHY: UNKNOWN PLEASURES

Joy Division's debut record *Unknown Pleasures* was recorded and mixed in three consecutive weekends in April 1978 and released on June 15, 1979, on Factory Records. The album was recorded at Strawberry Studios in Stockport, a suburb of Manchester, and produced by Martin Hannett, who was a proponent of using the studio as a creative tool and believed that punk rock recording was sonically conservative.

Hannett utilized new studio technology such as AMS 15-80S digital delays, the Marshall Time Modulator, and tape echo. He also incorporated unusual sounds, including a bottle breaking, someone eating chips, backwards guitar, and the sound of the Strawberry Studios elevator with a Leslie speaker inside. Hannett's goal was to produce a sense of sonic space in the recordings. Although the band was split on the more atmospheric sound of the album, fearing that it didn't match their more aggressive live sound, Hannett's production has been widely praised.

The album's cover was designed by Peter Saville and features an image of radio waves from pulsar CP 1919 from *The Cambridge Encyclopedia of Astronomy*. Saville reversed the image, originally created by astronomer Harold Craft from black on white to white on black. The image has become an iconic symbol of the post-punk era and has been parodied and referenced in other media in the decades since. The album's initial pressing of ten thousand was half-sold in the two weeks after its release, with the remaining copies filling the office of

Factory co-founder Alan Erasmus. The release of the nonalbum single "Transmission" helped sell out the initial pressing of the album, prompting additional pressings. The album garnered £50,000 in profit that was split between the band and Factory with Tony Wilson investing most of Factory's cut back into projects. At the end of a successful tour in November 1979 supporting Buzzcocks, the album had sold close to fifteen thousand copies. An auspicious start to a storied career.

SIDE ONE (OUTSIDE)

"Disorder"

Morris starts with a hybrid Jaki Liebezeit/Tony Chimes–type motorik beat, which even today signals the filling of any Goth club dance floor. It also includes the best end line for diehard romantics in the throes of capitulation. In my opinion, it's one of the best first tracks on any album of the era.

"Day of the Lords"

After a slowly climbing bass riff, a circular guitar arpeggio motif gives way to Curtis's stentorian vocals recounting the chilling horrors of war: "Where will it end?"

"Candidate"

Another slowly churning song with the snare marking the song's points while angular guitar and other weird sounds swirl about. A tale of a love gone awry portrayed as a political campaign, or is it the other way around?

"Insight"

The song opens with eerie sounds—like the machinery of a long-abandoned warehouse elevator descending to the doors of a hell that Curtis is just beginning to discover. The angels and judges of our past remembered. The driving beat punctuated by Morris's Syndrum slows down into an abstract flanged sweep.

"New Dawn Fades"

One of the album's great guitar riffs heralds the start of the song. Instantly memorable. The riff resolves with Curtis's vocals into a classic Jim Morrison–like verse. The bass pattern stays the same throughout with all the other instruments revolving around it. "New Dawn Fades" rises to a vocal crescendo that borders on the melodramatic, then slowly winds down until the drum's bleak fade.

SIDE TWO (INSIDE)
"She's Lost Control"

Probably the most instantly recognizable song on the first album. The Syndrum beat of Morris and Peter Hook's high bass riff identify this song immediately. As soon as Curtis's vocal comes in, there's no mistake.

"Shadowplay"

Another one of this album's anthems propelled by a circular bass riff that together with the drums' frequent snare fills gives the track its energy on which Sumner lays his most plaintive guitar riffs.

"Wilderness"

The song's quirky beginning is marked by the slap-back echo on the drums and rubber band–like bass riff. The lyrics are quasi-religious in nature, dealing mostly with the hypocrisy of organized religion and the pain it can bring.

"Interzone"

The most straightforward rock song on *Unknown Pleasures* with the lead vocal by bassist Peter Hook and a strange trill between verses.

"I Remember Nothing"

The album comes to an end with the atmosphere of Bernard Sumner's homemade synth and Stephen Morris's snare and kick drum joined by the sound of breaking glass and the bass riff just before the chopping guitar comes in with Curtis's atonal opening lines. The overall effect of the synth and sound effects and synth drums is similar to early Can and other krautrock groups as the record winds to an end slowly with a sizzling synth, which I feel is a nod to what is coming in the band's sophomore record *Closer*.

CLOSER

Joy Division's second and final album, *Closer*, is a masterpiece of Gothic-inflected post-punk. It was recorded at Pink Floyd's Britannia Row Studios from March 18 to March 30, 1980, and released two months after Curtis's suicide, on July 18, 1980. The album's tracks came from two distinct periods of songwriting. The more guitar-centered compositions ("Atrocity Exhibition," "Passover," "Colony," "A Means to an End," and "Twenty Four Hours") were written during the second half of 1979 and played live during that year. The other songs ("Isolation," "Heart and Soul," "The Eternal," and "Decades") were written during the beginning of 1980 and included the more prominent use of synthesizers.

As with their first record, *Closer* was produced by Martin Hannett. Hannett's experimental production on the album, incorporating extensive use of delays and reverbs, continues to be highly praised, though both Peter Hook and Bernard Sumner expressed dissatisfaction with how the record came out.

The album's cover was designed by Peter Saville and Martyn Atkins and featured a photograph by Bernard Pierre Wolff of the Appiani family tomb in Genoa's Monumental Cemetery of Staglieno. This image of a grave sets the funereal tone of the record; the sounds of *Closer* are cast in stark reliefs of grey, while also foreshadowing the imminent death of Ian Curtis.

Upon learning of Curtis's suicide, designer Peter Saville immediately expressed concern over the use of the image. This, combined with the dual meaning of the album's title as both something drawing nearer and the closing of a chapter, a band, and a life, serves to present the album as a final testament and a requiem to Curtis.

"Atrocity Exhibition"

The album begins with a rollicking tom-heavy beat, pugnacious and ritualistic. I think it's one of the least likely opening tracks on any album. Although Curtis's repeated intonation of "This is the way, step inside" invites us in, it is a twisted mindset, wracked by torment. Lyrically, the track seems to position the singer as a sort of carnival barker leading viewers to see the "atrocity exhibition" of the title. Maybe the "exhibition" is Curtis himself, as exemplified by a line in the first verse that refers to his epilepsy. The strangled guitar line that closes the song only seems to reiterate this pain.

"Isolation"

The track begins with an electronic drumbeat by Morris that gives the song a mechanical feel. The jittery and treble-heavy synth line is foregrounded, while Hook's bass locks in with the electronic groove. The use of various delay effects on Curtis's voice and the track in general lends a slightly psychedelic tone to a track that deals with the "isolation" of the mentally ill mind. "Isolation" is the closest thing to a pop single on this otherwise grim and foreboding album.

"Passover"

The stark drum intro and chorused Gothic guitar present "Passover" as a dirge. There is a lot of empty space on this track, allowing the reverbs to echo around the cold marble slabs of a cemetery or the interior of an isolated mind. The whole track is imbued with a feeling of hollowness and claustrophobia that is echoed by the lyrics of hopelessness and frailty, perhaps foreshadowing Curtis's own tenuous grasp on his life and reality.

"Colony"

The stuttered, jerky beat of "Colony" once again echoes the spastic torments of Curtis's epilepsy. The mood of the entire track is tense and frantic, like the twitching of a stressed muscle. Sumner's guitar is menacing, almost proto-metal, hacking away behind Curtis's plaintive lyrics that bring to mind images of war-torn Europe, the plight of refugees the world over, and connections to the dystopian visions of George Orwell and Aldous Huxley.

"A Means to an End"

The song starts off with a sinister octave bass line as the centerpiece of a strange, cold disco riff, punctuated by almost psychedelic Western guitar lines by Sumner. Curtis's ever more emphatic intonations of "I put my trust in you" give the whole track an atmosphere of paranoia. Visions of dogs and vultures eating at an abandoned house complete the scene. The track ends with a dismal slowdown of the tape, like the dying of some infernal machine, bringing Side One to an eerie close.

"Heart and Soul"

Curtis's vocals on this song are more whispered than intoned and this helps carry the tension of the track, along with Morris's tight, repetitious beat anchored around a repeated snare roll that goes off like a firecracker at the end of a four-beat loop. Above this, an eerie synth and a heavily chorused guitar float ghostlike above the song. The track feels haunted by the specter of Curtis's voice, with the lyrics of the last verse eerily foretelling his future.

"Twenty Four Hours"

This track starts at half speed before emerging into an explosive psychedelic gallop that echoes the most aggressive moments of The Doors. The song cycles back and forth between these frantic parts and the more subdued half-time sections that mirror the back-and-forth of the tormented mind. The song's lyrics encapsulate the search for meaning in a meaningless world, the loss of love and hope, and possible ways to create this meaning. The song recalls the stark realization of powerlessness in an unforgiving existence.

"The Eternal"

My personal favorite. The most slow-burning and atmospheric track of the record. Piano and icy synth oscillations float over a subdued kick and snare beat. Perhaps the most Gothic of the album's tracks, "The Eternal" never accelerates into anything approximating a rock song. Instead, it broods until it evaporates in a melancholy mist. The track's lyrics seem to describe a funeral procession where the speaker finds himself poised between emotion and dispassion. Its rich, imaginative sound canvas always makes me remember my own childhood, full of longing and mystery, never to be experienced again.

"Decades"

The album's closer rides the border between pop song and a sort of depressive klezmer with what sounds like an accordion rhythm pushing the song forward. The song then opens up with an ostinato synth line over a descending chord pattern that bears traces of a sixties-pop-writing sensibility. The lyrics once again seem to dwell on the horrors of war and the disappointments of the postwar world that Joy Division came of age in, living in a dark and depressing England in the late seventies.

Joy Division filled a particular aching void in the pantheon of late seventies British artists, being both a melancholy and powerful treatise on the human condition. Plaintive and passionate in equal measure and so desperately needed in the darkness that we found ourselves in.

BAUHAUS: UNDEAD

Bauhaus came out of the maelstrom that was punk. David J, the band's bassist, recalls his punk rock baptism. "I took my brother to see the Sex Pistols at the 100 Club in 1976. The Clash played one of their first gigs before The Pistols took the stage and it was as if the world had suddenly exploded! We decided to form our own punk band that night. A familiar story for our generation!"

Peter Murphy of Bauhaus in March 1980
Credit: Mick Mercer

His brother, Kevin Haskins, credits punk with giving him the push to pursue music. "Punk gave me the confidence to be the drummer that I wanted to be," Kevin said. "I was very fortunate to see The Clash and The Sex Pistols at the 100 Club punk festival. It was literally life-changing. The Clash came on prior to The Pistols and about twenty seconds into their first song I was captivated. It was raw, dangerous, sexy and really exciting. I thought to myself, *I can do this!*"

Sometimes where you come from is as integral to who you are as anything else. This was very much the case for Bauhaus, who all grew up in Northampton, England. Northampton is not the dark, mysterious Victorian streets of London town. It's not the cold, windswept Yorkshire moors of Emily Brontë's romantic Gothic masterpiece *Wuthering Heights*. No, it's a small grey industrial town in the middle of the country. "Northampton in the late seventies, early eighties was a very bleak, depressing, miserable place," David J said. "Everything seemed grey and rain-dampened. The sky was overcast and gloomy for months on end. It was perfect."

England in general in the late seventies was not a great place to live, but David J believed there were some advantages to being outside the capital, London. "It was good for us because of the feeling of being aesthetes in exile. We liked the idea of storming the big city, setting some fires, and then scuttling back to our dark stone."

Kevin recalled how early in their career they thought about moving to the capital to help their career but vetoed it because grey and gloomy Northampton was their muse. "After we had exhausted the Northampton workingmen's clubs and pubs, we wanted to play in the 'Big Smoke' and contemplated relocating there. However, after some consideration, we were concerned that if we were to move to London, that we would lose our sound and identity. It was probably hard living anywhere in the UK at that time, but Northampton I feel was particularly miserable and boring. The dead end feeling of living in that small market town gave us the motivation and inspiration to create and express ourselves."

These feelings of discontent were spreading like wildfire throughout the UK. Our mindset in The Cure was "us against the world." In some ways we felt like a gang, albeit a very well-dressed one. I asked David J and Kevin if they felt the same way. "Very much so," David J said. "We felt extremely alienated, especially in our hometown of Northampton, but we rather liked the feeling of being outsiders and relished opposition more than adoration. Kicking against the pricks would spark the fire of our personal revolution." Kevin agreed with his brother: "One had to grow a hard shell and stick close together in order to succeed. Especially so when we began to attain a measure of success and the British music press absolutely hated us. Their vitriol and venom was incredible. It had the opposite desired effect though, because it made us pull together even more, and sharpened our desire to kick down the doors and silence them."

Bauhaus was formed in 1978 by Daniel Ash, David J, and Kevin. The three had played in various incarnations since childhood. Bauhaus formed after the breakup of another short-lived group, The Craze. Ash tried to recruit his schoolfriend Peter Murphy. Murphy was working at a printing factory and had no experience playing music, singing, or writing lyrics, but he had the look. Initially, David J was not invited to join because Ash wanted a band he could control, but after a few weeks of rehearsing with another bassist, Ash gave in and asked David J to join. It was David J who suggested the name Bauhaus 1919, and the group played its first performance at a pub in Wellingborough on New Year's Eve 1978. The group took the typeface and the logo for the art school designed by Oskar Schlemmer. "I don't think we were scared of being arty," Kevin said. "On the contrary, three of us went to art school!"

The group initially recorded a videotaped performance to send to record labels with the hope of securing a deal. However, this approach didn't work as many labels didn't have home video equipment at the time. Instead, after only six weeks as a band, Bauhaus entered Beck Studios in Wellingborough to record a demo. The band's debut single, "Bela Lugosi's Dead," was recorded live in the studio in one take during a six-hour session. It was the first thing the band recorded together. The track clocked in at over nine minutes long and was released as the group's first single on Small Wonder Records.

The track is influenced by the band's interest in dub and reggae, experimenting with a sparse, open sound that utilizes partial barre chords as well as significant use of delay and reverb effects. Murphy's vocals don't enter until around the three-minute mark. This debut single is viewed as a forerunner of the Gothic rock scene that would emerge in the years following and is considered by many to be the first "Goth" release.

The rest of the tracks recorded in the studio that day failed to find official release with the exception of "Harry" and range from power pop to ska, illustrating a band finding its voice. "Bela Lugosi's Dead" lays the groundwork for Goth in all its myriad forms to come: the gloomy, haunted feeling of the track, Murphy's subdued vocals, the ominous bass line, and the horror imagery of the lyrics. Perhaps the track would've been relegated to just another aspect of post-punk experimentation were it not for the high camp of the lyrics and Murphy's funereal delivery.

The band shopped the acetate but were turned down as the labels felt the track was too long and uncommercial. However, according to Ian Shirley in *Dark Entries: Bauhaus and Beyond*, Peter Stennett of Small Wonder, who agreed to put it out, compared it to the classic Velvet Underground single "Sister Ray."

Fiction Records boss Chris Parry with Cure production manager Mick Kluczynski on the Orient Express
Credit: The author

Small Wonder, coincidentally, was the same label The Cure released its first single on before transferring to Fiction. As David remembers, "The Cure was one of the very few bands with whom we felt an affinity back in the early days. Because of this we sent an acetate of 'Bela Lugosi's Dead' to Chris Parry at Fiction before we approached Small Wonder. We received a letter back from Parry in which he declined the track, saying that he thought it was original but far too long."

However, "Bela Lugosi's Dead" received a positive review in *Sounds* as well as radio play on BBC 1 and John Peel's show, leading to a Peel session on January 3, 1980. After playing the single on his show, Peel was inundated with requests to play it again. Despite the success of this single, the band left Small Wonder for 4AD due to lack of touring support. On 4AD the band released two additional singles, "Dark Entries" and "Terror Couple Kill Colonel," before releasing their debut album, *In the Flat Field*, in November 1980.

In the Flat Field finds the band building on the sound of its first single, merging a glam-rock sensibility with the darker tones of the emerging post-punk music. "*In the Flat Field* was, in part, an expression of the numb-inducing boredom that permeated our existence in Northampton," Kevin explained. "It was very claustrophobic with a real feeling of no future and nowhere to go. We had all experienced low-paying, dead-end jobs, and I feel that all of this combined, fired our desire to escape the humdrum existence we found ourselves in."

The band toured the US and Canada in August 1980, playing four dates in New York, Chicago, and Toronto. Bauhaus began to outgrow the resources of 4AD and joined the roster of its parent label, Beggars Banquet. The band released the single "Kick in the Eye" as its debut on the label, followed by "The Passion of Lovers." The band's second album, *Mask*, was released in October 1981. *Mask* expanded the band's sound slightly with the addition of keyboards and acoustic guitars, and the cover featured a drawing by Ash.

For the title track the group produced a video, which borrowed heavily from German Expressionism, in a disused building in Northhampton. In July 1982 the band released the single "Spirit," which was produced by Hugh Jones. This was a departure as Bauhaus typically produced its own music. The band ended up re-recording the single later that year for its third album, *The Sky's Gone Out*. Bauhaus also scored its biggest hit that year with a cover of David

Bowie's "Ziggy Stardust." The band had chosen the song specifically to annoy those that accused the group of being Bowie plagiarists.

For what it's worth, although I have an enduring love for the perennial dark glam dub of "Bela Lugosi's Dead," I happen to love Bauhaus's stellar version of "Ziggy Stardust" much more than the original. It's vibrant, strong, and flexible in a way that the original was not. The snare drum rolls that Kevin inserts with precision are the very heart of the power I feel from the song. It's more punk and less seventies preening. The band's performance on *Top of the Pops* on October 7, 1982, captures the song's vigor. Peter Murphy prancing like a demented Rudolf Nureyev before diving into the audience comes across as wild and beautifully energetic. To me, it's everything Bowie's version could have, no, should have been. Taking no prisoners and storming the battlements. Beautiful.

Bauhaus, however, had many and varied influences. "Bowie himself was a great curator and champion of other artists," David explained, "and via him I discovered Scott Walker, Jacques Brel, Iggy Pop and the Stooges, and Lou Reed / The Velvet Underground—all of whom exerted a great influence. Also, Bowie's contemporaries such as Roxy Music, T. Rex and Mott the Hoople made a big impression. Patti Smith was a galvanizing force as well and she resonated with such literary influences like Rimbaud, Baudelaire, and Edgar Allan Poe. Also, talking of Patti Smith, her collaborator, Lenny Kaye's *Nuggets* compilation was another seminal influence on us."

"My early influences," Kevin added, "were The Beatles, The Modern Lovers, the Faces, T. Rex, Velvet Underground, The Sensational Alex Harvey Band, Roxy Music, and reggae. As a drummer, I picked up beats and fills by playing along to all of the above. It wasn't until the Joy Division and Siouxsie and the Banshees first releases that I found my strongest direct influences in Kenny Morris and Stephen Morris's drumming."

Bauhaus appeared in the horror film *The Hunger*, playing "Bela Lugosi's Dead." The final shot focused on Murphy, leading to resentment among the rest of the group. The group's fourth and final original album, *Burning from the Inside*, was marred by Murphy coming down with a severe case of pneumonia before recording. Consequently, Ash and David J spearheaded the recording of the record, even singing lead vocals on several tracks. The single from the

David J of Bauhaus at the Rock Garden in London
Credit: Mick Mercer

album, "She's in Parties," shot to number twenty-six on the charts and resulted in Bauhaus's third and final *Top of the Pops* performance. The band went on an extended international tour, before deciding to disband before two back-to-back shows at the Hammersmith Palais in London. The band played their farewell show on July 5, 1983, at the Palais, with David J ending the set with the words "rest in peace." *Burning from the Inside* was released a week after.

Both David and Kevin alluded to the intense, sometimes difficult nature of being in a band. It can be a fraught process full of ego and creation battling it out in close quarters.

"There was always a highly volatile chemistry in the band," David admitted. "Playing live was often something of an exorcism. Some of our best gigs were like blazing rows after which you feel better having vented. It was all very double-edged as that conflict added in great part to the edge that made the whole thing so exciting, but when it went too far, then it became unworkable. Having said that, Kevin and I always got on very well while we were playing with each other. Music was the first thing we really bonded over as brothers. That and a love of the *Batman* TV show!"

Kevin agreed with this assessment. "The tension that appears to exist within every band definitely fueled the creativity. That abrasiveness, that irritation that forms the pearl, was a very necessary element. Without that spark and sometimes fiery explosion, our live shows would have been rather dull. Having my brother in the band was, for the most part, not all that difficult. Most of the time we had fun and enjoyed the journey we were on."

The band's members all enjoyed significant solo careers after the initial end of Bauhaus. Murphy initially formed the short-lived group Dali's Car with Mick Karn of Japan before embarking on a successful solo career with albums like 1986's *Should the World Fail to Fall Apart* and *Love Hysteria* in 1988 and *Deep* in 1989. Ash had started Tones on Tail as a side project and Kevin joined after Bauhaus folded. They released an album and several EPs before breaking up in 1984. In 1985, Ash and David J began talking about reforming Bauhaus and went as far as arranging a rehearsal, but Murphy didn't show up. The Haskins brothers and Ash still rehearsed and ended up forming the group Love and Rockets, which experienced some success over the course of seven albums.

There have been several Bauhaus reunions since 1983, playing festival dates and multiple shows in larger cities. In 2022, the band was due to go out on their first American tour in sixteen years; unfortunately it was cancelled due to Murphy's health issues.

Bauhaus was able to tap into that mixture of strangeness and vulnerability that is at the heart of Goth. "I've heard many of our listeners recount youthful stories of feeling disenfranchised and lonely," Kevin said, "and our music provided a world for them to escape to, to feel embraced by. A secret world that didn't allow access for their parents, and provided a feeling of connection. A sense of, 'Thank god! I'm not alone after all.'"

Amen.

SEPTEMBER 1980: A NEW YORK KIND OF STORY

ONE OF MY FAVORITE BAUHAUS STORIES CAPTURES THE ALMOST ingénue quality of the young men of Bauhaus abroad for the first time in the

Kevin Haskins's passport photo in 1980
Supplied by Kevin Haskins

Big Apple. Just as many Americans fantasized about being in London between 1966 and 1976, many Brits felt the same about New York during this period, and Kevin confessed as much to me. Bauhaus arrived in New York a few short months after The Cure played its first shows there.

Bauhaus was staying at the infamous Iroquois hotel, which was not quite as salubrious back in the early eighties as it is currently. A $13 million renovation in 1997 turned it into a small luxury hotel, but back then it was run-down, a down-at-heel roach palace to be precise.

No matter, the chaps from Bauhaus didn't worry too much. "We were in New York for the first time!" Kevin said. As they were checking in, he noticed a small bar and popped his head inside to see what might be going on in there. He saw an old, worn-out crooner singing in the old, worn-out bar when suddenly in the gloom of the smoky room something caught his eye. He gasped and stared in utter disbelief at who was there. He ran back to the lobby where the others were still checking in.

"Guys, guys," he exclaimed. "You'll never believe who's in the bar!"

They stared wide-eyed with wonder and disbelief when Kevin revealed who he had just seen. Hurriedly, they finished up at the hotel desk and raced to the bar's entrance. Once inside, they squinted into the room's gloom. At the bar a familiar figure held court and they could hardly believe their eyes. It was Iggy Pop! Iggy-bloody-Pop no less!

They'd just gotten off a plane from England and had stumbled into the first bar they came across and there was David Bowie's friend, one of their idols for God's sake, sitting on a barstool just a few feet away from them.

Eventually the Bauhaus boys stopped gawking in disbelief, firmed up their courage, and tried to have a word with one of their teen idols. Surprise, surprise, they found that James Osterberg, a.k.a. Iggy Pop, was actually a pretty cool guy and enjoyed talking with these strange Brit boys from across the pond.

Peter, who was initially lurking in the back, got up his courage and moved closer to Iggy, who took notice of the slender figure now sitting beside him. Growing more animated by the minute, Peter suddenly started tickling Iggy! He was so astonished to be in Iggy's presence that he couldn't contain his emotions another moment. Iggy took it in stride, pro that he is. He'd seen it all before.

"'Hey, you're some fresh kid,'" Kevin recalled Iggy saying to Peter. "'Yeah, some fresh kid!'"

Finally, they explained to Iggy who they were and that they were staying in this little flea-bitten hotel to play their first show in the US on September 11, 1980, at Danceteria in Manhattan, which was a very hip place to play in the early eighties.

I find when I talk to other musicians from the eighties, there's almost always a connection with my own early experiences in New York City. As it turned out, Ruth Polsky, who helped The Cure book its first shows in New York City at Hurrah, was working at Danceteria as the talent booker when Kevin and Bauhaus first arrived in the US.

Ruth was one of the unsung heroes of the early eighties post-punk scene in New York City. She was responsible for bringing over so many English bands to play in America, which was hungry for the music from the UK. Sadly, she died in a traffic accident outside the Limelight night club in 1986 when she was just thirty-one years old.

Kevin told me that Iggy was so enamored with the boys from Bauhaus that he came to that Danceteria show. Iggy was at the front of the stage during the show, dancing about and daring Peter Murphy to push things further, exhorting the young singer, "C'mon, give me what you've got!" while Peter playfully pushed the mic stand toward Iggy. Afterward, Iggy invited them all out to a "really crazy S&M nightclub" he knew. Being good English boys at heart, and perhaps a little scared, they politely declined the invitation. We can thank Iggy Pop for giving Bauhaus a warm welcome to America.

SIOUXSIE AND THE BANSHEES: LIBERATION AND LAMENT
SEPTEMBER 1975

SUSAN BALLION AND STEVE BAILEY, A.K.A. SIOUXSIE SIOUX AND STEVEN Severin, met at a Roxy Music concert. They both shared an interest in glam but felt there was no new music that piqued their interest. This changed when Severin and Sioux began to follow the Sex Pistols. They and their group of friends became known as the Bromley Contingent, which also included Billy Idol pre–Generation X.

When the pair found out that a two-day festival organized by Malcolm McLaren, the 100 Club Punk Special, had an opening due to a band dropping out, they suggested themselves even though they had no band, no name, and no songs. (This was a ploy utilized by many bands, including The Cure in the early incarnation of Easy Cure. It's how we got our first gig at The Rocket in Crawley on May 6, 1977.) Siouxsie and Severin recruited Marco

Siouxsie Sioux on the cover of *Panache* in 1977
Courtesy of Mick Mercer

Pirroni, who would go on to play with Adam and the Ants, on guitar, and Sid Vicious on drums for what would be the band's first gig, consisting of a twenty-minute improvisation on the Lord's Prayer. Incidentally, Adam offered me one of the drum stools in his later version of the Ants, which I politely declined as we were going strong as The Cure by then.

The band initially intended to get together for this one-off gig but received additional invitations to perform. Siouxsie and Severin invited drummer Kenny Morris and guitarist Peter Fenton for the first incarnation of the Banshees. Morris had also attended the festival at the 100 Club and was impressed by the band's energy. After a few gigs in early 1977, Fenton was dropped from the band because he was too much of a traditional rock guitarist. He was replaced by John McKay in July, and in November the band made an appearance on Tony Wilson's show on Granada Television, *So It Goes*.

That same month the band also recorded its first Peel session for the BBC, debuting the song "Metal Postcard." By 1978, Siouxsie and the Banshees was

Siouxsie Sioux in Bournemouth in 1978—the year before The Cure played with The Banshees
Credit: Mick Mercer

filling venues and signed a deal in June with Polydor that offered them total creative control. The group released its first single, "Hong Kong Garden," soon after. With a bright xylophone hook and soaring vocals, the song reached the Top 10 in the UK. I recall the excitement of seeing them play on the television for *Revolver*, a UK music series that ran briefly in 1978 on ITV. The fact they played the track live as opposed to the normal practice of miming made it extra special in my mind.

Their debut album, *The Scream*, premiered in November 1978 with comparisons being made between the band and The Velvet Underground and Can. The record was recorded in a week in August and coproduced by Steve Lillywhite. Lillywhite was chosen for his unconventional approach to drums. He had Morris record the snare and kick first, followed by toms and cymbals later. Lillywhite also put a heavy echo on the drum tracks to give it a distinctive sound.

Lyrically, the album borrowed from the works of J. G. Ballard and William S. Burroughs. Ballard was a reference for the band because his stories often dealt with near-future suburban dystopias that resonated with their own upbringing in postwar British suburbia. The album cover was shot by Paul Wakefield and inspired by the 1968 Burt Lancaster film *The Swimmer*, based on the short story of the same name by John Cheever. The eerie cover photo of swimmers against a reverse-colored swimming pool, dark blue tiles and light blue stripes, was especially haunting and evocative to me.

John Peel generously played the record in its entirety one month prior to its official release on BBC Radio 1 without interruptions from a dubbed cassette. I listened to it on the Peel show that night and felt it heralded a big change in the punk manifesto. Later, critic Clinton Heylin argued that the addition of John McKay to Siouxsie and the Banshees, along with the formation of the bands Magazine and PIL in late 1977 and early 1978, marked the origins of post-punk in the UK.

The band released its second album *Join Hands* in September 1979. *Join Hands* took World War I as its conceptual inspiration and included references to the revolution in Iran in 1979, and other twentieth-century military conflicts around the world. Shortly after its release, the Banshees—as we had taken to referring to them—embarked on an extended tour in support of the album.

John Lydon of PIL in Los Angeles
Credit: Dina Douglass

However, after only a few dates, McKay and Morris left after an argument with the rest of the group.

The band's manager called Budgie, who had played for The Slits, and asked him to help them fulfill the rest of the tour dates. He was hired and the group invited Robert, as The Cure was the support group on the tour, to fill in for McKay.

Budgie became a permanent member of the band after the Join Hands Tour, and the group began working on its follow-up record, *Kaleidoscope*, which was released in 1980. The band also brought on guitarist John McGeoch, who at this point still played in the seminal group Magazine. The record saw the group working in new sonic directions, incorporating synthesizers, drum machines, and even sitars into their sound. The departure of Morris and McKay, and their subsequent replacement by Budgie and McGeoch, gave the band a new lease, and the resulting album was a departure from the stark, guitar-centered sound of the previous two albums.

The Banshees' fourth record, *Juju*, was released in 1981. It became one of the group's biggest successes, peaking at number seven on the UK charts. Budgie and Siouxsie became a couple on the subsequent tour and formed the experimental drum-and-voice group The Creatures. *Juju*, with the addition of McGeoch as a permanent member, saw the group returning to a more guitar-based sound. The band's fifth album, *A Kiss in the Dreamhouse*, was pyschedelic, with Severin describing it as "sexy."

John McGeoch had begun to seriously struggle with alcoholism and was hospitalized after returning from a Spanish promotional tour; he was fired shortly thereafter. The group spent 1983 working on various side projects: Budgie and Sioux recorded the debut Creatures album, while Severin worked with Robert on The Glove. Robert contributed to their sixth album, *Hyaena*, before leaving, due to the mental and physical stress of playing in two bands, in 1984.

The group went on to record five more studio albums before breaking up in 1996, having long cemented their role in the founding of UK post-punk.

In the same way that the old Irish banshee presided over the grave mounds found around the Irish countryside, wailing to announce a death in the family, Siouxsie Sioux heralded the death of the old guard and an outdated way of treating women in modern music.

The Siouxsie I first met in 1979 was the antithesis of the female singer archetype of rock music of the sixties and seventies. Previously, women were valued for their photogenic sex appeal over other attributes like singing, songwriting, or musicianship. Siouxsie was about to turn that equation on its head. She was neither demure nor eye candy. She was powerful and assertive, unconventionally beautiful, and undeniably attractive to men and women alike.

Women especially sensed that she was on their side, coming out of the heavily misogynistic ambience of the mid-seventies. She turned that particular trope on its head. Punk was the vehicle, and Siouxsie and the Banshees was there at the beginning of what would become post-punk.

AUGUST 2 & 3, 1979

Robert and I were at the YMCA on Tottenham Court Road in London for a series of concerts over four days. Joy Division, which had opened for us earlier in the year, played a wonderful set and we were excited to see in person the new Liverpool groups: Echo and the Bunnymen and The Teardrop Explodes.

It was a chance to see what all the fuss was about, and we wanted to see them play on our turf, so to speak. So we got on the train and went up to London. It was a great show. I remember Ian McCulloch and Will Sergeant as fresh-faced youngsters and, of course, Julian Cope with the Teardrops. Magnificent. A small crowd of the cognoscenti was there to appreciate them with us. I sang happily on the way home, hoping to return for the next day's event as Throbbing Gristle and Cabaret Voltaire were high on my list of bands to see.

The next day Robert was watching Throbbing Gristle and found Steve Severin in the gloom and darkness of the YMCA concert room. Robert and Steve got on straightaway. Within three weeks we were on tour with Siouxsie and her Banshees. Of course, there was also the other part of the equation that we would soon encounter: the chanteuse and dramatic persona of the Banshees, which was Siouxsie Sioux.

We were neophytes to the glamourous and sometimes riotous world of London's punk rock scene. We had heard of most of the front-runners and knew of Siouxsie and the Banshees' first album. The breakout single "Hong Kong Garden" had pierced our parochial home counties' Englishness with its happy but intense jinglejangle of xylophone. Robert told me we had been offered the opening spot on the Join Hands Tour. Within the week we were at a rehearsal room to meet with Severin before we would be introduced to Siouxsie herself.

The first thing that occurred to me was that, unlike our relatively cozy rehearsing situation at the Smiths' house—or if they couldn't let us use their extra room, the local church hall—being a band in the big city was decidedly more sleazy. The room we were first ushered into with Severin was small and cramped and had an unmistakable feeling of desperation and druggy dinginess. At the time, I mused this made Siouxsie and the Banshees tougher and more street-smart than us lads from Crawley.

Part of this desperation came from the band's early success and close association with the music business. The pressure the band was under from their label took away much of the joy of making music for its own sake. The odds of making it were long for all of us, but I had the sense that for Siouxsie and the

Banshees the stakes were higher. In the end, I think that led to the demise of the band. The music business presented many challenging pitfalls to navigate, and being in the belly of the beast destroyed many bands almost at their inception. The Sex Pistols being a very good example of that trajectory: one album and out. That's your lot, boys.

I don't think we were aware of how that particular scenario rolled out at the time, but I feel that our naivety and parochialism very likely saved us and helped us live to fight another day.

The home counties might not be the most exciting place to be in, but it was also not the bleeding edge of destruction that we often rubbed up against in the capital. The egregious frisson of punk had brought out the best and the worst in England.

Because there was the opportunity to make money and get somewhere, that meant competition was very high in Chelsea and Camden and the other hot areas of London town. We had no such imperative where we lived. We were literally the only show in town, and it was a town that was brutally uncaring about us anyway. We were ignored and left to our own devices and that gave us the space to carve out our own groove. This was the first time we had thought about the greater world and what we might have to gain or lose by trying to fit in and succeed in the heart of the old empire here in London.

Everything was harsher in London. No green trees outside the windows. Just a dark and endless maze of Victorian alleys, their black smoke walls dripping with the eternal drizzle. It's true we found excitement in the bright lights of Piccadilly Circus, Kensington High Street, and Soho's inviting alleys, but underneath it all there was the unmistakable feeling of degradation and dissolution inherent in the poisonous reality of postwar England. "Don't expect to see your dreams realized" pulsed the neon signs of Soho's sex shops and theaters.

No wonder then that we first found a home in the Marquee, a club right in the middle of all the chaos of sleazy Soho. Because we didn't live there, I suppose it was more exciting than depressing. All it took was a trip to Victoria Station just south of the Thames River and a cheap rail ticket out of town and we'd be out of the misery back home in the semi-bucolic burbs in thirty to forty-five minutes. Every time I got on the train and passed through Clapham Junction (the biggest train junction in the world I believe at one point) and peered intrusively into the projects alongside the rail line, I mentally heaved a sigh of relief that I was not trapped in that particular vortex of despair. My life might have been rough, but I had opportunities to do something with it, opportunities that had been denied a great many of my countrymen and women.

Our first meeting with all of Siouxsie and the Banshees took place at the end of August in Bournemouth at the Stateside Center. I recall little about the actual show. Bournemouth on the south coast of England was a sleepy seaside resort. I had visited as a teen as my older sister lived there with her husband and children in nearby Poole. I recall one lonely summer as a teen strolling around the empty streets of Poole and then catching a bus down to the seafront at Bournemouth to sit on the beach and talk to no one in my tie-dyed grandad shirt and pink loons.

I reasoned this first show with Siouxsie and the Banshees would be quite a different experience and I wasn't wrong. After the show we decamped to the Banshees' hotel. I don't recall if we were staying there as well, but we had been invited by our hosts to come join them after the show for a drink back at their hotel bar. Being just twenty, we understood the chance to get a drink after the

Siouxsie Sioux at The Vortex, London, 1977.
Credit: Mick Mercer

pubs shut at 10:30 p.m. was an opportunity not to be missed. We rolled up in our vehicle, a green Maxi if I remember correctly, to the hotel. It looked a little quaint, I mused, as we parked our car. Our equipment had been kindly transported around by the Banshees' road crew, which was a luxury for us, so we didn't have any items to pack away or stash safely somewhere. We were free to accept the invitation.

As we walked inside the slightly run-down English seaside hotel, we immediately noticed the bar, a small affair with a few tables and chairs. The sort of bar that your grandparents might have in their own house. Very quaint and hardly the picture of rock and roll excess, but appearances can be deceiving. We spent a few hours getting to know the band, including Sioux, and drank until the wee hours courtesy of the owner of the hotel, a small, balding, middle-aged man who probably had never experienced a gaggle of very thirsty rockers and their attendant crew. My main memory of the evening is of the owner running back and forth, contently ferrying trays full of pints and shots for all and sundry as his small seaside hotel bar saw the most action it had probably seen ever.

As with most evenings with the Banshees (and in all fairness, it has to be said The Cure as well), it eventually dissolved into nonsensical jabbering and slopping lager and gin everywhere before we made our way to our rooms. The next two days of the tour were when I really got to see the Gothic metal machine that was the Banshees.

A second warm-up show was in Aylesbury, a bustling provincial town that, judging by the procession of creative people that have emerged from this market town over the years, was the sort of place where it was okay to express yourself. Aylesbury's been home to a very English type of eccentric country bohemian—John Otway, for example. This bit of bucolic countryside was far enough away from the madness of the capital but close enough to the capital that one could feel its vibes. I supposed it was a little bit like where we lived. Crawley, it has to be said, was a tad more urban and violent. In short, Aylesbury was the kind of place where it was okay to be a weird teenager drinking scrumpy, reading strange books, and listening to even stranger bands without the threat of a good kicking by the local wankers lurking about.

At the heart of this was the dearly beloved Friars club, which has been in existence in one form or another since 1969 and is still going strong today!

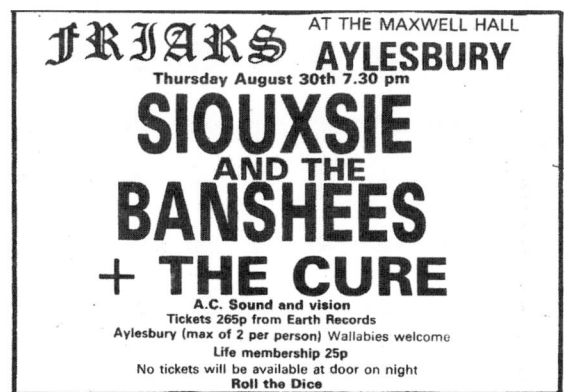

Siouxsie and the Banshees and The Cure at Maxwell Hall in Aylesbury in 1979. "25p—roughly a quarter—for lifetime membership!"
Credit: New Musical Express, September 1, 1979. Supplied by JC Moglia

Friars had a reputation for a good audience of serious music lovers, so was a popular place to play on tour. Being just the second gig of the tour, there were some hiccups with the gear and such and a segment of the audience was intent on heckling Sioux, but I thought we all pulled through pretty well. Apparently not, according to the write-up in *New Musical Express*.

As stated by an article written by Deanne Pearson that appeared shortly afterward on September 8, 1979, The Cure had "technical know-how but lacked imagination." My drumming was deemed "flamboyant," which contributed to an overall "bare, basic sound, void of excitement or real feeling." The Banshees didn't fare much better in this harsh review. "The band just didn't seem to be trying," Pearson concluded.

Saying it was a great gig, which was true, it was also the kind of place where visiting thugs from the neighboring towns, places like Hemel Hempstead, might come to cause trouble, especially once word got out that a punk band with a female lead singer was in town. Every English band in the eighties will tell you that the violent gigs were nearly always in the satellite towns of the metropolis, never in London or Manchester or such. Something about being part of the scene but not completely inside it seemed to foment trouble.

Aylesbury was the exception that proved the rule, a great gig town that could be hazardous on occasion.

I recall Sioux was forced into a situation of being both the provocateur and the provoked, which is a place where there's not a lot of room to maneuver. Such was the unfortunate dichotomy of the music industry in the late seventies and early eighties. If you were a woman in music, you not only had to be better than the men, you often had to prove you were tougher than them too. Unlike today, where the performer's gender is less of an issue, back then artists like Sioux were outliers and she had to forge her own difficult path.

I watched her from the side of the stage with Robert and Michael. We were amazed at Sioux's command of the misogynistic Neanderthals taunting her and at the same time completely in awe of her, and it must be said a little scared of her too. She was something they hadn't seen before: a woman in complete command of her environment, and they were a little perplexed to say the least. Of course it was much more primal than that. The skinheads crowded the front of the stage and tried to provoke the singer by grabbing her and staring up her skirt. She responded by stomping on their fingers and whipping the mic cord in their faces. Mostly this revealed the skinheads at the front to be nothing more than prepubescent schoolboys who slunk away when confronted, especially when Mick Murphy, the head of the Banshees' security who bore a curious resemblance to Henry the Eighth, stepped purposefully out of the darkness of the wings and poked a baseball bat their way.

We of course had never seen anything like this, and it was with a mixture of awe and a frisson of fear that we watched these proceedings. Gradually the audience settled into a musical truce of sorts and the show went on. I never forgot what I saw on that tour and at that show in particular, where Sioux as the Valkyrie of a new day's royalty commanded her audience and finally made the idiots behave. It was quite something to witness. As kids from the sticks, we were suitably impressed.

The Banshees as a band had a sort of monochromatic power that mostly came from Kenny Morris's drums and John McKay's guitar underpinned by Steven Severin's bass pulse. It helped that the drums were big and black as most of the instruments were. No sunburst hippie instruments for the Banshees!

After the show, which had been good and hectic in equal measure, we sat in the dressing room area backstage, contemplating the slightly scary thought that moving forward we would have to embrace a hard-edged approach in our own presentations. Although Crawley had toughened us up a little and we had already experienced some of the shaven-headed brethren on the London pub circuit, this was a whole new area of impossible for us to navigate. We definitely weren't in Kansas anymore!

The next show, the first proper show of the tour, was in Belfast. We had a few days' break after the unsteady warm-up at Friars, and we travelled over to Belfast on the ferry to Northern Ireland for our first gig outside mainland Britain. This was during the time of the Troubles between the Catholics and Protestants, and evidence of that struggle was all around in the bombed-out pub opposite our hotel and the heavily fortified city center patrolled by the British Army. For some reason that was never explained to us, our gear was held up at the port and we had nothing with which to play for the youth of Belfast.

Chris Parry, our sometime manager, had made a quick call to Terri Hooley, the owner of Good Vibrations records store that had a label of the same name. Terri was the promoter and most prominent face of the Belfast punk scene and had put many Northern Irish bands—most famously The Undertones—into the national spotlight.

Terri put the call out and The Outcasts, a band on his label, came to our rescue by providing us their backline for the night. Thus, we were able to play the Ulster Hall gig to at least a few people. As the gear was arriving quite late in the day, the decision had been made that the Banshees should go on first in order to let the audience get the last bus home afterward if they wanted. So our first official show on the Join Hands Tour was to a few hardy stragglers in the Victorian grandeur of the Ulster Hall, built a hundred years before my birth in 1859.

Despite the minimal audience who braved a late-night walk home to see this new band, the show was a small success. Afterward, we adjourned to the bar of the Europa Hotel, which has the distinction of being the most bombed hotel in all of Europe, for a few beers. There, we were treated to Terri Hooley's famous glass-eye trick, when it's popped into a glass of beer. We shrieked in horror and had a few more drinks. The rest is a muzzy blur . . .

The next date on the tour was in Aberdeen, which meant a journey back across the sea to Scotland. We all assembled in the lobby and drove to the ferry port with hangovers and delicate stomachs being tested on the choppy waves of the Irish Sea.

We rolled into Aberdeen late afternoon to be greeted by sharpshooters on the roof of our hotel. The then prime minister Margaret Thatcher and her cabinet were in attendance, hence the tightened security. A sense of foreboding crept over our party, especially me, who was literally spotted by the little red dots of the sharpshooters' rifles while I was having a pee in the car park.

I don't recall much about the first part of that show except that things changed rapidly when we got offstage after our set. There had been some weird tension backstage before we went on and during the afternoon sound check. In fact, I remember only Sioux and Severin were there for that. That seemed strange to me, but being all of twenty years old and having never been on a big nationwide tour, we were pretty oblivious to the way things were supposed to work.

"John and Kenny did a runner," was how one of the crew explained the situation to me.

It seemed that guitarist John McKay and drummer Kenny Morris had both just disappeared after an in-store appearance at a local record store to promote their new album. It wasn't until later that we found out they had caught a train to London and left their tour passes pinned to their pillows in their hotel rooms.

Back in Aberdeen's Capitol Theatre, the crowd was getting restless. We had been offstage for about thirty minutes and there was no sign of the Banshees coming onstage. The more-seasoned concertgoers in attendance were alert to the fact that nobody had moved The Cure's gear out of the way in preparation for Siouxsie and the Banshees. What was happening?

The Banshees' tour manager, Dave Woods, came to pay us a visit in our dressing room. "The crowd's getting ugly," he informed us. "You chaps better get back on and play something."

Stunned by this development, we began to prepare for a second set when Sioux and Severin walked onstage, went right up to the mic, and told the confused crowd what had happened.

"John and Kenny have just disappeared, so we can't do the show we want to do for you, but The Cure will play again," Severin said.

"Two art school students fucked off out of it. You have my blessings to beat the shit out of them!" Sioux said, somewhat sarcastically.

At this point I, Robert, and Michael sauntered back onstage and stood ready behind our instruments. We started to play some songs that we hadn't already played, including the beginning of what was to be our new album *Seventeen Seconds*. Eventually Sioux and Severin returned to the stage and joined us. Severin turned to us and said, "We going to do 'The Lord's Prayer,'" which was the song that they played at their first gig ever in 100 Club with Sid Vicious on drums no less. Michael later told me that the only instruction he was given was Severin telling him, "It's in E." Michael thought that must be the key of the song, but that wasn't quite it. Severin meant it's just an E note!

We went on for what seemed like an eternity, improvising what we didn't know. Improvisation has always been The Cure's strong suit, born of many years of practicing in Robert's parents' house while we honed our craft. We knew how to jam, man!

The restless crowd became less restless after they finally got to hear some old stuff by Siouxsie and the Banshees, new stuff by The Cure, and were treated to the spectacle of the curious hybrid of both—the one and only time we played together like that.

It was a somewhat chastened Sioux and Severin that met with us back at the hotel after the show. We had been through an emotional wringer for the last few hours, not really sure of what was going to happen. It was our first big tour, and faced with the prospect of going home after just four shows, we felt terrible.

The night wore on as we commiserated with the two remaining members of Siouxsie and the Banshees. All these years later I still don't understand what would make John and Kenny leave after the tour got off to such a promising start. Disagreements between band members is a mysterious area sometimes. Sometimes the slightest things can lead to bad arguments, and other times serious confrontations completely blow over. You can never know from the outside looking in what might be going on with a band's dynamics and how things will all turn out. It's such a high-stakes occupation and subject to so many slings and arrows of outrageous fortune that even if you talk to all the parties involved, you never really find out the truth.

That's the magic and the mayhem all in one package. Just as you can't construct the best band simply by getting the best musicians and singers together. Once you've got the right chemistry, you can't really mess with it because that's what makes the band tick. We spent a long night together talking things over with plenty of drink to keep the conversation flowing until everything turned into a blur and eventually sleep came. As I recall, Robert and Severin were deep in conversation that evening, and it turned out that Robert had offered his services as a fill-in guitarist for the departed John McKay. Obviously, this had serious implications for both bands, but it didn't solve the problem as to who would replace Morris on drums. The next day we were back home with no real idea what was going to happen with the tour.

A few days had passed when we heard from the Banshees' manager, Dave Woods. He informed us they had hired Budgie as the new drummer and were busy auditioning new guitarists to replace McKay. Curiously, they were holding these auditions in the same rehearsal studio The Cure used to rehearse in London. Now that we were a professional band, we needed a place in London to practice and keep our gear.

It was a dark warehouse-type affair next to the women's prison. We found ourselves there rehearsing our set in the event that the tour started up again so we would be prepared. Since we were already there, we went along to the auditions and sat at the back with scorecards. After each candidate auditioned, we would hold up one of the cards—just like in the Eurovision Song Contest—to indicate what we thought of the performance. At the end of this process, Robert was clearly better than any of the candidates who'd auditioned. As a gesture of goodwill toward the Banshees, Robert agreed to play two sets each night—one with The Cure and another with the Banshees.

That was all well and good for the Banshees, but there were unintended consequences for the rest of The Cure, meaning me and Michael. Since the Banshees were headlining and were expected to sound check, that meant for the rest of the tour Robert would travel with the Banshees and Michael and I would follow along behind in the green Maxi. I couldn't help but wonder if this was an ominous indication of what the future might hold.

At the time, it didn't occur to me that Robert might join Siouxsie and the Banshees as a full-time member of the band. I always felt that Robert would want to have his own band and that was The Cure, but I don't think Michael shared in that certainty and his relationship with Robert was never the same.

Two nights stand out in my mind from the rest of the Join Hands Tour. The first was the show at the Odeon Theatre in Chelmsford on October 11, 1979.

I was backstage after the show when I heard a weird sound like a scrabbling of hands and feet against the wall of the dressing room. The sound came again, stronger this time, at the window, which was about shoulder height. It was late and we had no idea what was going on out there because we couldn't really see. It was also miserably cold outside. Eventually one of us mustered the courage to go investigate and found a very small and very distressed teenage girl outside trying to climb through the backstage window!

We pulled her in and she breathlessly told us her story. She had no money to see the show and desperately wanted to talk to Sioux. Although she was clearly in a great deal of anguish, we let her stay. Someone found her a pass, and after the show she did indeed get to speak with her. Sioux talked earnestly with the young woman, and I believe helped her see her own life and potential differently. That was the night I saw the best side of Sioux. She had a great deal of fame and influence, but that night she used what celebrity she had in the service of another young woman who sorely needed it. If she hadn't spoken to Sioux that night, I shudder to think what might have become of her.

The other night I recall from the final leg of the Join Hands Tour occurred a few days earlier but remains crystal clear in my memory—or at least parts of it do. It's also a signpost of things to come in my own life, though I couldn't have known that then. We played at the City Hall in Hull. The venue was a large edifice in the Baroque Revival style. It had been built in the first few years of the twentieth century as a concert hall. During World War II it had been badly damaged. Hull sits on the east coast of Britain and was exposed to Hitler's blitzkrieg bombing campaign. The structure was finally repaired and restored to its former glory in 1951.

It seemed like a suitable place for the Banshees to play its World War I–influenced album *Join Hands*. To be honest, I don't recall much about the concert, but it's what transpired afterward that sticks in my mind for reasons that did not become apparent to me until many years later.

OCTOBER 8, 1979: HULL BY THE RIVER HUMBER

Damp. That was my first sensation while coming to. This was immediately followed by a strange sharp feeling across the palms of my hands. I didn't want to move, yet I felt remarkably calm even though I wasn't quite sure yet where I was or how I got there. I tried an exploratory maneuver and moved a finger out into the air, where I felt a wet sensation. Was it water, perhaps?

Yes, that was it. Water! My vision came back into focus and I could see that I was lying on my back, staring upwards at the moon. It was a small crescent moon obscured by clouds scudding across the sky. It was obviously nighttime and I was surrounded by long grey stalks with slightly bulbous heads swaying rhythmically in the wind. It was starting to feel cold, a damp penetrating cold, and I became aware of more pain in my hand. I propped myself up out of the wetness to get a better view of my surroundings, and my hands squelched into something soft and yielding. Mud? Where the bloody hell was I?

I stretched my legs out and cautiously tried to stand up amongst what I could now see were bulrushes. I almost immediately slipped and was thrown down among the bulrushes again. As I continued to slide I could see where I was. I was at the edge of a river, the dank, muddy, disintegrating banks of a river. The River Humber, to be precise. How did I get down here, I wondered.

I remembered a door. I remembered running down a corridor. I remembered lights and laughter and a tussle of hands and legs and feet followed by more laughter. It was all a bit blurry, but I could clearly make out a door. I was running to the door but it was locked. I was pushing on it with all my might when it suddenly gave way and I was flying out into the darkness and the chill night air.

I ran like a fox being pursued by hounds hunting me, the spittle flying from the corners of my mouth as I pounded the ground harder and harder with my feet, faster and faster to escape someone behind me. Then, suddenly, the ground dropped away and I was tumbling down a steep hill over and over and hitting something that knocked the wind out of me. Still I continued to fall. I flew past long stalks of what I suddenly realized were bulrushes that I desperately clutched at in an attempt to stop my fall. The rushes ran through my hands, but they were sharp and stung my flesh, until I finally came to a stop and the darkness settled around me again.

I don't know how long I lay there unconscious. When I came to it was quiet—not like the last time I remembered. As I retrieved myself from the river's edge, I remembered more. Robert and Severin drunk and howling as they ran after me down into the bowels of the hotel. It felt light and fun. Just stupid drunk stuff. At some point, as it started getting darker, I could see my hands start to swing. What had I done? And to whom?

I don't recall Sioux or Budgie there, down in the bottom of the hotel. I felt invincible in that drunk kind of way, but also there was something else. Maybe, just maybe, I was mad at Robert for spending so much time away from us, away from our band, away from The Cure. Primitive, instinctual strains of something like jealousy flooded my drunken mind, and now I had nothing but my own shame to show for it.

I dragged my battered body and burning hands back to the hotel. The dim glow of dawn was coming, and I could see the eerie fog coming off the water. I made it back to my room to tend to the rope burns on my hands, wash the dirt off my body, and fall into my bed to sleep for a few more hours before the trip to the next town and then the next town and then the next one after that. This was my pattern for the next ten years. Never dealing with my problems, only occasionally lashing out and then running away.

The new Humber suspension bridge, across the Humber estuary, by which our hotel was positioned, was not yet open, but the cables had just been spun for the bridge, ready to attach to the deck and make it the longest-span bridge in the world. It was a marvel of modern engineering. I, on the other hand, was busy burning my bridges.

In Daniel Defoe's novel *Robinson Crusoe*, the protagonist sets sail from Hull via the Humber estuary and ends up shipwrecked on his *island of despair*, which eventually he escapes—however, it would be some years before I was able to leave mine.

In later years, I recall two more times when I bumped into the Banshees. I had become friends with Budgie on the Join Hands Tour. All drummers are friends by virtue of their shared experiences. We had not kept up with our friendship as we had both been very busy during the first post-punk era. But we met again on two other occasions, bookends to a shared life.

The first was during the making of *Pornography* in the winter and spring of 1982. We were at RAK Studios in St. Johns Wood. The area was famous for Lord's Cricket Ground, and it was where my son would be born a few years later. Meanwhile, the Banshees were at Workhouse Studio across town on the Old Kent Road in another part of London that was famous for pie and mash—a local gastronomical delicacy, if you can call it that.

After work one night the Banshees came to visit us and discovered that our sessions at RAK were not all cricket, as they say. Budgie was somewhat concerned to see the state we were in. The work was getting done, but as a group we were in a bad way. I think what he was witnessing was the end of that version of The Cure that made those three Gothic albums. Everything changed after that—and not just because I changed instruments. It was never the same band again. Never.

Budgie and I would not cross paths for another thirteen years. In April 1995, the members of Siouxsie and the Banshees were in Los Angeles to play their last album, *The Rapture*. The last tour before the Banshees disbanded after twenty years of working together. I now lived in Los Angeles and was a changed and different man. I had left The Cure six years before and was several years sober and in recovery. I went to see the Banshees play on April 14 and afterward we decamped to a club down the street to chat and reconnect. I don't

Siouxsie and the Banshees in LA in 1984. L-R: Steven Severin, John Valentine Carruthers, Siouxsie Sioux, and Budgie
Credit: Dina Douglass

recall where we were, I was just happy to see my old friend Budgie and catch up with everything.

It was the antithesis of the old nights together. I was clean and sober and had even learned how to drive. Budgie was a new driver too as I soon found out. More synchronicity. We had a warm and joyous conversation, but it would take almost another quarter of a century for us to connect again in 2019.

My friend Joe Wong told me that he was meeting Budgie to have breakfast one day and then interview him for his podcast, *The Trap Set*. I turned up at the breakfast. The next stage of our relationship started anew, and it hasn't stopped since. Across the years and through all the tears, we both emerged as older men and, hopefully, a little wiser too. Sometimes you have to go the whole of your life to find the connections that you were meant to make.

"PHIL SPECTOR IN HELL": THE COLD PSYCHEDELIA OF THE CURE

I HAVE KNOWN ROBERT SMITH SINCE WE WERE BOTH FIVE YEARS OLD and attending elementary school together. At age eleven we both transferred to Notre Dame Middle School, where we met Michael Dempsey. The Cure began as schoolfriends in Crawley, England.

Our middle school was perhaps a little radical for the times in that they were open to the students expressing themselves through art and music ideas. For instance, I was allowed to hold an impromptu lunchtime "disco" at which I occasionally sneaked in such ungodly LPs as the first Black Sabbath record. More importantly, school officials allowed us to use the music room at lunchtime in inclement weather and that's where it all started for the three imaginary boys—the music room of our middle school is where the group that would become The Cure began to take shape.

We first played live together at an end-of-year show in 1973 as The Obelisk. This "band" consisted of me on percussion and Robert and Michael on guitar. Marc Ceccagno was our lead guitarist and Alan Hill our bassist. The Obelisk wasn't really a group in the formal sense but the genesis of our musical journey. We spent the next couple of years after that "show" learning how to play properly.

In January 1976 we formed a five-piece group called Malice that included me, Robert, Michael, and Porl Thompson. We finished up our quintet with Martin Creasy, a local journalist, on vocals. By this time Ceccagno had formed his own band, Amulet, a jazz-rock group that was much more his style. Malice played some gigs in December 1976, including the infamous and terrible St. Wilfrid's show on December 20, 1976, during which Martin played his one and only gig with us. He departed in January 1977, and we changed our name to Easy Cure. The show at St. Wilfrid's was such a fiasco that a name change seemed like a good idea, and the name was taken from some lyrics I had written. Despite all the usual ups and downs, we had the bit between our teeth. We were becoming a *real* band.

We were further encouraged by the emergence of punk rock, and in May 1977 we won a talent competition advertised on the back of *Melody Maker*. As a result, we signed a contract with the German label Hansa Records. In September 1977 the group's then vocalist Peter O'Toole left to live on a kibbutz in Israel. We auditioned several other vocalists before Robert assumed vocal duties—a decision that changed all our lives forever.

Now we were a four-piece of me, Robert, Michael, and Pearl (né Porl). We recorded several demos at S.A.V. Studios in London between October and November of 1977, none of which were ever released by Hansa. Our contract with Hansa eventually dissolved after the label refused to release any of our own songs, suggesting cover songs instead. That wasn't going to happen.

We played our last show under the name Easy Cure on April 22, 1978, before Pearl left as he wasn't feeling the new stuff we were starting to write. He was going off to art school anyway. To mark the change, we dropped the Easy and The Cure was finally birthed.

Musically, we had two main rivers (and many tributaries) at our core: the two p's—punk and psychedelia. More importantly, we had a different outlook on the world we found ourselves in at the end of the seventies, a world of industrial strife and despondency as England hurtled headlong into a very bleak era. Dismal outcomes were expected for most people we knew. Of course, in that atmosphere you are set free in another way. Given the facts of our meager experience, we assumed it didn't really make a tremendous amount of difference if we followed a more traditional route in our adult lives—go off to college, then find a career—or try to find a different way. There were, as The Clash sang, not many career opportunities available to us as teens in Thatcher's Britain. So we chose the other way, and I have never once regretted it.

The impetus to do something, anything, to get out of this stagnating place came from punk; but the other part, the more poetic part, the thing that filled us with yearning, came from psychedelic music and books of poetry. We always had our heads in the clouds and noses in books. We wanted to express the things we felt in this solemn world of desolate despair in much the same way that Dylan Thomas had expressed his outlook in poems like "The force that through the green fuse drives the flower." We weren't dumb. Punk had liberated our voices, and to us Dylan Thomas was as punk as Joe Strummer. We took the elements that we liked from artists that came before us, the melancholy and the strange, the romantic and the profane, and used them to create something new and different.

We made a demo tape as The Cure that we handed out to a dozen major labels. The tape found its way to Chris Parry, an A&R man at Polydor who

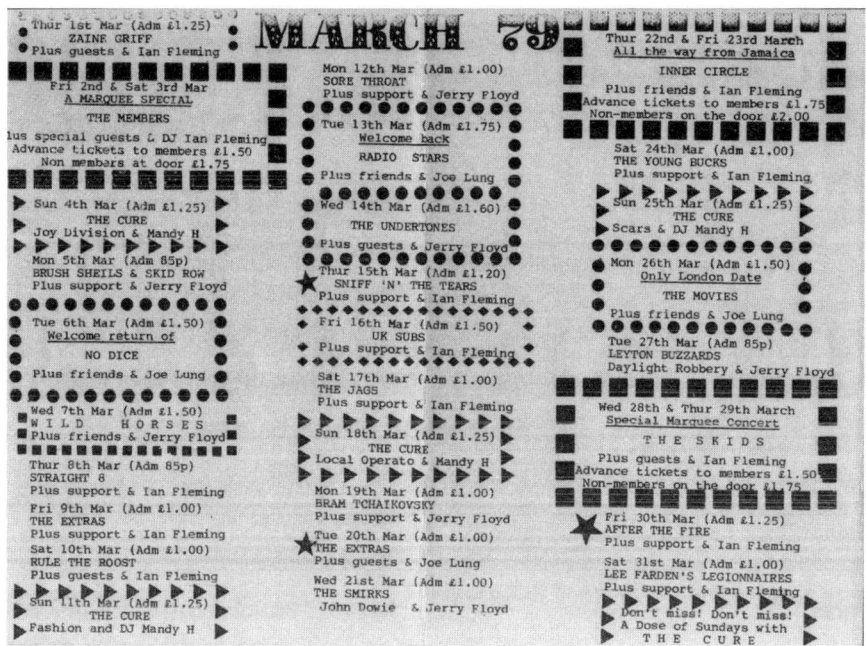

Flyer for The Marquee in March 1979
Supplied by the author

signed us to his newly formed label Fiction. Fiction released our debut single "Killing an Arab" backed with "10:15 Saturday Night" in December 1978. The single, inspired by the novel *The Stranger* by Albert Camus, attracted both acclaim for its fresh sound and controversy for its wrongly perceived racist connotations, which we fervently denied. We were existentialists, not racists.

We released our first album, *Three Imaginary Boys*, in May 1979. The record was engineered by Mike Hedges, and due to our inexperience in the studio, Parry and Hedges took control over the sonic direction. Parry also chose the songs and the cover art.

In the very beginning we weren't any good at crafting anything longer or more complex than a three-minute bash or a rock and roll pop song. *Three Imaginary Boys* started the whole process, and one can surmise from the wacky album cover that we had little say in our presentation as a new untested band.

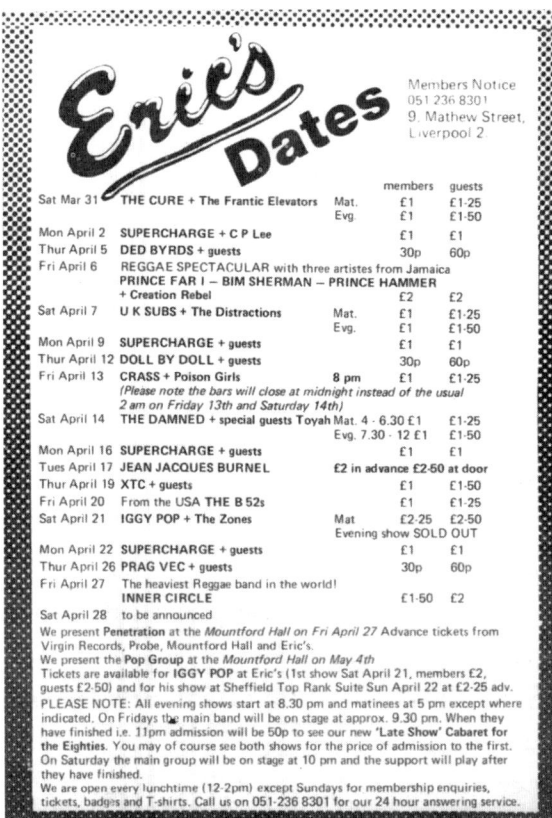

Flyer for shows at Eric's in Liverpool in March and April 1979

Supplied by the author

That record didn't really convey the angst that was to come, but there were hints of a future foretold.

The title track came from a weird dream I had full of shadows and statues and the dark of night, all the emphatic imagery we were to employ on later works. I have said before that I consider us one of the fertile fields that Goth arose from. It was actually a process that we initiated with ourselves and used to carve out the template for our further adventures in this realm. If you think I'm overstating that one track's importance, consider the fact that The Cure continues to play it, including in 2019 at the thirtieth anniversary of *Disintegration*, which is its own genre but also a grander more royal version of Goth. The force that through the green fuse still drives the flower.

From this point on, however, things changed rather dramatically. We were beginning to write different kinds of songs that were thoughtful, somber, and spare. We felt these songs accurately reflected the world we inhabited and our place in it. We realized if we were ever going to really get across what we wanted to say, we couldn't let record labels make creative decisions for us. We would need to take hold of the reins ourselves. It was the start of a darker path for us.

By the time we had finished promoting the first album and joined Siouxsie and the Banshees on the Join Hands Tour, we were ready to explore new dimensions. Well, at least Robert and I were. Michael was not as keen on the new songs, even though we had started to play an early version of "Play for Today," and so fell out with Robert about the different direction we were going, which was starker and more minimal. This suited me just fine as the bleak soundscape reflected my own personal feeling. I identified with the music more and contributed lyrics for "Play for Today" as I felt totally in tune with this new direction we were taking.

It can be argued that The Cure is both the progenitor and the antithesis of Goth. Both are valid arguments. As Hamlet said, "There's the rub!" On one hand, it's undeniable that spiky black hair, heavy makeup, and dark clothing combined with sonorous, doom-ladened songs are the calling cards of Goth. However, The Cure also famously cuddled polar bears and cats. Is The Cure the Schrödinger's cat of Goth?

I'm certain, however, of one thing. The roots of The Cure's Gothic résumé come in the shape of three albums: *Seventeen Seconds*, *Faith*, and

Pornography. I was deeply involved in the making of all three albums and looking over them forty years later, these records form the story of The Cure's darker inclinations.

Goth historian Dr. Tracy Fahey says, "Gothic is a mode that responds to *crisis*." I would say that the time those three albums were made, when we were in our early twenties, was definitely a time of crisis for us—personally, emotionally, and economically. The UK had been going through a time of deep recession from the early seventies onwards. High inflation and high unemployment meant that for most young people leaving high school the outlook was pretty bleak. When I look at those three albums, I see a very clear route brought about by our shared childhood and teens. The Cure needed a way out of the situation that we found ourselves in, but first we had to undergo a quest to fully understand who we were and where we came from.

The first of the three albums, *Seventeen Seconds*, is a kind of smudged sadness. Next came *Faith*, which is both questioning and challenging. Lastly, *Pornography* is a declaration of anger and melancholy and a surprise glimmer of hope. Three steps to heaven or hell.

To me, they are like a Francis Bacon triptych painting in that although they are connected by themes of belief (and its opposite nihilism), they do not form a straightforward narrative. They are freeze-frames of our lives. Stories glimpsed in their defining moments. The dictionary definition of triptych is "a picture or relief carving on three panels, typically hinged together side by side and used as an altarpiece." Looking back now, it's obvious to me that what we were doing with these three albums was constructing our own altarpiece. It was something we had to do.

Robert and I were both brought up as Catholics, and I believe that is a very important key to understanding the shadowy side of The Cure. Catholicism is, at its heart, a very intense religion full of dark theatrical symbolism and guilt. Robert's parents were devout Catholics. My mother was a Catholic convert and converts are known to be extra zealous. From the time I was seven years old until I was fourteen I was an altar boy, serving mass three to four times a week. I spent as much time at the church as I did at home. When I was thirteen, I was going to pre-seminary training every week at the rectory to see if I might be suitable priest material. It turns out that I was not, but this wasn't so obvious to me when I was younger and soaking up the teachings of the church like a sponge.

At fourteen, all the normal teenage trials and tribulations were arriving at my door full force with an extra dollop of guilt ladled on top, courtesy of the Vatican. I had started to realize that the religion we had been brought up in was mostly about control and not about spirituality or even love. For many aspects of human sexuality and other human behaviors, the church had a strict set of rules and demanded that "good Catholics" follow the edicts that were relayed to us by male priests who were, of course, all bachelors. The point where I personally parted company with the church was over the idea of "papal infallibility." Basically, church dogma says that the pope as the descendant of Saint Peter cannot possibly make an error on doctrine. That seemed suspicious to me—now and then.

Something needed to change, and it did. I discovered girls, music, and drinking at about the same time. I didn't dive headfirst into sex and drugs and rock and roll, but they were looming in my future. Fast-forward a few years to when we went on tour with our first album. We returned late in 1979 having played well over a hundred shows, toured with Siouxsie and the Banshees, and changed our band from a three-piece to a four-piece. The changes I went through as a person were even more dramatic.

Touring helped us see more of the world outside where we lived, and it didn't really look like the world we had learned about in the church. That's not to say that we were as sheltered from the world as some religions insist, but our minds had been forced into a kind of straitjacket that we had to shed to actualize as adults. Our first big trip outside our limited environment convinced me that other people enjoyed a much different approach to things like love, romantic relationships, and humanity in general. Thanks to the church, my information was muddled and distorted. It was all about things being forbidden, that sex was somehow wrong and would bring you untold calamity rather than accepting normal desires as something inherently human that we all experience. When we returned to suburban England, we became even more aware of our "outsiders" status. First as Catholics, second as explorers who had gotten a taste of what the world outside Crawley looked like.

Flyer for The Cure in Ghent, 1979. "I'll be home for Christmas and we just made it!"
Supplied by the author

With this in mind, I can look at *Seventeen Seconds* and say that this was the first album where we took the feelings and fears we had relating to our Catholic upbringing and specifically put them into the lyrics. To me, the songs are about guilt and longing and the emotional distress brought on by that guilt. This is where you can find the roots of The Cure's angst, what we were about to become famous for.

There is, however, another observation I've had since that time that has become more apparent to me as the years drag on. For all the similarities in our outlook, Robert's homelife was completely unlike mine in several ways. His father was a successful businessman. Mine was not. His house was in the posh area of town. Mine was not. Overall, his homelife was much happier and his family more involved with each other, whereas mine were not. My experience of life was disjointed and glum at best. So where did Robert's angst come from?

The conclusion I reached might be thought of as self-serving, but I can't shake it. Artists of every medium usually take an informed reflection of life around them as material. Grist for the mill. With The Cure, we spent most of our time together. I have to believe that the combination of our lives was what we drew from to create. It's a theory that makes sense to me and I can explain it no other way. I don't mean to suggest I was a muse or something of the sort. Mary, his girlfriend and then wife, was always that for Robert.

Rather, it was what we talked about and what was going on in our shared experience of the world that became the fuel for our art. My life was pretty damn bleak, which I'm sure Robert was aware of. It was very natural for us to feed off each other's lives. I think that a certain unity of thought and experience created these records. More than we all care to admit or reveal. Time both exposes and distorts the truth of our memories.

Seventeen Seconds has three instrumental or quasi-instrumental tracks: "A Reflection," "Three," and "The Final Sound," which appear to me now as slightly precocious attempts to be artful. The album starts with one, "A Reflection." However, it's when I listen to songs like "Secrets" weaving in amongst the melancholy bass line that I hear the real sound of The Cure emerging from the effects of our Catholic guilt. Robert described "Secrets" in *Cure News* #6 as "hopelessly wishing to have the courage to seize missed opportunities." (*Cure News* was The Cure's official newsletter published by the International Information Service from 1986 to 2000.) To me, that's a central tenet

Listing for shows at The Marquee for March 1980
Supplied by JC Moglia

of Catholic thinking: because desires are forbidden, do not indulge your emotional instincts. Naturally, we were opposed to that.

On "Play for Today," for the first time words I had written for a song by The Cure came from my direct experience about how I felt abused by duplicitousness in relationships. Suddenly, not everybody had an honest agenda, I realized. To me, it was a revelation that I could put my feelings in a song in such a precise fashion. My attempts before were more abstract or flowery like "Fire in Cairo." These were not.

"In Your House" best exemplifies the overall effect of *Seventeen Seconds* for me. Its metronomic beat locked together with the arpeggiating guitar line produces a hypnotic, almost swooning sensation. But it's the words that make "In Your House" so essential to me. The lyrics were about being at my then girlfriend's house late at night. The feelings I felt being there. Both guilt and desire. Guilt because I knew I was probably leaving her. The band had changed things so radically in my life and this relationship no longer worked for me. A selfish desire also to keep things going the same way. To have her love when I wanted it. I was "pretending to swim" in two worlds at the same time.

Her father was a dark, formidable figure. He kept a multitude of mechanical clocks in the house, which he would wind up late at night with little keys on returning from his nights out drinking at the pub. His Sisyphean struggle to try and get all the clocks to chime the hour at exactly the same time both fascinated and disturbed me. When he had a few drinks, he would interrogate me, eyeing me suspiciously, quizzing my intentions with his daughter. "If anything happens to her, I'll crucify you," he said to me on more than one occasion. That felt like a very Catholic response.

Later, after I had left and everyone had gone to bed, including her father, I would secretly return to my girlfriend's house and meet her in her room alone. I kept returning to her even though I knew our relationship would end soon. I felt guilt at not being a good and honest person to her. This story still feels poignant to me now, forty years on, and brings back memories of that house full of clocks. The song is full of Gothic themes: darkly romantic but unresolved love (*Wuthering Heights*), a lurking monster (*Frankenstein*). Feeling unfulfilled and unsatisfied no matter which course I chose.

I know this story will surprise many readers who think of Robert as the sole lyricist for The Cure, but that simply wasn't the case. It's not so much a secret as a reclaiming of my past. Over the decades, assumptions have been made about the band's creative process, and after I wrote *Cured* I thought it was time to speak up. It's about repossessing my art. All of us in recovery are accustomed to denying our truths because of crippling self-loathing and feelings of unworthiness. Getting clean and sober means we don't have to hide behind that fear anymore. I believe that the creative process is often the sum of many psychic streams converging and reinforcing each other. This was especially true in The Cure during the period we created our Goth trilogy as we were in each other's pockets for long periods of time. With our lives so intimately entwined, we were naturally a self-reflecting feedback loop. When something happened to one of us, it was felt by all of us.

For "A Forest," perhaps the most famous track from *Seventeen Seconds*, I played a type of motorik beat that rocks as much as it stays in place, something that I learned listening to Can's drummer Jaki Liebezeit. It was a new way of drumming for me, and its mesmerizing power is something I'm most proud of. I think we created a whole different atmosphere and sound with that beat alone.

"A Forest" showcases the deeper, darker feeling that was taking hold in our music after our first album. I remember Robert playing the idea he had for the track at his house at the end of a rehearsal one day. I loved it immediately. Everything fit perfectly from the bass to the synth to the guitar line. I thought of the title right there at rehearsal: "A Forest." Such a primeval title with a cool psychedelic vibe just felt *right*. Lyrically, it evokes that helpless feeling one would have being lost anywhere, but especially in a dark, foreboding forest. I extrapolate that as an acceptance of vulnerability that permeates the whole atmosphere of *Seventeen Seconds*, which was a 180-degree turn away from the macho lyrics of rock bands in the seventies. This, to me, is what changed the conversation about The Cure.

"M" starts with a lone strummed guitar segueing into a backwards electronic drum hit. My favorite part is the end, with the chiming motif of Robert's guitar and the evocative Synare drum synth that sounded somehow like the sea.

It's one of the few songs Robert wrote that mentions his wife in such a straightforward way.

"At Night" was inspired by an existential short story of the same name by Franz Kafka that Robert had become enamored with. You might think my drums are programmed, but listen carefully, and in the first part of the song the beat turns around and then back again, which is a real good trick, but I have no idea how it happened. By the time I realized it we didn't have the time or money to record my part again, so it stayed. A happy accident. There are more than a few of those in The Cure's records.

The album ends with the title track and features one of the most recognizable guitar and bass intros in The Cure's catalog. I especially liked playing it live when it lifts up into the full beat just before the vocals—magical! The bass is very sexy and fluid here. Naturally, any album that ends with the drumbeat sounds good to me. I think it gives the album a finality. Lyrically, Robert told *Cure News* #6 in 1989 that it was about "an arbitrary measure of time—one that seemed to be suddenly everywhere once the song was written." Perhaps he was alluding to the various explanations people came up with for the enigmatic title, but to this day I have no concrete idea what it refers to.

The Cure's lyrics have always been on the more mysterious side without being deliberately obtuse, as we were accused of being from time to time. I have always felt that old maxim "Show don't tell" is a better and more artful way to communicate what I wanted to get across. Much of my life was surrounded by grim reality, so music and words have always been a necessary relief from that. A different, more poetic way to make sense of the world.

With *Seventeen Seconds* everything changed for us—and not just the music. We had a whole new band, adding Simon Gallup on bass and Matthieu Hartley on keys. Those dates with Siouxsie and the Banshees in October 1979 with our original trio had not been easy. Because Michael and Robert weren't communicating, I had to act as a go-between, a role I accepted but didn't like as both parties were my friends. The final shows of the Join Hands Tour had been very challenging. We all knew something had to change. In the end, it was down to me to let Michael know that it wasn't working with him in the band, something I never felt comfortable doing. Then Robert and he had a follow-up conversation and just like that the three imaginary boys dissolved forever.

We started rehearsing with Simon and Matthieu shortly after that and imperceptibly the mood started lifting. We were excited and passionate about making music again. Even though our themes were darker in subject and approach, it felt like a truer, more authentic version of us. We entered Morgan Studios in North London with new hope and a feeling we had something special to record.

We pretty much lived in the studio making *Seventeen Seconds* for one simple reason: we didn't have money to stay anywhere else. We slept on the floor of the studio most nights. Mike Hedges was a willing collaborator and helped us get what we needed onto tape. It wouldn't have been the same without him.

I don't think having a good work environment is at odds with creating something that is darker and more cerebral like *Seventeen Seconds*. Mike told Richard Buskin in an interview for *Sound on Sound* that "it was so introspective and so depressing, it did us all in." But I actually remember it being a very positive experience in its own way. I've always thought that way about *Seventeen Seconds*, believing that out of the darkness came light. I see this reflected in the album cover in the way the artwork is smudged from dark to light. That motion always strikes me as moving upward.

I vividly remember all of us sitting in the studio intently listening to the songs during playback because we believed in them in heart and soul. It was the first time I felt like a real artist, and it was an intoxicating feeling.

Robert has mentioned before that he was listening to Bowie's *Low* back then. I too had *Low* on constant play. Listening to Dennis Davis and that great drum sound the producer Tony Visconti got informed my playing, but more than that the melancholy vibe of *Low* transported me to a strange and beautiful world in my imagination like a dream of perfect longing. It entranced me and helped my understanding of the world as it appeared to a twenty-year-old boy who was both a man and not quite one at the same time.

There are other clues you'll find if you look hard enough. Robert venerated Nick Drake and his album *Five Leaves Left*. It's an album full of loss, longing, guilt, and emptiness. It's a very British kind of melancholy. A melancholy drawn from the dark, dank countryside and probably exacerbated by drug use and maybe mental health issues like depression or even schizophrenia.

There's another influence here that's not often mentioned but I believe should be: John Martyn, another British songwriter and guitarist. He had an album out in 1977 called *One World* that we all liked at the time. It was experimental but still pop and had dub ambient effects. It has an almost proto-trip-hop kind of sound. Martyn also made a previous album, *Solid Air*, in 1973. The title track was dedicated to his friend who was none other than Nick Drake. We felt these records were all in conversation with each other and we wanted to be a part of it too.

To my mind there is a rich vein of English musicians like Bowie, Drake, and Martyn that shaped the making of *Seventeen Seconds*. It didn't just spring up out of nowhere. It was also the distillation of a lot of other threads of the British and American music we heard growing up, especially the more psychedelic stuff. We were the natural successors to that lineage even if you can't hear it immediately. It was in our bones.

For instance, I remember seeing a program for a concert by The Incredible String Band, a psychedelic folk rock group, in my brother's closet when I was ten years old. I looked over its photos and words and ran my fingers along the pages. It was like a magic rune to me. I wanted to be part of that thing that was this "other music" even at that early age.

Music writer Simon Reynolds calls *Seventeen Seconds* "translucent sounding with ambient, echoing vocals, crystal-thin ethereal guitars and driving drums by Tolhurst." *Seventeen Seconds* is the on-ramp we took toward the more Gothic sounds of *Faith* and *Pornography*. The album was released April 18, 1980. "A Forest" became the group's first hit single, reaching number thirty-one on the singles chart. Meanwhile, our first album *Three Imaginary Boys* was repackaged for the American market as *Boys Don't Cry* with new artwork and a modified track list.

We embarked on our first world tour in support of *Seventeen Seconds* after which Matthieu left as he wasn't as interested in the dark and melancholic music our band was now pursuing. By this time Simon was firmly entrenched in The Cure, contributing to the music and the words. We were expanding our artistic palette, painting ourselves out of our corner and into the larger world.

Things turned bleaker and more colorless in 1981 with the making of *Faith*. Once again, we worked with Mike Hedges to craft the funereal sound of the

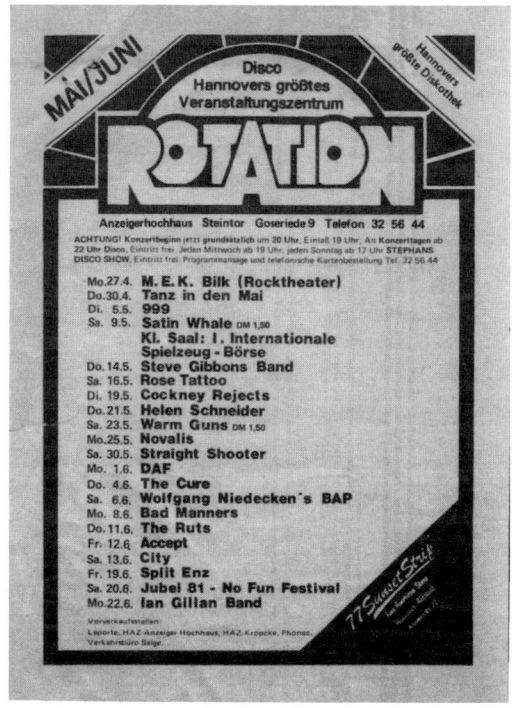

Flyer for The Cure at The Hannover Rotation in Germany, 1981
Supplied by the author

record. For *Faith*, life handed us a lot of material that affected the lyrics and the mood of the music. My mother, a lifelong smoker, was diagnosed with stage-IV lung cancer. The prognosis was dire; we were told she had three months to one year left. She told me on a visit I made to her before a string of shows, "I don't want to hang around and lose my dignity. I'm going to say goodbye to everyone I need to say goodbye to, then I'm gone." I didn't blame her for this outlook. She was in a lot of pain and I didn't want to see her suffer. I wanted to be strong for her, but at night when I thought about her on the road it was more than I could bear sometimes. All that got poured into what would become *Faith*.

My life was delineated by several things: a love of music but also of reading and literature. My mother was a big influence on the latter. She went back to school at fifty years of age and finally got herself the English degree she had always wanted but had been unable to pursue during the postwar years. The view toward education for women was not particularly enlightened. My mother told me the options for women back then were much starker: "Get married or go into service." Her perseverance against those odds helped me. Still does, actually.

We spent the first months of 1981 doing the bulk of recording for *Faith*. We had already started sporadically in September 1980, but nothing turned out right. Sometimes that's the way it goes. We had been on the road all year touring. Despite what people might tell you, I've found that writing on the road can be difficult because there's simply not enough time.

It was a troubling period for me. My mother, now terminally ill with no chance of recovering, would die later that year while we were on tour in the Netherlands. Robert's grandmother would soon pass away as well, so the atmosphere during recording was particularly dour. More than that we were starting to question the ideas we had been indoctrinated with growing up at school and in church. The teachings of Catholicism were deeply ingrained in me. The fact that my mother was about to be taken away from me as I turned twenty-two was the catalyst for working out those ideas in a creative way about what exactly I believed in with regards to my faith in God.

At this point our references were becoming more internal. We learned we could pull from our own psyche the essence of what we wanted to reveal about ourselves and our world. We had at a very young age started to experience these more painful aspects of life. I realized only much later that it's not entirely normal to lose a parent in your early twenties. Most have that experience much later in life. The fact that it was happening to me became the energy I used to drive my creativity. I think that was perhaps true for Robert as well. After that there was no turning back. The Cure had turned inward and become self-referencing. We started to create a world for ourselves.

Certainly, there were traces of other influences that various reviewers tried to attach to us. Remember "Punk Pink Floyd"? But we had created our own style and our own music. We were beyond doing anyone else's version of anything. Music, like people, doesn't really fit into neat little packages. Musicians are not one-dimensional characters in some music supervisor's categorizing dream. Fuck off with your pigeonholes.

We had all manner of influences that surfaced in our music. It came from a heady mixture of psychedelic and punk music, strained through existential literature and confessional poetry, and stamped by our depressing upbringing in Crawley. When asked the inanest of inane questions by hapless

The Cure Picture Tour poster in Hamburg in 1981
Credit: Porl and Undy

journalists—"What do you call your music?"—Robert would say something like "It's not punk or rock, it's Cure music. That's what we play."

That was certainly the case with *Faith*, starting with "The Holy Hour." The straightforward religious reference marks the mass as a performance, with the church serving as its theater and the mass its gloomy ritual. Yet, as Robert sings, the promise of being saved "makes me stay." This is at the heart of the paradox: wanting to believe in the rewards of salvation but unable to give one's self over to "devour the sacrifice." Longing for forgiveness is at the center for me. Forgiveness is big with Catholics. There are a lot of sinners in the church.

The next track, "Primary," is just bass, drums, and vocals: a stylistic change that became a trademark of The Cure. The song features twin bass guitars played by Robert and Simon. Robert used a Fender VI bass that had six strings rather than the normal four, which gives the track a very particular low-end sound that became identified with us. Incidentally, Robert often wrote on that

The Cure Faith Tour in France, 1981
Supplied by JC Moglia

bass as opposed to a regular guitar. I believe this gave him a more rhythmic approach to songwriting than if he'd used just a straight guitar.

In "Other Voices," I started to get into the idea of tom beats and making a more rolling drum pattern. Some lyrics came from my new life on the road. I was drifting apart from my old friends from Horley and Crawley. Any touring musician will tell you that life at home takes a big hit when you're on the road as much as we were. Relationships, and not just romantic ones, start to lose their hold, which is painful any time of year but especially around the holidays as the song makes clear. Call it the loneliness of the long-distance drummer.

For "All Cats Are Grey," I wrote about my mother's impending demise from cancer. Full of despair and pain anticipating that coming event, I couldn't bear to wait for the end. So I wrote a song about it. The first verse is about the surprise at waiting in the anteroom for death, imagining what's coming next. I saw it as a vast, empty place where no one is allowed to leave just yet. According to Roman Catholic doctrine, the souls of those who die in God's grace may make satisfaction for past sins and become fit for heaven. Those who aren't in a state of grace go to purgatory, a kind of eternal waiting room, which is a very Catholic notion.

For the second part I used the idiom "in the dark all cats are grey," which means that in darkness appearances are meaningless. My mother told me this was an expression they used during the blackout of World War II. When Hitler's bombers came to London, the whole city went dark to avoid giving them easy targets. The insinuation was that during a romantic tryst in the dark you might not know what the other person looked like or even know who they were, but it didn't matter. In wartime, there is only now.

The next part is about disappearing into the next world imagined in the afterlife. Sound, vision, and touch being very different senses toward the end of life, without normal earthly boundaries. Imagining the last thing you hear before passing is "a single note" that rings forever. I wanted to get across the idea that it's as much about my feeling of *imagining* this happening as me *imagining* what her experience going through the end might be like. I wanted

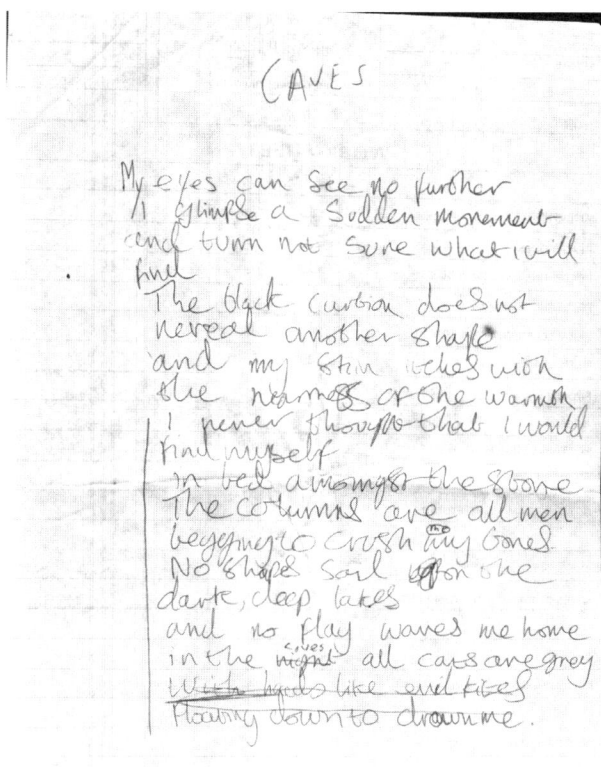

"My handwritten page of words on the back of a studio worksheet that some of the lyrics for 'All Cats Are Grey' were taken from."

Supplied by the author

to feel what she felt. The only way to accept or acknowledge the pain she was going through was this profound act of empathy, which in retrospect was very Goth of me, though that word wouldn't have occurred to me then.

My mother's death wasn't a fantasy. We actually played "The Funeral Party" at my mother's funeral service. I was glad that she would be honored by us in that way. The song is about the rituals of death, which both Robert and I experienced. As he said during an interview in *Rockerilla* in 1983, "When someone you know dies, you suddenly realize what death is. Something takes shape in your mind. It's not an indefinite, abstract entity."

The song "Doubt" came from a musical idea of Simon's, and then Robert and I developed the lyrics together. A true collaboration. As most of *Faith* was written in the studio, it was by its nature collaborative. At this time very rarely did anyone bring songs into the studio that were fully formed from soup to nuts. We were the real definition of a band. We all had our parts to play. Usually, we got basic tracks down—drums, bass, rhythm guitar—before we added further embellishments to the arrangement. Also, we had an unsung hero in the studio. Our labelmate and dear departed friend Billy Mackenzie would drop by and offer suggestions, usually by singing a melody idea from the back of the control room in his unmistakable high tenor.

For "The Drowning Man," Robert had read Mervyn Peake's *Gormenghast*, a sort of Gothic-flavored *Lord of the Rings*, which I admit doesn't do it justice. So that is where the reference to Fuchsia in the lyrics comes from. I won't spoil the story with my description; you should read it for yourself. Personally, I always felt life was about not assigning your life power to others; to live your life with some hope, however you find it. I hoped what we were doing by playing these sad and questioning songs was helping others that felt disconnected from this world.

Julianne Regan of All About Eve told me how "The Drowning Man" was helpful to her in a time of crisis when she was nineteen:

> Fortunately, I'd discovered and was able to take solace in music that in some way chimed with how I felt while also offering a kind of muted warmth, ultimately throwing me a rope. *Faith* was one such album. I was lost, often isolated, and intermittently disconnected. Music was a medium wherein I could

psychologically curl up and within which I could nestle. "The Drowning Man" was perhaps the song that afforded me the most warmth and the most hope. I related to the drowning, lonely, frozen girl, and took comfort in the sense that it would matter to someone if she—and by extension I—slipped into an ocean, be that an earthly or metaphorical one. This wasn't a misguided glamorous ideation of suicide; it was about hoping that someone might care, even if that were just the narrator of a song. It wasn't important *who* cared, but just that someone was capable of caring.

A very powerful statement about the ultimate healing power of music and lyrics. A great many of The Cure's listeners found our songs in much the same way that Julianne describes. Our songs were always more of a solace than destructive or depressing. That's always been a false notion that people hurled at us. That somehow this intense music made its listeners' anxiety or mental problems worse. I beg to plead exactly the opposite. Very often it's the panacea. We weren't the problem but the cure.

We put "Faith" at the end because we felt it was a summation of the album's themes. In this song, we make our feelings about the religion of our childhood plain. It is the song of someone at the end of their rope. The lyrics were composed collaboratively between Robert and me, which Robert then trimmed to fit his vocal style. Lyrics are not poetry: you have to be able to sing them in a way that fits with the music. Whatever words I gave Robert, he would, of course, need to have the last say in what was used and in what way he would sing them.

This album brought to the surface some diametrically opposed ideas between Robert and me about our respective beliefs in a higher power, which I think was partially responsible for later events. Not because we disagreed about organized religion—we were both on the same page there—but with respect to God, Robert chose not to believe. I had a fear that if I didn't know what I believed I would cease to exist. Although I, too, had turned away from organized religion because it felt like a man-made system of control, I still had belief in something outside myself. That belief was what guided me during the making of *Faith*. It gave me something, however tenuous, to attach to my ever-more chaotic reality.

It would only get more intense as the inevitable passing of my mother and Robert's grandmother transpired. The slightly soft-focus blur of *Faith* approaches this idea with a velvet feel and soft, misty specters. I don't think we were being coy, but a lot of sadness colored our outlook and informed its bleakness. Songs like "All Cats Are Grey" and "Faith" mapped out our new gloomy landscape of fractured belief.

The cover of *Faith* is our most overtly Gothic with the Bolton Abbey photo. It always reminds me a little of the first Black Sabbath album, which is a circle of sorts. It was time to move out of our old life and into something more suitable for the way we felt, but it turned out *Faith* was the calm before the storm and the clouds were gathering on the horizon.

Pornography is where the seeds of Goth grew, and we started to fully embrace bleaker themes in our songs. Subjects that would explode on our fourth album, snarling and punching their way through the darkness. For me,

The Cure fans in Brussels, 1981
Credit: Richard Bellia

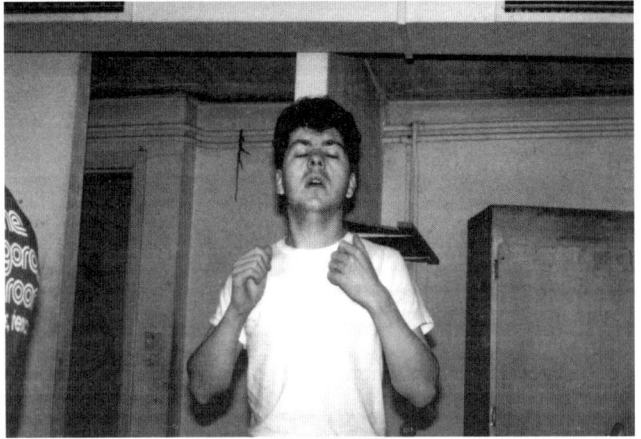

The author in Brussels in 1981. "Just over one year later we played the same place and it was the end of that version of The Cure. Does it look like I have a premonition already?"
Credit: Richard Bellia

Pornography is the pinnacle of The Cure as a three-piece unit and represents my proudest moment as a musician. Is it strange that the best creation comes from the darkest times?

I think not. It's only when you are the most vulnerable that you can pull everything out of yourself to create. *Pornography* was a furious mass of sound, especially the drums. Phil Thornalley, our new producer and just twenty-two years of age when he recorded us, put the drums in the big room of Studio 1 at RAK London. The whole effect was immense sounding. It wasn't easy to make this album. There were some drug issues, some infighting, and just general madness. Robert spent several nights at the record company office where we were staying, sleeping on the floor behind the couch in a makeshift camp made out of old sheets and bits of furniture like a homeless person, isolating himself to cope with the situation.

As I said in *Cured*, we wouldn't let the studio cleaner remove any of the cans of beer or empty bottles of liquor that we consumed during the weeks making *Pornography*. We kept them as a sort of Dadaesque sculpture in the corner of the studio control room. We also only worked at night, so we never saw the regular studio personnel who only worked days. We were like the studio ghosts. Except for the Banshees and our friend Gary, no one was allowed in the studio while we made *Pornography*. It was peculiar and intense.

But also right there at the junction of all that we found the massive sound we needed for *Pornography*. It was, as Dave Hill of the *New Musical Express* noted, like "Phil Spector in Hell." These factors culminated in an album that bristles with an intense anxiety and nihilism that positioned The Cure as the foremost purveyors of Gothic rock.

The drum machine intro to "One Hundred Years" heralds just how different this record was going to be. It was also the first song I played keyboards on for The Cure. We used the Boss Dr. Rhythm DR-55 drum machine for the drums. We fed it out into two amplifiers (guitar and bass) for the snare and kick drum, respectively, then recorded that martial beat, which gave it its grim atmosphere. Playing this song live was dangerous too. I used to come off the kit to play the keys at the lip of the stage. I had to duck under a descending screen that isolated the drums for this song. If I timed it wrong on the darkened stage—concussion! Appropriately, the album's first lines touch on themes of blood, war, freedom fighters, and death mixed in with our own desperation and pessimism. A swirling crucible of angst and pain.

I loved the pounding drums on "A Short-Term Effect" and the swirling hallucinatory effects, which were happening quite a lot at the studio at that time. We had to postpone the first two days of recording because of "hallucinations" that I suspect were brought on by drug use. I'm surprised that Phil didn't want out of the project after that auspicious beginning, but he had a bigger—and more sober—vision.

As I recall, "The Hanging Garden" evolved initially from the drumbeat. Normally the songs came differently, maybe from us playing together or someone playing a riff. The first time we played it live in France was before we recorded it, so the fact that I slowed right down in the middle and then stopped wasn't noticed. Nobody knew the song yet. Robert said in *Cure News* #9 in 1990, "'The Hanging Garden' is something like about the purity and hate of animals fucking."

One of my favorite guitar lines by Robert appears on "Siamese Twins," *especially* with the flanged effects on it. I added a few lines to the lyrics. "Is it always like this?" was inspired by reading *The Bell Jar* by Sylvia Plath. In the book, the protagonist Esther Greenwood (a thinly veiled Plath) plans to seduce a young professor to lose her virginity to, but afterward she starts to hemorrhage. "Is it supposed to hurt?" she says to him. "Sometimes it hurts" is the reply from her unconcerned lover.

Earlier in the book, Esther, who is in New York as an intern at a women's magazine, stands on the roof of a building after a harrowing experience of sexual assault. She decides to leave New York there and then and throws all her wardrobe one by one off the building to float down over a predawn New York City: "Piece by piece, I fed my wardrobe to the night wind, and flutteringly, like a loved one's ashes, the gray scraps were ferried off, to settle here, there, exactly where I would never know, in the dark heart of New York." I found the sad story of casual brutality and emotional pain that's inflicted on her especially distressing. In love with Plath and her words, I willingly lived in the shadow of her poetry. It explained so much to me about how I felt.

It's strange that when I think of *Pornography* I think of hard music, but "Siamese Twins" is almost soft in comparison and very sad and confessional. In

Polaroid of the band taken for the *Pornography* cover photo shoot in 1982
Credit: *Michael Costiff*

the Catholic world, confession is good for the soul. Understated and mournful, "Siamese Twins" is a heartbeat of hurt.

To me, "The Figurehead" is the best example of how tight as a band we were. In a three-piece you need to be almost perfect when you play to prevent the music from falling apart. It's a strange almost baffling contrast to me because as people we *were* falling apart—emotionally and mentally—but the music had become very precise. I think it was the only thing that kept us somewhat sane. Budgie remembers coming to the studio when we were recording *Pornography* and he felt this dichotomy too: the great music coming from us but as people not being quite right.

Robert says in *Cure News* #9, "'The Figurehead' was about a grotesque skull sculpture I discovered in the disused asylum we used in the 'Charlotte Sometimes' video. I took it home to talk to—to confess to? And this song is about guilt." I also have a weird sculpture from that shoot: a strange green dog that sits by my bed to this day. I recall thinking of the title. "The Figurehead" from these bizarre bits of sculpture we had found in the abandoned asylum art rooms. It's a song about sins committed and the guilt they create. I remember looking at the murals on the walls of the hospital and they were full of devils and demons! It seemed to me that the asylum's message to the patients was that somehow you might be responsible for your own illness because of your sins.

Robert in Bourges, 1982
Credit: Richard Bellia

The connections between madness and guilt seemed very close in the unforgiving world of Catholicism.

"A Strange Day" is about the end of the world. The mixing desk was used as an instrument. Phil recorded lots of drone loops and placed each on a separate fader on the desk. Then we played them like a rudimentary sampler of sorts. That's the sound you hear at the beginning that swells up into the song and the most gorgeous guitar motif. If you think this is all doom and death, you're not paying attention to what "A Strange Day" has to say. It's more ecstatic than that. Perhaps religiously ecstatic.

"Cold" is the most Goth track on the album and perhaps in our entire catalog. Maybe this is where the reputation comes from? I remember Robert played the cello intro with it on his lap like a very large guitar. Lyrically, the song contains some drug references, such as "crawled across the mirror." It's The Cure's cocaine song.

When making *Pornography*, rather than the repressive sexual mores of the times, I considered man's inhumanity to his fellow man and the subjection and oppression of others to be the real pornography of the world. In forty years, nothing seems to have changed much. In fact, it feels worse as we spiral into war in Europe and authoritarianism closer to home here in the US.

I think for me, as well as being the musical pinnacle of The Cure as a three-piece, *Pornography* also is the height of our lyrical output in terms of subject. At the beginning of the track "Pornography," we had recorded some late-night TV discussion shows in the studio and then reversed and manipulated that. It was, as I recall, a program with Germaine Greer about sex. Then the drums come galloping in like the horses of the apocalypse while Robert sings some of The Cure's most disturbing and chaotic lyrics with disconnected, violent images. But at the end a tiny ray of hope appears through the fog of war. We might not have been prophets, but *Pornography* is a prophecy.

We put everything we felt into that record. It was our therapy and our salvation. Listening to it all these years later, I still feel it is the best record we made. Period. It is the most authentic and honest record The Cure ever created.

So where does that leave us with the idea of The Cure as the kings of Goth? We started with gently smudged colors and ended up with slabs of darkness. We are Goth and not Goth and that's the truth *and* the conundrum. You are what we think we are.

But there is something else that I realized when thinking about the album *Pornography*.

The author in Bourges, 1982
Credit: Richard Bellia

"Set the controls for the heart of the sun!" The author behind his kit in Bourges, France
Credit: Richard Bellia

Yes, most of the music is uncompromisingly bleak. Even the cover is like a Francis Bacon painting. Life imitates art. The first line of the album *Pornography* revels in nihilism and negation galore, but then consider the last line's determination to fight. Underneath it all, as much as death swam by, I found hope.

Taking the path these three albums dictated was, I now realize, teaching me. It still is. A transcendent light compressed into a pinpoint that then flooded and washed the known and unknown universe. Out of the gloom comes salvation.

What a blessing I was given.

THE FOUR DRUMMERS OF DESTINY

WE LIKED THE ANARCHY OF PUNK BUT MOSTLY WE WERE JUST TRYING to stay afloat and weather the storms of post–World War II life. In modern music, two things grab you first: the rhythm and the voice, but underneath both is the beat. It's about the percussion: kick, snare, toms, hi-hat, and cymbals. The magical formula to release the id without the idiocy.

So it is with Goth. The vox reigns over all with the tones from baritone to tenor to soprano, but the drums are the signature of the genre, the primal impulse. Listen to the first few bars of "Hybrid" by Siouxsie and the Banshees or "Cold" by The Cure. The beat tells you it's about the dark, the sad, and the strange. The rhythms of night and desperation lifting you up if you're down, especially if you're down. That's their purpose, to free you from the bonds imposed by existence. Whether you hear them or play them, or both.

From Morris to Budgie to Haskins to myself, the drums give the music authenticity, the rhythm of our lives. We owe a debt to Moon and Starr and Baker and Watts but most of all to our time. Marching onwards. We were the first set of drummers not to come out of the typecast swing era (Watts and Baker), pop and skiffle (Ringo), or the teen anarchy of rhythm and blues (Moon). We took something from them all, but punk fused it together and propelled us forward.

We might not have been trained musicians in the traditional sense, but that's never been a prerequisite in rock and roll. In fact it's usually a hindrance blocking the untamed creative soul with rules and regulations. Anyway, we knew we wanted the drums to help splatter the picture of our art. So, we learned what we needed and painted with the rest of the music.

I played with the urgency of punk and the sadness of Plath. I learned to play the hi-hat from Charlie Watts, with a metronome I borrowed from Jaki Liebezeit of Can. I followed that voice, rather than bars on a chart. So it was with the other three; we all found a way. Budgie's tribal rhythms were gifted by Jerry Shirley's technique and Ringo's feel. Kevin Haskins fused the toms of Kenny Morris with a dash of Ringo too. For Stephen Morris it was the art-rock simplicity of Moe Tucker and krautrock motorik gleaned from Can's Jaki L. Truth be told, we all had a little bit of each of these shades of rhythm and every one of us owes a debt to Ringo. He showed us all that feel was more important than virtuosity, and this led us in surprising ways back to the mutant disco of Cabaret Voltaire and onward to the Cocteaus' blurred machines and the industrial noise rhythms of Nine Inch Nails.

In the end it's all about the music and the instrument we played that brought us here in the first place. It's about the means to an end. How to liberate your soul and have a happy-sad time doing it. It's been about not following the crowd and not allowing the forces of repression and normality to drag us down to ordinariness. It's about escaping all that and also, more importantly, about finding out who we are.

This is what Goth has given me. It didn't ask that I subscribe to anything definite in particular; rather, Goth was a way of looking at the world that I was familiar with from the art, literature, and music of the past. It crystalized via punk into something I could believe in that held me in the bosom of darkness and at the same time set me free.

Modern life eschews looking too closely at things for any length of time, especially if they are in any way disturbing. My life in Goth served as a kind of communal reverse meditation. By exploring the darkness of books, films, music, and paintings together, we escaped for a brief moment to better understand the place we all found ourselves in time and space. We kept floating but now a little more liberated.

PART THREE

LEGION

CHAPTER FIVE

SPIRITUAL ALCHEMISTS

COCTEAU TWINS: ETERNITY'S SONG

Siouxsie Sioux is the Empress of Goth, but only Elizabeth Fraser made me cry.

"Only Elizabeth Fraser made me cry."
Credit: Mick Mercer

The Cocteau Twins (actually a trio) was formed in 1979 in Grangemouth, Scotland, by guitarist Robin Guthrie and bassist Will Heggie. The young singer Elizabeth Fraser joined in 1981. Heggie was replaced by Simon Raymonde in 1983. They pioneered the then nascent subgenre of dream pop, but their early roots were influenced by Siouxsie and the Banshees and Joy Division. Fraser even had a Siouxsie tattoo.

I met them only once but it's that meeting many years later that explains to me my emotional reaction to her work, my tears. Brought on by more than just the exquisitely beautiful tones of her voice.

Spending most of one's adult life as a performing artist can leave one either too accustomed to hearing new material or not receptive enough to other artists' work. The very nature of the beast encourages influence but also dictates an enormous amount of reflection on your own thoughts and processes. As a result, it can cut you off from experiencing art the way fans do. In other words, instead of relating the artistic experience directly to you or your life and your own feelings, you start deconstructing it to figure out how it was made and what instruments and effects were used to produce certain sounds.

During the eighties I heard many songs by the Cocteau Twins and enjoyed them for what they represented: a beautiful, yearning slice of Gothic-inspired dream pop. However, it was harder to deconstruct the Cocteau Twins because the lyrics fit together in impressionistic collages, sometimes without using actual words. Or maybe it's not harder at all if you remove the barrier of conventional speech and go with your feelings instead. Simpler and closer to the source. I realized with the Cocteau Twins the sound and the emotions don't need to be explained with another set of constructs brought on by formalized language.

But I digress. I wanted to tell you about the day we met. The Cure had been going for a while and we had already been a little successful. Both Robert and I had bought small apartments close to each other in North London. Much of our band life was centered in London studios or rehearsal rooms. So, it seemed like a good idea to get our own places rather than living at Fiction's office or at a hotel. At twenty-three or so it was also the right time to finally leave our hometown and start something approximate to adult life. As things progressed, within a few years of living in London, I upgraded and bought a large house and moved out of the confines of my small apartment.

However, there was one caveat as to where I was going to move. I had a good friend, Peter, who was a restaurateur and wine bar owner who had a place mere steps from my flat. I found my way to Peter's place, very aptly named La Folie ("madness" in English), the first night I moved into my flat and realized the electricity hadn't been turned on yet. I was there most nights when not on the road. It was a short walk down my street and a more complicated stumble back, but at least I didn't have to drive. It was my home away from home during that crazed period of my life.

So, when I moved to the bigger accommodations, I stuck a pin in the map at the bar's address, and drew a circle representing a mile's distance around it. I gave this map to the Realtor with instructions to "Find me a house within this range." Obviously, I was not yet ready to be removed from the madness.

Sometime in 1988 I was at my usual spot in La Folie, nursing a large something or other and talking with the regulars, when I saw a younger couple enter the bar. At first, I wasn't sure if I knew them, or if they just looked familiar somehow. Then I realized who it was: Robin Guthrie and Liz Fraser of the Cocteau Twins. We introduced ourselves and the normal sort of night

Cocteau Twins at The Venue in 1982
Credit: Mick Mercer

Robin Guthrie and Elizabeth Fraser of Cocteau Twins in 1984
Credit: Mick Mercer

(for me at least) ensued in that place of madness. Sometime later we wended our way back to my house and continued listening to music, chatting, and of course drinking more. A very pleasant evening was had by all, and years later what I recall the most is Robin and Liz's quiet demeanor and low-key presence. Remarkably interesting and agreeable companions is my abiding memory.

Over the following years I occasionally heard some Cocteau Twins material, and at one point both Liz and I were on an album together, albeit without coming into actual contact, which is the way it often goes for percussionists. That album was Massive Attack's *Mezzanine*. Liz was the vocalist on three songs on that album, whilst Massive Attack sampled "10:15 Saturday Night" for their version of The Paragons' "Man Next Door" with Horace Andy. My hi-hats and her vocals on the same record.

Even though I had been aware of their music, admired them for their alternative stance, and had gotten to know them socially, it really wasn't until some years later when I heard Liz and Robin's version of Tim Buckley's "Song to the

Siren," performing as This Mortal Coil, a collective led by Ivo Watts-Russell, the founder of the British label 4AD, that I finally got it.

I had heard the song before, but it wasn't until I finally climbed out of the madness of my alcoholism that I at last felt the great emotion inside the performance and marveled at Liz's beautiful Indian-influenced vocals. Suddenly it all clicked. From their other great songs with no words but phonetic sounds to the more impressionistic word shades of the more traditional offerings, it all coalesced into a grand and wondrous tapestry.

It was, of course, the purest emotion from music. From a small, magical Scottish lady came this miraculous connection to the collective unconsciousness of feeling in vulnerable emotional beings.

Unlike the way of most singers, which is to attach their id to the words to give them instinctual power, she was tapping straight into the subconscious and dredging up visions that when I first met her in my mid-twenties were beyond my comprehension. The hardest to elucidate, those strangest emotions of life.

Occasionally, we meet a soul in this world that's been here many times before either consciously or unconsciously and can filter out the dross and stupidity of everyday life and present us with the real and true essence of existence

Elizabeth Fraser in 1984
Credit: Mick Mercer

in their work. That is what I finally was able to hear in her voice and that's why I cried. I cried for the death of my mother, I cried for the death of my daughter, and I cried for myself. I'd finally been released from my being because in that voice I had at last heard eternity.

WIRE: WIRED

WIRE WAS FORMED IN 1977 BY SINGER AND GUITARIST COLIN NEWMAN, bassist Graham Lewis, guitarist Bruce Gilbert, and drummer Robert Grey. Wire's sound drew on the cultural explosion of punk but always had an artsy, forward-thinking bent that prevented the band from being pigeonholed. In this way, Wire can make a legitimate claim as one of the first "post-punk" bands. It had what is now recognized as one of the most original debuts in the first wave of UK punk, *Pink Flag*.

Wire engaged in a period of intensive twelve-hour rehearsals that polished their sound to razor sharpness. A mix of punk energy, angular and unexpected chord changes, and oblique lyrics characterize Wire's early sound. My good friend Budgie remembers seeing Wire in the early days from the side of the stage at Eric's in Liverpool. "They played so many songs in such a brief time—each song was super short with minimal presentation. I think they played with no stage lights! But it was obvious even then that they were moving toward something different and less punk, something beyond the fast and hard sound, moving into what was really post-punk."

The Cure had snagged a gig opening for them as they promoted their second album, *Chairs Missing*, which departed from the starkness of their debut and added more atmospheric sonics with synthesizers played by producer Mark Thorne. The single "Outdoor Miner" became a minor pop hit. The departure from their early sound showed that Wire was willing to experiment and push the boundaries of the stereotypical punk sound. Wire's sound was informed by the fire of punk, but had more avant-garde touches to display and utilize. It was also the first band I saw with a Syndrum, which is basically a synthesizer that produced drum sounds. Strangely enough, it was not to be found on the kit of Robert Grey's drums! Rather, it was held like an African talking drum under the left arm of singer Colin Newman and struck occasionally with a single stick.

We had a support slot opening for Wire at the University of Kent. It was a revelation to us as a band. Up until then we had only played with groups that were fairly "normal" punk bands like Charlie Harper's UK Subs—and that was one of the better gigs. We had a few where we were entirely mismatched with a bigger, straight-ahead pop or rock group. Such is life in the trenches when you're what's referred to nowadays as a "baby band."

I remember two things clearly about that show. Running into Wire's bassist Graham Lewis in the backstage hallway and being shocked in my home counties, suburban male ingénue kind of way when I saw the long rattail hanging from the back of his otherwise very normal haircut.

The other thing I remember was their very minimal and stark presentation. The band wore black and white and had very simple stage lighting. They had moved forward from the straitjacket of the punk ethos but had brought with them that which still worked. For instance, the stark minimal drumming of Robert Grey was almost hypnotizing.

That kind of approach was both inspiring and influential. It helped me appreciate the earlier works of drummers like Jaki Liebezeit of Can. Jaki was the pioneer of the "motorik" beat. *Motorik* is German for "motor skill" and is the 4/4 beat associated with German bands of that genre. To me, it felt appropriate for our new songs that would become the basis for our sophomore album, *Seventeen Seconds*. They were studies in repetition, so it became a style that I soon appropriated into my mode of playing. Like Jaki, I believed you must "play monotonous" to the point of being half man, half machine. I related to the mantra-like feel of simple beats played consistently with no fills or ornamentation, allowing the pulse of rhythm to act hypnotically in a repetitive but musical way.

We internalized the lessons we learned from Wire's outré presentation but got even more from the way the band combined art and music in one package. It liberated for us the notion of what we could be and what we were expected to do. In other words, it made us a little freer. Wire showed that we could experiment—even if we weren't completely sure what direction we wanted to go. I believe that Wire's influence helped set the stage for our next three albums: *Seventeen Seconds*, *Faith*, and *Pornography*. Not in a straight facsimile of style or sound. Rather, it was the fact that they were doing it

1979 Summer nights with The Cure—The Lyceum, London and Friars, Aylesbury
Supplied by JC Moglia

and appeared to be getting somewhere with a more challenging approach to music. Up until that point we had been somewhat constrained in our thinking of what a pop song could be. We wanted to reach a level of success where we could finally quit our jobs, do this music thing full-time, without sacrificing our art.

Playing with Wire demonstrated that we could take some of our more radical ideas and be successful doing them. This was really the Holy Grail for us. We wanted to be artists and not just copycat purveyors of this year's pop fashion. Even at our relatively young age, we realized that if we hitched ourselves to a style of music, we wouldn't last long. Jumping on someone else's train was not what we aspired to do.

It proved to be the right course. We distilled our core values and musical strengths through our own sense of creation. Although the UK especially has always been a hotbed of instant fashion takes for music that are here today but gone tomorrow, by not sacrificing a long career for easy fame with a vapid pop song, we escaped to live another day, then another day after that, and so forth, for a long period of time.

The same has been true of Wire, although they have travelled quite a bumpy road in their long career. Consider their third album, *154*, which continued mining this vein of experimentalism. However, the band, in typical punk fashion, had a falling-out with their label, EMI, over promotional strategies that the label considered unorthodox. Newman's solo album *A–Z* was supposed to be Wire's fourth record, but failed negotiations between EMI and the band led to cancelled studio time and the band was dropped from the label. Wire staged a series of unusual concerts to demonstrate tracks that would have made up the band's fourth album. The shows, punctuated by performance art interventions that were decidedly confrontational in nature, divided audiences and perplexed potential labels. Lacking a recording deal and funding, this initial period of the band ended in 1980.

Wire reformed in 1985, incorporating more electronic instruments into their sound. To continue their forward-looking mentality, the band decided against playing any early songs, instead hiring a Wire cover band, The Ex–Lion Tamers, to open with their older material while they played only new work. The band signed with Mute Records and released the EP *Snakedrill*, followed by *The Ideal Copy*, recorded at the iconic Hansa Studios in Berlin. The record found the band experimenting more with sequencers and utilizing the studio itself as an instrument, which was a technique pioneered by Brian Eno.

The band continued releasing with Mute; 1988's *A Bell Is a Cup* featured pop single "Kidney Bingos." Wire's sixth album, *It's Beginning to and Back Again*, mined live recordings and reworked them heavily in the studio. 1990's *Manscape* continued to interweave the electric and electronic, and *The Drill*, released the following year, presented eight different versions of a single song. Drummer Robert Grey, feeling that there was increasingly less of a role for himself in the band, departed. Wire changed its name to Wir and released *The First Letter*, after which the band again went on hiatus.

Wire returned in 2000 with Robert Grey now back in the fold, initially as a live-only project, playing songs from every stage of their development. Soon, however, the band began releasing new material beginning with *Send* in 2003. Bruce Gilbert left in 2004 to focus on his solo work and collaborations with other experimental musicians. Since that first foray back into the studio the band has released eight subsequent LPs, with two in 2020. Wire has weathered the slings and arrows of outrageous fortune even with their influence being much greater than their fairly modest record sales. Perhaps proving the theory that art in the end has much more longevity than commerce!

The band's sound influenced artists as diverse as The Minutemen, Big Black, Sonic Youth, Guided by Voices, My Bloody Valentine, and the Washington, DC, hardcore scene. The band interjected an artistic sensibility into the economy of punk that continues to resonate in the music of indie rock and electronic acts alike.

SISTERS OF MERCY: SISTERS ARE DOING IT FOR THEMSELVES

THE SISTERS OF MERCY WAS FORMED IN LEEDS IN 1980 BY GARY MARX and Andrew Eldritch. They took their name from a song off Leonard Cohen's *Songs of Leonard Cohen* that was featured in the Robert Altman film *McCabe & Mrs. Miller*. The duo released their first single, "The Damage Done," backed with "Watch" and "Home of the Hit-Men" with Eldritch on drums and Marx on guitar, with each sharing vocal duties. The duo shortly after regrouped with Craig Adams on bass and the addition of a drum machine that the group named Doktor Avalanche. Each of the successive incarnations of the machine would also be named Doktor Avalanche.

Ben Gunn was shortly added on as second guitarist, forming the core of the first classic Sisters lineup. Gunn left in 1983 over conflicts with Eldritch about the direction of the group. He was replaced by Wayne Hussey, who focused on twelve-string and acoustic guitars. In 1984, the band began to work toward recording its first album and the subsequent tour cemented the group's cult status.

Marx, Hussey, and Adams predominantly composed and rehearsed the songs on the group's first album, *First Last and Always*, with Eldritch coming in toward the end to write lyrics and sing. The band embarked on a supporting tour for the album, which Marx left after the UK leg due to an inability to work with Eldritch. The tour continued with Hussey shouldering all guitar parts. The band played the final show of this incarnation at the Royal Albert Hall on June 18, 1985.

Eldritch relocated to Hamburg, where he was soon joined by Hussey, and they began working on a follow-up to their debut album, but these ideas were soon scrapped. Hussey and Adams formed a band called The Sisterhood, which eventually became The Mission after Eldritch released a single with the band name, thereby prohibiting Hussey and Adams from using it.

Eldritch followed up with *Floodland*, which he mostly wrote with Larry Alexander and some contributions from Jim Steinman, most notably "This Corrosion." The album was a move toward more keyboard-oriented productions and away from the guitar-based compositions of the earlier work. Eldritch then formed a new incarnation of The Sisters with Andreas Bruhn and Tim Bricheno on guitars and Tony James on bass. *Vision Thing* marked a transition back to guitar-based rock. Unfortunately it brought to a close the most productive period of the band and the start of an ongoing feud with the band's label East West, after which the band would release no more music under The Sisters name.

Eldritch has at times been referred to as the "Godfather of Goth," a label he rejects for both himself and his band. The Sisters of Mercy, however, continues to have a large following in the subculture and play at festivals associated with Goth. Eldritch's dark baritone vocals and the combination of propulsive drum machine and swirling guitars laid a blueprint for many post-punk and Goth groups of the coming decades. Eldritch himself cites Siouxsie and the Banshees, Suicide, and The Psychedelic Furs as major influences on the Sisters' sound, though first and foremost he considers the group a rock band.

THE MISSION: WAYNE HUSSEY'S MISSION IN LIFE

Some people are seemingly born Goth, while others find their way to the tribe. Such was the path taken by Wayne Hussey of The Mission. Like millions of kids around the world, when he was growing up all he cared about was football. He envisioned a place for himself on the world stage even though it was obvious to his PE teachers that he would never make the grade.

"I always loved the stories of the players that weren't particularly outstanding as kids," Wayne told me when we talked in 2022, "but persevered and practiced fanatically and ended up playing in FIFA World Cup finals. That would be me. Blind belief and dedication would get me there."

Wayne Hussey with The Mission at The Marquee in 1987
Credit: Mick Mercer

It was the classic dream of many a young man in postwar England, including my own band of friends. Football was Robert's first life goal—no pun intended. Truth be told, Robert was a pretty good footballer. With The Cure, the worlds of football and music were intertwined in a way that Liam Gallagher hadn't even thought of yet. As noted, one of Robert's earliest lyrics was a tribute to Rodney Marsh, the English footballer.

However, Hussey's dreams of football fame were soon to be derailed by a more powerful urge for music stardom. When Wayne discovered the lure of playing music, his football fantasies began to recede. First came T. Rex, which opened the door for Bowie and a host of others. Instead of aspiring to be a footballer like Kevin Keegan, he wanted to be Marc Bolan. He'd always loved listening to pop music, and his parents were fans of The Beatles, The Animals, and The Walker Brothers, who were their favorites. While his father was on holiday in Spain, he bought an acoustic guitar for Wayne.

"I would play and practice until my fingers bled. I started writing my own songs because I couldn't play anyone else's. My own songs would invariably start off as vague assimilations of my favorite songs by my favorite artists. That rule still applies today. Very early on I decided I was gonna be a musician. That's all I wanted to do now that I had put my dreams of being a footballer aside. I was obsessed with music, listening, playing, and reading the weekly inkies."

Growing up in a Mormon family, Wayne found himself outside the norm. He was one of four or five Mormon students at a school of two thousand–plus pupils, which made him the subject of unwanted bullying and ridicule. Being a good athlete spared him from serious bullying, but once he started playing guitar in bands he enjoyed a different kind of status. His belief in himself and his dedication to his craft helped propel young Wayne into the music business.

Nevertheless, Wayne was very much a musical outsider with lots of trial and error. In many ways, Wayne's "pilgrim's progress" as a musical outsider mirrored my own, but in at least one respect his experience was very different. In 1978, Wayne moved to Liverpool and his education began in earnest. "I didn't really start reading literature as such until I left home and moved to Liverpool in my late teens. Once I got to Liverpool, though, and was introduced to all kinds of new culture—books, films, music—then I became a voracious reader."

A key component to this education in the arts was a club called Eric's, where Wayne saw The Cure play. Eric's was a veritable breeding ground for aspiring young musicians. He started hanging out with cool bands that were going places, such as Big in Japan, whose members included such future notables as Holly Johnson and Budgie, but he always felt like he was on the outside looking in.

"Like all youth movements, there are the cool ones that lead the way and others, like me, that aspire to be accepted by the elite. I never really ever felt I was until I joined The Sisters of Mercy as a guitarist and moved to Leeds. But that was to disappear again once I formed The Mission in late 1985 with Craig Adams."

The Mission was formed from the wreckage of The Sisters of Mercy, the band that made Wayne cool. After a disastrous recording session they parted company with Andrew Eldritch, who carried on with The Sisters, while Wayne's new band signed a seven-album deal with Phonogram in July 1986 and released their debut album, *God's Own Medicine*, in November 1986. The band embarked on a three-month World Crusade Tour around the UK and Europe. World Crusade II brought the band to North America.

It seems to me, even in the naming of tours and records, there is a strong undercurrent of belief—if not outright spirituality—in The Mission's work. The name stems directly from Wayne's conflict with his own faith.

"In my mid-teens I started questioning the religious beliefs that I had grown up with and started to go to other churches to see what they had on offer compared to Mormonism. I think that questioning eventually led me to being agnostic. I have gone through my life *wanting* to believe but not really finding anything to believe in—apart from living in the current moment."

Wayne's education is actually quite in line with the philosophy of existentialism and follows the trajectory of many a young person leaving the rigidity of their belief behind and searching for answers. Wayne eventually came to realize that he has no idea if God exists and what happens after death—and that's okay.

"I have become really quite comfortable not knowing," Wayne said. "My wife is a quester, a searcher, and I marvel at her determination to find the truth, but just watching what she puts herself through exhausts me. That being said I do think that spirituality comes in many guises and doesn't necessarily have anything to do with organized religion. There have been times I've been tripping and it's been spiritual and sex has sometimes felt that way too."

I agree with Wayne's view about organized religion, and the psychedelic experiences he shared with me cast him as a kind of shaman of Goth. With The Mission there was always a strong undercurrent of that—especially if you look at live footage of him playing with their trademark sound, blending glam sensibilities and hard rock guitars with emotive vocals and dark themes. It became something of a mystical and transcendent blueprint for many Goth bands that came after them.

Wayne is a symbol of the healing and redemptive power of music, especially in these dark, divided times. Music has been for me a salvation and a path, a Tao to help escape the worst impulses of humanity and move into a better, brighter day. This might seem counter to the darkened corners of Goth, but it really isn't. Goth has always been about belief one way or another.

For Wayne, music is the path out of the toxic mess we've created, especially with the internet. Despite its many benefits as a communication tool—one that would have seemed like science fiction when we were children—it's also used to drive a wedge between people and make the world we live in more divisive.

"Music is the one big hope," Wayne said. "There is music everywhere in every culture, and everyone has access to music. Music can be healing, soothing, and unifying—a balm for sure. The sense of communion that we sometimes feel with our audience when we're onstage can be elevating, spiritual, shamanistic, and it is a privilege that we should never take for granted."

A salve indeed.

THE DAMNED: WAITING FOR THE BLACKOUT

WHERE WE GREW UP, WAY SOUTH OF THE RIVER, PUNK WAS ALL AROUND us. Michael Dempsey's mother was a schoolteacher, and one of her colleagues was the mother of The Damned's drummer, Christopher John Millar, a.k.a. Rat Scabies. We did wonder if we were to meet her, should we call her Mrs. Scabies?

Dave Vanian of The Damned at Hammersmith Palais in 1983
Credit: Mick Mercer

The Damned formed in 1976 and was the first UK punk band to record a single, record an album, and tour the US. Dave Vanian, Captain Sensible, and Rat Scabies had all been members of the Masters of the Backside, a short-lived proto-punk group that never recorded and never performed live (well maybe once in a church hall?) but included members that would later go on to fame in punk rock circles including future Pretenders member Chrissie Hynde. The fourth member, Brian James, knew Scabies from a failed audition for another short-lived group called the London SS.

The four became The Damned and began to write and work on a live set, playing their first show opening for the Sex Pistols on July 6, 1976. October 22 of the same year, The Damned released "New Rose" five weeks ahead of the Sex Pistols' "Anarchy in the U.K.," giving them the honor of being the first UK punk group to release a single. The band supported the Pistols for their

Dave Vanian of The Damned at Godzilla's in LA in 1982
Credit: Edward Colver

December tour, but they were kicked off by the Pistols' manager, Malcolm McLaren, ultimately playing only seven of the twenty scheduled dates.

The Damned released its debut album *Damned Damned Damned* in February of 1977, embarking on a tour supporting T. Rex that March on what would be T. Rex's final tour, symbolically taking the torch from the earlier wave of UK rockers. The Damned also toured the US that year, and their brand of punk with fast tempos and short, succinct songs would be hugely influential in the American punk scene, particularly in Los Angeles.

The band tried to get Syd Barrett to produce its second LP, but ended up settling on his bandmate Nick Mason. The resulting album, *Music for Pleasure*, was poorly received, and the band was dropped from their label, Stiff. Scabies left shortly after and the band broke up in early 1978. The group reformed in 1979 and released *Machine Gun Etiquette*, which was informed by sixties garage rock with heavy use of the Farfisa organ. The band released *The Black Album* in 1980, which saw Vanian moving toward a darker vocal style, with more overt Gothic influences. From the beginning of the group, Vanian had adopted a vampiric look with white face paint and formal dress but the next two albums, *Strawberries* and *Phantasmagoria*, made this predilection clear, especially the latter with its single "The Shadow of Love." The group's follow-up *Anything* was a critical and commercial failure and the group went on hiatus, though it continued to record the occasional single.

The Damned forms a critical link between the glam and pub rock of the mid-seventies and the punk rock and new wave of the late seventies and early eighties. It has the honor of being the "first" in many aspects of British musical culture while also producing what amounts to one very good album and a handful of important Gothic singles. Vanian's striking stage presence earns The Damned an unlikely place in the pantheons of punk, new wave, and Goth.

AND ALSO THE TREES: CUT FROM THE SAME CLOTH

IN 1980, THE CURE NEEDED A SUPPORT BAND FOR OUR PRIMARY TOUR, so we put out an ad and asked bands to send a cassette of their music to our label. We found one particular band, And Also the Trees from Inkberrow in Worcestershire, very intriguing. They had a style somewhere between Gothic

And Also the Trees in 1980: Justin, Nick, Graham, and Simon
Supplied by the band

romanticism and general melancholy, which we found attractive. In fact, the band's music was so appealing that we invited them to open for us on tour, beginning a friendship between the bands that has endured over many years.

The Trees was (and is) a peculiarly English type of group. They came from a small place and sprouted in isolation, far away from the influence of the big city. They followed their own path and distilled that experience into their art. This made the band both charming and unique, characteristics that you need not just in music but in life.

Originally the band featured two sets of brothers: Simon Huw Jones on vocals and Justin "Jo" Jones on guitar, with Graham Havas on bass and Nick Havas behind the drum kit. Simon, the singer, cultivated a look that would not make him out of place in a Victorian romance novel. Jo told me that when they were growing up, "Simon discovered literature and lived in a Thomas Hardy reality."

For our first show together we travelled up to Loughborough University in early November 1980. And Also the Trees was a relatively new band and it was only its fourth show. Coming from such a rural setting, its previous shows were in village halls. One time it played a pig roast on a farm, which turned into a riot with skinheads. Despite the rural setting, skinheads were still a problem in those days.

I asked Jo about his initial impressions of playing with The Cure in front of a larger audience of about a thousand or so people. "Our set at Loughborough University was surprisingly well received," Jo said. "We'd never really had a proper audience before and these people seemed to really like us. Peeling off from the stage toward the dressing room, I noticed all three members of The Cure watching us in the wings and you were applauding. *This is going well*, I thought."

Afterward, we all went to dinner in a small, dark restaurant somewhere in the town. We shared a similar sense of humor and laughed a great deal that evening about current events. The tour hadn't started yet and each band returned home. "We got home at 4 a.m.," Jo recalled, "and my father was still up, pretending that he normally walked around the kitchen in the middle of the night moving cups around. I had school the next morning. I suppose things would never be the same for me. This changed the course of the rest of my life."

In the beginning, given And Also the Trees was composed of two sets of brothers, I wondered if that unusual dynamic of sibling energy helped or hindered the creativity of the band.

"When we started," Jo said,

> we were two sets of brothers which, by the law of averages, was going to cause trouble somewhere down the line. It was the Havas brothers who had the most trouble with one another, but actually the breakup of And Also the Trees was finally triggered by my sometimes obstreperous nature, which eventually caused one of those brothers to leave. I've always got on with my brother Simon. We have a shared understanding of what is artistically "right" and thankfully we have nearly always managed to leave ego out of it. I'm sure there have been times when he has wanted to punch my lights out but, generally, we get on well. Probably because we were very close when we were boys.

When I was a teenager in Crawley, the things that helped me escape small-town English life were music and books and art. I wondered if it was like that growing up in a small English village like Inkberrow. "I liked being an outsider and being different," Jo said, "but it doesn't make one very popular in a small village as people are suspicious. Simon could get away with it because of his good looks. All the girls loved him. But we created a reputation of being reclusive and odd. There was a rumor going around that 'Those Jones boys who live under the hill are weird. They only eat rice!' That was how it was."

Inkberrow may have been rural and remote, but it wasn't a total cultural desert. They watched films and listened to John Peel on the BBC and would venture out to Malvern or Birmingham to see bands as no one ever came to Inkberrow. For The Cure, it was our relative isolation that gave us permission to start something new. Was it like that for The Trees in rural England?

"Yes, completely," Jo said.

I followed the path of boredom, which led to buying a secondhand guitar, which in turn led to Simon having the idea of forming a band with our friends. We kept it a secret from everyone we knew. I'm not sure why but when we did tell people that we had a band and we're playing at the weekend it created some interest and I suppose meant that there was little expectation, so we didn't have far to fall. We were fortunate to grow up in the post-punk era. The explosion of punk created a vacuum, so after the revolution there was fertile ground for new ideas.

When we were on tour and everyone was locked into the same mindset, we were like a gang. It was us against the world. Did the Jones brothers feel the same away about And Also the Trees?

"'The brotherhood' is what we came to know it as," Jo said. "Even when we had sisters, it was known as this. It's touring that cements the bond between the members of the band and small crew. You live in a kind of bubble with one purpose: the show. You eat, drink, sleep at the same time and certainly with The Trees there was a real camaraderie. Being outsiders, this brotherhood was all the more important. So, for a while in 1980 and again in 1981 when we toured together as bands, travelling in the same small minibus, I felt that the 'brotherhood' was extended."

After the tour, And Also the Trees asked me to help produce their debut album at Southern Studios in North London—the favorite studio of the art collective punk band Crass. They were slightly more eccentric in the studio than they had been onstage. For example, Jo showed up with an amp fronted with chicken wire.

In the studio, I found them to be earnest and willing to learn all they could about the process; they were intensely involved in the making of their record. Helping them produce their debut album remains one of the best experiences I've had in a recording studio to this day. In the years since its first album, And Also the Trees has found an appreciative audience in Europe, especially France.

One of the aspects I always found special about And Also the Trees is that the band's music is a reflection of where its members grew up in the English countryside. "I think this is another reason we got on so well with you, Robert, and Simon," Jo said. "Our backgrounds are similar. The Trees are a few years younger and certainly students of The Cure, but cut from a similar cloth."

ALL ABOUT EVE: GOTHS WITH GRACE

Julianne Regan moved to London to attend the London College of Fashion. After interviewing Gene Loves Jezebel for *ZigZag* magazine, she was invited to join the band as the bass player. "I was very fortunate,"

All About Eve at The Marquee in 1987
Credit: Mick Mercer

Julianne said, "because they were very enlightened young men. They were very egalitarian. That was their thing. Everybody's equal. And so I was never *the girl*."

After Gene Loves Jezebel, Julianne formed The Swarm with Manuela Zwingmann of Xmal Deutschland. After a little shuffling of members, Julianne, Tim Bricheno, and Andy Cousin formed the core of All About Eve. They had a softer sound that drew on folk influences but maintained a melancholy mood. Call it Pastoral Goth.

I first met Julianne during the book tour for *Cured* in September 2016 in Bath, where she now teaches a course in songwriting at Bath Spa University. I'm always interested in how one's religious upbringing affects people that write music, especially in the Goth subculture. Whether it's presented positively or negatively, religion and belief are at the heart of so much of our music. So I asked Julianne about her experiences in All About Eve and her life in music.

"I was raised Roman Catholic," Julianne told me.

> This meant that from an early age I was exposed to paintings, statues and stained-glass windows depicting an almost naked man wearing a crown of thorns and bleeding from a wound where a spear had pierced his side, his eyes closed in agony, his brow furrowed, a man nailed to a cross through the palms of his hands. Add in the exotic aroma of incense, the flickering votives, and the whisper of prayer, and there you have a seedbed for a future fascination with all things dark and uncanny. Yes, we had Santa Claus, but we also had a Holy Ghost, and as a child I believed in both, equally.

Julianne moved away from Catholicism when she was fifteen. In her latter teens she began to read books about mythology and the occult, such as *The White Goddess* by Robert Graves. She began to experiment with tarot cards and automatic writing in the hopes of getting in touch with her own spirituality. Her education began in earnest under the tutelage of a local witch.

"For a brief while," Julianne said,

> not much more than a couple of months, I was taken on as a kind of apprentice witch by a woman in West Hampstead, London. I was part of a small group

of apprentices that would convene at her place each Tuesday evening. It wasn't weird; in fact it was very genteel. There was tea and cake. We'd draw, in charcoal, what we felt were our spirit guides, and we'd do psychometry on each other's belongings, such as bracelets, keys, etc. Seemed I had a gift. One Tuesday I couldn't make it because I went to see Echo and the Bunnymen at the Hammersmith Palais. The witch lady wasn't pleased and berated me for putting something so apparently earthly above something so unearthly, and said that I clearly wasn't "ready." And so ended my apprentice witchhood.

Much of Julianne's experience seeking out the spiritual found its way into All About Eve lyrics. Julianne's co-writer, Tim, even went so far as to ask if she could put together some lyrics that weren't quite so obsessed with God, though you'd never know this from the title of the band's third album.

"Calling our third album *Touched by Jesus* was a very dumb move," Julianne admitted. "It was assumed by some that I'd 'found God.' I hadn't. I wasn't looking for Him. God, Jesus, that Holy ol' Ghost, the saints, the angels, the

All About Eve's Julianne Regan in 1987
Credit: Mick Mercer

archangels, well, they'll always be a part of me, just like Santa Claus, just like Batman and Robin. They don't have to be *real* for them to have shaped me."

All About Eve rehearsed at Julianne's flat in Tufnell Park in North London. They recorded on a two-track reel-to-reel at her place. I lived in Central London early to mid-eighties, and our crowd, the punks, Goths, and other alternative people, were more free-thinking and informed for the times, but some people in the city were not. Being a woman in a rock band in London presented many challenges.

"It was kind of hard getting on the night buses," Julianne said. "You were fair game for being harassed, especially if you looked a little bit Gothic."

As a Goth guy with dyed hair and makeup, I would get grief from people when I was trying to get home late at night, so I generally avoided the buses and took taxis if I could. For Julianne and other Goth women, there was a perception that no matter what they wore, their colored hair and heavy makeup signified they were no better than prostitutes. She recalled a minor TV personality who made a rude, sexist comment to her at the tube station.

"*'Look at you! You red-tighted demon!'*" Julianne recalled the man saying.

You needed to be a little tough if you were a girl in a band back then. I've seen Sioux deck a guy for saying such disrespectful things to her. Some people couldn't understand that there were *real people* under the unusual clothes and hair, so Julianne did her part to change perceptions.

"I remember being at a bus stop in Tufnell Park one day. There was an old lady standing there with me and she was petrified. I started talking to her and she realized I was a nice young girl. We were scared, but we were also scary!"

At the heart of it all was a naive yet passionate bravado. We were all outsiders in the middle of the gloomy metropolis, but we had each other. "We were this little gang of misfits," Julianne said. "There was a kind of solace in that. I wonder if London was scary because we took a lot of risks, because we were young and daft and in love with music, but I never did it on my own!"

Julianne moved around quite a lot as a child, including spending time in semi-rural locations in Ireland before her family settled down in Coventry. Tim's family came from Huddersfield. London was very much "the big city," and in Julianne's early lyrics one gets a sense of how the capital was both the center of excitement and a source of unease.

We were poor and living in one of the world's most expensive cities, and I think that's where some of my more romantic lyrical notions came from, in that they were almost a compensation for what I didn't have, who I couldn't be. I'd moved to London, feasted on what it had to offer, went to as many gigs as I could afford, but felt overwhelmed by the anonymity of the place, of the sprawling ugliness of some of it, and writing songs allowed me to escape to somewhere else. This feeling of disconnectedness, of so often wishing to be elsewhere, I felt it then and still feel it now. This sense of otherness, of the uncanny, that sensation of never quite feeling at home, it runs through me and much of what I do, like veins in marble. I'm stuck with it. Sometimes it's wonderful and at other times it's horrific.

This feeling of otherness can be a great source of inspiration, but when everyone in the band feels like an outsider, it can make the dynamics challenging. Though our music was somewhat different, one aspect The Cure shared with All About Eve was the frequent turnover as members cycled in and out (and sometimes back in again). Julianne has always been up-front about the challenges of being in a band.

"All About Eve has broken up and gotten back together on several occasions," Julianne said,

> and there have been a couple of line-up changes along the way. At some points it felt like family, and for much of the time, a pretty dysfunctional one. Adults aren't really supposed to spend time together 24/7, in groups, working and socializing, being business partners, but that's what bands do, and it can impact negatively on different individuals at different times. Just when I didn't think things could get any more claustrophobic, my sister went and married the band's then drummer. Stupidly, and he and I both agree it was pretty stupid, or at least misguided, Tim and I then entered into an ill-fated romantic relationship. Looking back on it all, I don't know how we did it, how we spent all those hours stuck in little tin boxes driving up and down motorways. In fact, maybe I do know, and it involved alcohol. Whether that was to fire us up or wind us down, there it was. In the van, in the dressing room, at the venue, in the hotel: alcohol everywhere. Band glue.

All About Eve offstage at The Marquee in 1987
Credit: Mick Mercer

I know that story. Alcohol was band glue, but it was also the band dissolver in my case! For Julianne, it took her many years to learn that although she plays well with others, ultimately she's a lone wolf who needed to cut herself off from her dysfunctional family. She compared the experience of being a member of a touring band to being in a cult in that it takes time and distance to process the experience. When All About Eve had lost its magic, she needed to step away.

"There are individuals I've worked with that I'm still fond of, and others that I am far from fond of. However, we grew up together, were poor together, got a little famous together, and then drifted off from one another in opposite directions."

One of the things about growing up in England at that particular time was there were still vestiges of an older, more "proper" version of English life, with tea and cakes and suchlike. Even if it was tea with a witch! This way of life fades with each passing generation, but it still had a profound influence on our imaginations and our music. I sometimes wonder if this influence was lost on listeners outside the UK, especially in America.

For instance, I recently went on Google and "walked" down the streets of our youth, and it was astounding to me. I understood immediately why we were compelled to express our emotions the way we did. It was all there in the dark, dank English countryside. Growing up in surroundings that were so small and insular helped us focus on things with a high intensity. It was like looking down the wrong end of a telescope. Not surprisingly, Julianne was all too familiar with these echoes of the past.

"I spent a lot of my life staring out of windows; still do. My family moved house several times and so there were many different windows and numerous views, but I think the Irish windows offered the richest. At one time in Ireland, we lived on a stretch of road between the town of Sligo and the village of Strandhill, right across from a cemetery, the one in which my dad now has his grave. That's about as Gothic as you can get."

Yes, I've been there! I visited W. B. Yeats's grave there in 2017. Just a few miles north of Sligo. Very Gothic indeed.

The author at W. B. Yeats's grave site
Credit: Cindy Tolhurst

Adjacent to the house there was a row of tall trees that seemed perpetually populated by raucous corvids. My junior school—or National School as they're called in Ireland—was situated at the top of the hill in the village. From the playground you could see the Atlantic Ocean—about a kilometer in the distance—and I remember the sea as grey and the sky as a slightly different shade of grey, with tankers and cargo ships hinting at where a horizon might be. Reflecting on this puts me in mind of theories of the sublime put forward by the philosopher Edmund Burke, who wrote that "the cloudy sky is more grand than the blue" and that "the ocean is an object of no small terror."

For Julianne, the ocean was not a bucolic backdrop for her village, but a source of potential violence. It was more of a mysterious but Gothic symbol of something deeply unknowable lurking at her back door.

"Perhaps for me," Julianne said,

it was more to do with this strange juxtaposition of the apparent calm and predictability of village life against the untamed vastness of the ocean and the surrounding mountains that resulted in a feeling that even when wrapped up in assumed safety, there was potential danger. Yards from the shop that sold ice-cream and picture postcards, the waves would rise and bash mercilessly against the shore with terrific might. This wasn't a bucket-and-spade kind of seaside. Stories of shifting sands, drownings, and shipwrecks added to the sea's dark mystery. I feel certain that this all fed into my attraction for the uncanny, and this is a theme that has appeared in some of my music and song writing over the years. I only wish I'd expressed it with more coherence.

Goth, by its very nature, is obsessed with the past, but what about the future? We live in a divided and polarized world right now. However, I have always felt music, especially intense music, to be a liberating and unifying force. I've seen people with deep emotional problems who were healed in the heart of this movement and have become who they were meant to be. There is beauty in Goth, but it's also been destructive and chaotic. Julianne has had her share of both extremes.

"Certain genres of music will always appeal to what might be called misfits," Julianne said.

Reading *The Outsider* by Colin Wilson aligned with a time in my life when my young brain was perhaps at peak plasticity and the book led me to read several related works. I was nineteen and it was the early eighties. I was living in a squalid flat-share, and Karen, my best friend from school days, had just moved in. She came home from work one November evening to find me in my room literally gripping the arms of the chair in which I was sitting. That grip was white-knuckle tight because I felt that were I to let go, I might descend into irreversible madness. The book she found on my lap was *Thus Spoke Zarathustra* by Nietzsche, and the lines that had petrified me were, "I say unto you: one must still have chaos in oneself to be able to give birth to a dancing star. I say unto you: you still have chaos in yourselves." I'd read the entire book, followed by *Twilight of the Idols*, and those books had royally screwed with my view of the world and my place within it. The concept of nihilism consumed and damaged me.

Without music, Julianne's life would have been quite different—both personally and professionally. Making music gave her hope that somebody was listening, and if they were listening, they were capable of caring. That, in turn, made her a more careful listener.

"I don't know that I ever felt healed by listening to certain music," Julianne said,

> but it did salve the pain. It patched me up sufficiently to limp on to the next hurdle, at least. Of course, my late teens and early twenties weren't a total gloom fest, but for some reason it's the more melancholy and bittersweet memories that seem to hold the most significance. Perhaps when a person is happy they're so lost in the moment of happiness that it just is what it is. Although I've managed to do so, I've always struggled to write happy songs. It seems fitting to quote Tim here, who said of us: "Sad is what we do best."

I understand that viewpoint. It has always seemed to me that the sadder aspects of experiences are the most poignant and maybe the most helpful in the long run. Julianne Regan helped change perceptions for women back then, and her work and music are certainly worth our attention now.

CHAPTER SIX

INFINITY'S WINDOW

THE BATCAVE AND BEYOND

In 1983, The Batcave was yet to become the stuff of Goth mythology. But it was well on its way.

The Batcave was always packed in 1983.
Credit: Mick Mercer

"It's the people that make the atmosphere. It's not, 'Suck your cheeks in and pose in the corner,'" Olli Wisdom once said of The Batcave, where he was both host and purveyor. His catlike presence in the club was accentuated by his kohl-painted eyes, and he favored wearing fishnet stockings as shirtsleeves and belts made of lipstick tubes instead of the standard-issue, punk rock bullet casings. "It's about having your tongue firmly in your cheek and being able to laugh at the realities of the day-to-day existence."

Every Wednesday night, patrons queued up to enter the upstairs floors of 69 Dean Street—otherwise known as the Gargoyle Club—in the Soho neighborhood of London's West End. We had to squeeze into a tiny lift that held only two people at a time, passing trench-coated women who were exiting the place following their afternoon striptease performances. Meanwhile, those still in line down below sometimes waited in a drizzling storm that threatened to flatten their extravagantly styled hair and dissolve their equally elaborate makeup.

One such patron was once interviewed by a reporter from London Weekend Television. The young interviewee wore black shades, a grey blazer over a black

Southern Death Cult in 1982
Credit: Mick Mercer

T-shirt, and black hair meticulously combed back from his powder-white forehead. The front of his shirt was concealed, but it was entirely possible that it bore the name of one of the moody post-punk bands that partied and played at The Batcave. Maybe it was even The Cure.

The list of The Batcave's past performers was already impressive, but it also included many musicians that left a footprint far outside the walls of the Gargoyle: Bauhaus, Joy Division, Siouxsie and the Banshees, Soft Cell, Nick Cave's pre–Bad Seeds group The Birthday Party, Southern Death Cult (which would later become The Cult), Sexbeat, and of course Alien Sex Fiend, and Wisdom's own band, Specimen.

More conspicuously, however, the kid with the black T-shirt and shades was clad in an aura of cold, detached indifference that he wore like a suit of armor.

"This is where I can do whatever I want," said the young man. He admitted that it took him five hours to prepare for The Batcave's phantasmagoric, midweek suspension of workaday doldrums.

And yet, his look was relatively understated compared to those in line next to him. Some sported close-cropped mohawks dyed omnipresent black. Others

Nick Cave with Nik Fiend in Birmingham in 1984
Credit: Mick Mercer

Specimen in LA
Credit: Dina Douglass

boasted a similar coiffure, only grown out, bleached white, and sprayed up so that it resembled—deliberately or not—a mushroom cloud. For a splash of color in the otherwise monochromatic crowd, there were occasional flashes of fuchsia bangs and leopard print. A few flaunted their allegiance to the club with membership cards clutched in their hands.

These cardboard badges of honor were adorned with the club's logo. There were two versions of the logo, I recall, featuring either a coffin or a bat—the latter reminiscent of the campy *Batman* television show of the sixties—that circumscribed the words "The Batcave." Those words appeared in scratchy letters that might have been drawn by sharp claws in skin.

It's understandable why this grey-blazered young man craved a place of freedom. He said his father, a miner, had come to accept his unconventional sartorial choices—but that he had physically assaulted his son the first time he came home wearing makeup. In the early eighties, choosing Goth was not done lightly. Or even safely.

When The Batcave's patrons stepped off that rickety lift, however, they may never have known a safer space. Or a weirder one. Just to get inside the place one had to pass through an actual coffin with the bottom knocked out.

Inside, the people passed through the darkest looking glass. As advertised, it was cavernous—but not in a spacious way. The Batcave's low ceiling loomed over the dance floor, needing only a few scattered stalactites to complete the illusion. It was dingy. It was loud. It was a parallel universe where death resembled life and doom resembled hope.

Wisdom once described his imposing club as "very friendly. Basically, it's about fun." To him, "fun" meant tolerance. Better yet, it meant inclusion. There was a large overlap back then between Soho's Goth scene and its gay scene. The two were kindred spirits, opposed by mainstream society—often violently so. But The Batcave welcomed all.

Wednesday night proved it. Yes, there were women in flowing black dresses that seemed more apropos to a funeral than a dance floor. There were sinuous men in ripped tights and Flux of Pink Indians shirts writhing like serpents to the DJ's thunderous rhythms. And there were spiky-haired people of indeterminate gender who glided between or outside them both. But

Christian Death's David Glass at The Batcave in 1984
Credit: Mick Mercer

that was not everyone. There were also kids in blue jeans, button-up plaid, and plain brown hair, dancing alongside these pale, otherworldly figures.

That said, not everyone was white. One of the DJs, Hamish MacDonald—also of the band Sexbeat, a staple of The Batcave's stage—said, "Many Black people were part of the vibe too. We always played some reggae, some dub."

Black DJs such as Don Letts spun plenty of reggae and dub records at the original London punk clubs in the seventies, which helped push bands like The Clash and The Slits toward Jamaican influences in their own music. And to be honest, Goth's first big anthem—Bauhaus's bass-heavy, echo-haunted opus from 1979, "Bela Lugosi's Dead"—is, for all intents and purposes, a long, skin-crawling dub song.

The policy at The Batcave was clear: anyone could enter. No matter how packed it got, there was no gatekeeper at the door admitting the cool kids while turning away the plaid shirts. If you had three pounds to enter and seventy pence for a can of lager, that was it. You're in. At play was a basic truth: when outcasts start casting out others, they've basically become their own kind of establishment.

The Batcave was savagely radical, but it was also traditional. Its music and fashion may have jarringly confronted the notions of commercial shallowness, rigid gender roles, and bland conformity—but at the same time, it was just the latest in a long line of kids redefining style, identifying with a tribe, cutting loose with sex and substances, and collectively creating a make-believe realm for one night a week to escape the humdrum of life on the dole or at the shop counter or behind a desk.

The difference was, never in history had youthful rebellion looked and sounded so pensive, so poetic, and so brutally elegant.

Style can be mischievous and magnetic as well as mysterious and menacing. Or as my old friend David J of Bauhaus is fond of saying—in the words of the transgressive painter Francis Bacon, himself a former patron of the very building where The Batcave existed—"The job of the artist is always to deepen the mystery."

The paradox of Goth, though, was just beyond the horizon. From the way the music establishment viewed Goth as a flavor of the week, albeit an acidic one, you couldn't have blamed anyone in 1983 for predicting that Goth was a

Batcave fashion
Credit: Mick Mercer

fad, fated to sputter out like so many fads before it. But Goth wasn't born in The Batcave, nor would it die there.

The perceived wisdom is that Goth proper originated in The Batcave. I beg to differ. I was living in Central London in the early eighties, and I hung out with London clubgoers at the capital's nightspots, including The Batcave—with people like Steven Severin, Siouxsie Sioux, and Budgie of Siouxsie and the Banshees; Marc Almond of Soft Cell; Boy George of Culture Club; and so many others. In my mind, there were several clubs where Goth started, and not all of them in London, either.

The Camden Palace was definitely where some seeds were sown. It was an old BBC radio theater that in the late seventies became a rock music venue. By the early eighties it had transformed into the home for the new romantic club run by Steve Strange and Rusty Egan. Madonna played her first London gig at the Camden Palace. The new romantics were the natural reaction to Thatcher's

Britain of austerity, basically saying, "It's the end of the world, so let's dance and look good doing it!"

Of course, punk exerted its influence on this post-punk world. Strangely and almost imperceptibly, a whole group of people took a left turn instead, and this darker, more gloomy music started to emerge. The Camden Palace, with all its eighties contradictions, was where it became a little more focused for me.

I had been a regular at the Palace for a year or so. My bona fides were marked by my photo in the "club night" picture case that adorned the old theater's ancient, red velvet wallpaper. It was kind of a rogue's gallery, mostly featuring young women in various stages of dishabille. Oh, plus their consorts, skinny men in their own states of undress, marked by a distinct lack of sensible clothing—ripped T-shirts and plastic pants.

Everyone was usually quite inebriated too. My picture on the wall was extra special, I felt, as it showed me bursting through the venerable theater's ornate glass doors, obviously three sheets to the wind—exhibiting a certain bon vivant quality, I thought, like Oliver Reed or any other bad boy on late-night TV.

I was, of course, quite proud of it, and I made a point of showing it to anybody I happened to enter the club with who didn't know yours truly was enshrined on that legendary wall. Most of them remarked politely along the lines of, "Wow, did you hurt yourself falling down those stairs?" Luckily, I could tell them that God looks after drunks and babies, and a little tumble down the heavily carpeted Palace stairs in my usual one-in-the-morning state was not too problematic.

More than anything, it really was the place where the two big rivers of early eighties alternative culture met. The old, austere punk (and post-punk) types with the raincoats, leather pants, and spiked-up hair rubbed shoulders with the new romantics with their emphasis on outlandish fashion. What rose out of that was the newly blossoming alternative dance culture.

The Palace was the first place I had been where I saw punks really dancing, not just pogoing about or slamming into each other. It was the melding of the sexy dance floor with nihilistic anarchy—something a little more stylish than regular punk and definitely not the horrid, smooth discos we had in our hometown of Crawley. But the Palace and new clubs like it were places where you

Christian Death's Gitane DeMone
Credit: Mick Mercer

were definitely going to get your head kicked in if you went in anything less than mob-handed.

"Remember when we used to have to come here with at least four of us if we weren't going to get stabbed afterward?" a Batcaver recently asked me.

He was only half joking. It was probably only 25 percent joking if we were going to Heaven, a club tucked underneath the arches at Charing Cross station.

Heaven was the most prominent gay club in London; it also held club nights for the other outsiders to which obviously we belonged. It's still there, and it's still the most prominent gay club in town, so there are obviously still lots of outsiders left in London. It wasn't that getting into Heaven was dangerous—it was one of the least violent clubs to attend—it was the fact that back then, the area around it, which is now quite gentrified and booming, was very run-down and derelict.

And that was the problem. Drunk people coming out of Leicester Square's pubs and clubs would invariably pick fights with the more outré-dressed club-goers from Heaven. Such is English life. Heaven had evolved from another club in Old Bond Street, The Embassy, which was sort of like London's Studio 54—only London didn't have the money of New York City in the late seventies, so it was never going to be that decadent. More Viking longship than ancient Rome. Which, come to think of it, is awfully Goth, isn't it?

By the time The Batcave carved out its niche in '82, Goth was already an established, if nascent, subculture. And that subculture's tomorrow was already dawning. That same year, the members of Bauhaus were miming "Bela Lugosi's Dead" on a movie set, rubbing elbows with their hero—and one of Goth's godparents—David Bowie. New Order, the band formed from the ashes of Joy Division after the suicide of its front man Ian Curtis in 1980, was recording "Blue Monday," a game-changing single that would bridge the gap between their bleak past and their bright future. And in The Cure, we were putting the final touches on our fourth album, *Pornography*, which would rise above its initial lukewarm reception to one day be embraced in a way I could never have imagined.

Flyer for The Cure in Brussels at the end of the seventies
Supplied by the author

There was a difference that was going to rise out of this post-punk world, a severe new strain that combined both the rush of teen angst and the romanticism of the bedsit poet. This darkly beautiful view encompassed both punk and Plath, and I knew I wanted this more than anything. It lifted my normal twentysomething feelings to a more intense and, dare I say, reasonable level, granting it a realness I never knew possible.

We loved this music. It was our art. But there was more than a flimsy statement, here today and forgotten tomorrow. This had a seriousness of intent, and it cried out for validity.

This was where the magical part came. Goth wasn't just for the kids in London. It wasn't just for the hipsters around the globe in New York City, Paris, or Berlin, who were picking up on our dark Soho vibe. Young people worldwide in less than perfect circumstances, from the deep, dark heart of the American Midwest to the forgotten villages of England, could find something in this music, this movement. It spoke to them and a way of life, a form of being, that they could believe in.

They did. And they still do.

DEPECHE MODE: THE PRIORY

It's said that God has a sense of humor. A macabre one maybe.

At the time it didn't seem funny. Necessary, but not particularly amusing. I left The Cure in Christmas 1988 due to my ongoing mental health problems. Whilst that didn't really come as a surprise to me, it heralded a complete sea change for my life. No longer roaming the world playing to larger and larger audiences, I found myself alone without my band family. Left to my own devices, I holed up in my predictable rock star mansion on the bleak and wild expanse of Dartmoor National Park in southwest England.

With no real idea of what to do, I carried on until I couldn't carry on anymore. Finally, I made my way back to the doctor I had talked to the year before about my "problem" and I at last agreed that enough was enough. I was sick and tired of being sick and tired. He gave me the address of a private hospital in southwest London called The Priory. I had heard of it, but I had no idea what to expect. The doctor said he would make the necessary arrangements to admit me there after I detoxed at the Lister Hospital in Chelsea.

It was a warm summer afternoon in early August when my taxi pulled into The Priory Hospital, Roehampton in London. I had spent the last night before rehab packing my belongings up at the Lister Hospital, grateful that I was no longer suffering symptoms of withdrawal. I was calm and fairly lucid and in a small, uncertain way, looking forward to what this next part of my journey would be like. *It sure as hell couldn't be worse than the previous year*, I mused bitterly as we pulled up to the big white building.

The sight that greeted my eyes could have been straight out of Mervyn Peake's *Gormenghast*: a white Gothic mansion complete with pointed arches, spikes, and battlements. For a moment I was unsure if I had finally crossed over the apparently permeable barrier between reality and fantasy. My still-fractured mind whirled and wondered if this was it, if I was finally mad and gone. The Goth guy ends up at the "Strawberry Hill" Gothic palace of The Priory. The irony of the moment was not lost on me as I took in the all-too-real hospital, the end of my journey of desperate destruction. It was a cruel twist to my fragile mind, mocked by the gods for getting so out of line. I felt I deserved whatever was coming. I should man up and take whatever punishment was going to be dished out to me for falling so far from grace, but the very fact I was even thinking along those lines was the main thing that was wrong with my soul.

The morbid atmosphere changed rapidly, however, once I was inside and was greeted by the friendly and efficient staff. I realized I was in the right place, a sanctuary where I could learn about what was wrong with me and fix it. Lord knows I needed fixing at that point. Once I settled in my room and arranged my few possessions, I ventured out and met the staff nurses and other hospital workers who gave me the necessary information about what I could expect at The Priory. For the next few days, I started the long process of crawling out of my own personal hell as the possibility of a new way of living slowly revealed itself to my shattered psyche.

On most days, during breaks between therapy sessions, meetings with counselors, and lectures on our condition, all the patients came together at the hospital's large dining hall for meals. At any given time there were close to a hundred souls in there; about a third of them were in the unit with me. We tended to sit with each other to discuss what we had learned that day as we ate. It was a bit like high school in that regard.

Besides my fellow sufferers, there were those with other reasons for being there, getting treatments for their mental health. Mostly depression and related maladies, I was told. About a week after I arrived, I started to feel like my old self a little bit as I ventured out of that terrible place I had been hiding in. I felt I was on the road to recovery at last.

One morning in the dining hall during breakfast, about a week into my stay, I was idly glancing around. I admit some of the other inmates intrigued me. I speculated wildly as to why they might be there. In the chemical dependence unit, we pretty much knew why we were there. We fitted a certain pattern of maladjustment to life. Sipping on my coffee, I had to do a double take, because but ten feet from me stood Andy Fletcher!

I dimly recalled once drunkenly thinking I had seen the great train robber Ronnie Biggs one night during a wild bender in Rio de Janeiro, but this was different. I was stone-cold sober, and thus not prone to delusions or strange impressions. As my initial shock receded, I was certain it was him. I got up and walked over to Andy, and a smile of recognition crossed his face. He was as surprised to see me as I was him.

I knew Andy because we had crossed paths on the road a few times. I had frequently seen him at my local pub in London, where it seemed quite a few well-known or up-and-coming bands would hang out. I immediately liked his self-deprecating manner and felt a connection with this gentle pop star. I met his bandmate in Depeche Mode Martin Gore there too and noted there were many similarities between The Cure and the Mode because we came from different places that were exactly the same. The members of each band grew up in a new town: us in Crawley to the south of London and Depeche Mode in Basildon to the east of the capital. Both these towns were created after World War II to house Londoners who had been driven out by Hitler's blitzkrieg. Crawley and Basildon shared a grim drabness and bleakness of design. They felt like places where nothing ever happened, and if it did, the apathetic locals mostly ignored it. We both had similar reasons to get out of town and start up in the big city, to change our futures, a future that started after the end of the seventies with the punk revolution. Our bands were two sides of the same coin, products of a drab suburban existence.

The structure of a new town was almost guaranteed to either imbue you with apathy or fire you up to change. It's a strange truth that despite the bleak surroundings and general malaise of the areas around Basildon and Crawley, these small towns have been the birthplace of quite a few artists, writers, musicians, and sportsmen of note. A partial list includes The Cure and Depeche Mode, obviously, but also the boxer Alan Minter and Olympic decathlete Daley Thompson. To the list we can add Caroline Haslett, the electrical pioneer, engineer, and champion of women's rights; Mark Lemon, the first editor of *Punch* magazine; and YA writer Theresa Tomlinson. Several actors, including Natasha Pyne, lived in Crawley (with none other than Dame Judi Dench living nearby in Outwood). The extremity of life seems to foster a desire to escape the chains of despondency.

Meanwhile, in the hospital dining hall, Andy and I were reacquainting ourselves over a cup of cafeteria tea. I had followed Depeche Mode and Andy's career. They were international pop stars by this time, but lately their music had taken a somber turn. Depeche Mode's more Goth-influenced phase began midway through the 1980s, after it had already begun to achieve some international success with singles like "People Are People" and "Master and Servant." The band received significant college and alternative radio play in the US and was shifting away from the "industrial pop" sound of its mid-eighties records.

The band's aesthetic had turned darker and more pessimistic with the release of their fifteenth single, "Stripped," and its accompanying album *Black Celebration*. The album's subsequent singles "A Question of Lust" and "A Question of Time" further cemented this darkening direction.

In this era, both The Cure and Depeche Mode had reached a level of success that meant we were both asked to play the most important festivals of the time. One such festival being Rock in Athens, which was part of the massive celebrations honoring Athens as the European Capital of Culture for 1985. It was important enough for the Greek minister of culture Melina Mercouri to make a personal appearance.

It was also a societal flash point I now realize. Punk was a part of the general musical language, but youth culture was moving on, and so this was a fitting place for The Clash to play their last show ever. Afterward, as Joe Strummer told *Record Collector* many years later, he had "fucked off to the mountains of Spain to sit sobbing under a palm tree." The new guard had become the old guard, and the passing of the torch transpired right there in the dusty streets of Athens.

For the times they were a-changing! Culture Club, with their androgynous vocalist, was introduced to a somewhat perplexed and antagonistic Greek crowd, some of whom threw rocks at Boy George for daring to be himself.

Both The Cure and Depeche Mode represented something darkly different, and I recall the night we played in Athens at the ancient Olympic stadium as being one of the highlights of my tenure in The Cure. If you look closely at the videos of the show, you'll see I wore a bat insignia on the back of my silk stage shirt that night in a curiously prophetic nod to this darker music that was taking wing.

Music for the Masses from 1987 expanded sonically on this darker direction for Depeche Mode. It was also the first time the band worked with a producer who did not have a relation to Mute Records. David Bascombe had been brought in to replace Daniel Miller due to growing tensions between him and the band in the studio. Things were changing for Depeche Mode. The band once again found themselves using extensive sampling and synthesizer experimentation on the singles "Strangelove" and "Never Let Me Down Again."

I remember meeting Martin Gore in London around this time and talking excitedly with him about the new sampling technology that both bands were using. The early eighties had many firsts in the area of modern music, and we were both eager to see what these new instruments would add to our musical palates.

That record was supported by an international tour that began in October 1987 and saw the group playing East Berlin and Prague—both Communist at the time—as well as selling out the Rose Bowl in Pasadena in one of the most successful concerts of the band's career.

The band returned to the studio with Flood, who had worked with us in The Cure as an assistant to Mike Hedges, and producer François Kevorkian. The sessions in Milan produced the single "Personal Jesus." Prior to the single's release, the band took out ads in UK personal columns advertising "Your

Own Personal Jesus" with a number that played the track. The ad campaign aroused such great interest that the single shot to number thirteen on the UK singles chart and hit gold in the US. "Enjoy the Silence" was released in February 1990 and also rocketed to the top of both UK and US charts, earning the band another gold record.

Andy had been recording a new record with Depeche Mode in Denmark when he was overcome by depression. His bandmates Martin and Dave Gahan thought it would be best if he sought professional help, which was really the wise thing to do. In The Cure, Pearl Thompson took me aside during the *Disintegration* recording sessions and suggested that I should seek help when I started to, well, disintegrate. Unfortunately, I wasn't in a particular frame of mind that I could hear that from him, or anybody.

A band has a strange dynamic. On one hand, it requires very close and personal relationships with which to create stuff together. It has to be this way so its members can tolerate and be with each other for long periods of time. On the other hand, it is fraught with ego and delusion, and it's not always obvious who is deluding whom. In the beginning, you're generally so young and inexperienced in life you don't really have the tools to deal with mental health problems. I recall Joe Strummer saying something to that effect about bands in The Clash documentary *The Clash: Westway to the World*. When drug or other mental health issues come up and it starts to drive a wedge between people, you don't understand how to deal with it and that's the way bands fall apart. "Don't mess with the chemistry," as Joe had it.

Luckily for Andy, he was able to get the help he needed. While preparing the album *Violator*, he had anxiety and depression. At The Priory, he told me he was affected by the death of his sister in her early twenties and had some other problems that he felt might be inherited. We both agreed we were in the right place, regardless of how we had got there. We spent many lunchtimes chatting, and it was great to see my old friend improving. I hope he saw the same in me. The Priory has some beautiful and pleasant grounds to walk around in, so we were able to stroll and talk that summer of rehabilitation.

Although we were in different parts of the facility, we saw each other most days. While Andy was there, Martin Gore came to visit him with photographer and filmmaker Anton Corbijn. As I knew both of them—the music business being a very small world—we chatted in the hospital corridors. I imagine we all sensed the unique strangeness of the situation but also the wonderful fact that a necessary healing event was taking place for both Andy and me.

The days passed into weeks, and both Andy and I left the hospital at different times but comrades in arms having lived through a very unusual situation. This was especially true for English people with our stiff-upper-lip mentality, meaning that no matter what troubles befall you, one should keep going and not make a big deal out of it. Keep calm and carry on. While this idea is often held up as a virtue, I find it bloody silly when you have places like The Priory that can help you. I feel very strongly about mental health as we live in a time and a world that has made treatment more accessible. So why not talk about it?

While I was recovering from a career that I'd slaughtered, Andy was in the process of making *Violator*, the band's seventh studio album, which was finally released on March 19, 1990, about six months after he left The Priory. This release marked the peak of the band's Gothic pop sound where Martin meshed elegant melodies with dark, neurotic, sexual themes often referencing elements of BDSM and religious devotion in the same lyric.

A sad footnote: In 2022 Andy passed away, in his sixtieth year, a kind, gentle man and someone I shared a friendship with in rather unique circumstances that probably neither of us had envisioned when we started playing music. When I met him in the years after our stay at The Priory, either on the road or elsewhere, he seemed to me to be much happier and on a better path. I was definitely placed on the road to recovery after my time with him at The Priory. We were men without a cure who found one in that strange Gothic palace.

DEATHROCK, CA

DEATHROCK IS THE GENERAL NAME FOR THE DARK PUNK AND POST-punk scene that developed in Southern California in the early to mid-eighties. The music grew out of hardcore bands like Germs, Black Flag, and T.S.O.L., but took on a decidedly darker tone and progressed in a more theatrical direction.

Christian Death's Rozz Williams at
Al's Bar in LA in 1981
Credit: Edward Colver

The term "deathrock" came from a genre of fifties-era songs that dealt with teenage tragedies such as "Leader of the Pack" by The Shangri-Las. These songs took a romantic yet morbid view of teenage death that would later inspire death-obsessed lyrics of many punk and post-punk groups. The name was used to describe the LA bands of the early eighties scene most likely either by Rozz Williams of Christian Death or Nick Zedd in his 1979 underground film, *They Eat Scum*.

The emergence of deathrock as a genre in the late seventies ran parallel to darker elements of the post-punk scene in the UK. Elements of both these emerging genres were reflected in the music of deathrock and were embodied in the music of 45 Grave, which was formed in 1979 by the drummer Don Bolles of the Germs with Dinah Cancer on vocals, Paul Cutler on guitar, and Rob Graves on bass. All these musicians had been in the band Vox Pop, which opened for Throbbing Gristle's first LA performance.

As Dinah Cancer succinctly put it in an interview with Alice Bag,

The first prowlings of deathrock came in the early eighties before we were labeled as our other counterparts—the gothic movement. There were no Goths. The deathrockers were splintered off from the punk/hardcore scene that was going on at the time. We played punk rock but we loved Halloween and we looked like vampires. So the phrase "deathrock" was born. . . . At the time when I was performing with 45 Grave, we were just playing music and we didn't consider ourselves a pioneering movement. We were playing with bands like Christian Death, Black Flag, and T.S.O.L., to name a few. And it wasn't until later that we were named as part of the pioneers of the deathrock culture.

Deathrock took punk's riotous impulse and combined it with the experimentation of bands like Throbbing Gristle and PIL, as well as the tawdry glamour of decaying Hollywood replete with monster movies, vampires, and other kitschy trappings. Deathrock also skewed away from what many artists viewed as the rabid machismo of hardcore into something that embraced experimentation in sound and gender expression. In his book *Phantoms*, Mikey Bean traces the end of LA's initial punk wave to the death of Darby Crash of the Germs,

Christian Death in 1984
Credit: Mick Mercer

which fostered the birth of the new scene that exploded into myriad, incestuous directions.

The Cure arrived in Los Angeles the summer after Darby died. We came to California in July 1981 to play our first shows on the West Coast. Everything was very different, but there were some elements that reminded me of the scene we were part of in the UK. Dinah Cancer is correct: there were no Goths in LA back then, but there was something in the air that was drawing experimental artists to LA like moths to the flame, people like Lydia Lunch, who had recently moved from New York.

That first time in LA we met both Lydia and her friend Marcy Blaustein. They looked like our tribe. Black clothes, black hair, and black eyeliner. Marcy drove me up and down Sunset Boulevard and through Hollywood in a big old black Cadillac as a kind of cultural ambassador to show me just what was happening at the birth of the new cool.

We went to a club after our shows at the Whisky. It was most likely Club Lingerie, which was owned by the same guy who was one of the owners of the Whisky, Elmer Valentine. Back then, the club scene on Sunset Boulevard, and in Hollywood in general, seemed to be a self-referencing feedback loop where all the emerging styles would eventually bubble over into the more mainstream rock world. At Club Lingerie we could sense the emerging Goth and deathrock scene. In the dark room of the club, if we weren't surrounded by American accents we might think we were back in London.

The shows at the Whisky were sold out for two nights, and we were very pleasantly surprised that so many people knew our songs. We had played on the East Coast a year before and had garnered mixed reactions. New York and Boston were great as people understood what we were trying to do. In Cherry Hill, New Jersey, less so. But in California people *got it*. Something was changing.

We were staying on Sunset Boulevard in a kitschy little motel whose name now escapes me. It had a kidney-shaped pool and Joe Jackson was staying there too. Joe represented the new wave movement. Oh dear.

Lydia and Marcy were definitely outsiders to the current LA look, which was much more colorful and tanned. Thankfully, as our unofficial guides for our first trip to California, we got the real deal. The true underground.

Stylistically, deathrock took inspiration from seventies shock rockers KISS and Alice Cooper as well as horror films and fifties teenage death ballads. The groups were also inspired by bands like Bauhaus, The Cramps, and The Misfits. SoCal bands such as Christian Death, 45 Grave, and T.S.O.L. added horror camp and religious iconography to create a darker image that corresponded with the sounds they created.

A few groups merged hardcore punk with the deathrock sound, including T.S.O.L. on their EP *Beneath the Shadows* and full-length album *Change Today*, which added a layer of atmospheric synth effects to what might otherwise be fairly straightforward punk songs. But a glimpse of T.S.O.L.'s eagerness to shock can be found in "Code Blue" on its debut album *Dance with Me*, in which the protagonist of the song gleefully engages in necrophilia.

Only Theatre of Pain by Christian Death is widely considered to be the first American Gothic album. Christian Death was formed by Rozz Williams in

Gitane DeMone of Christian Death
Credit: Mick Mercer

1979 and originally called The Upsetters. In 1982 the group signed to Frontier Records, which had put out punk rock records by the Circle Jerks, Adolescents, and Suicidal Tendencies, and released Christian Death's debut record *Only Theatre of Pain* to wide acclaim. By 1983 the band was breaking up due to a number of reasons, including Williams's desire to move in a more experimental direction.

Williams merged Christian Death with members of Pompeii 99, who counted Valor Kand and Gitane DeMone as members. In 2017, I had the opportunity to speak with Gitane. I was interested in her experience as a long-time Goth, and she was gracious enough to talk to me about the birth of death-rock and her own journey into it.

"I actually got into Christian Death by mistake!" Gitane told me. "I was in an early post-punk band called Pompeii 99. We were kind of arty and rebellious; Rozz liked us a lot. He was hanging around our shows, and we would open for Christian Death."

Gitane was a keyboardist and backup vocalist, but by her own account she stumbled into singing. She lived with a lady who was looking after a child whose mother was a singer. She urged Gitane to join her band because she liked the sound of her speaking voice, but Gitane had her doubts.

"I was in a talent show for the school when I was six, and I won for the whole elementary school. Then I tried again when I was eleven and I got stage fright. I thought, *Okay, well, I'm not supposed to be a singer.* I didn't have any training or any support to do that, but I sang all the time anyway. I just thought it wasn't for me."

I recall thinking much the same way when I first had a desire to dabble in music. I felt that since I wasn't innately talented, I would need formal training if I was going to accomplish anything. Punk changed that premise for me. I realized I didn't need formal training or specialized gear. All I needed was something to say and a desire to say it. Like so many young people around the world, I had plenty of both.

Even though Gitane didn't know how to sing, she started practicing an hour a day and immediately fell in love with singing. "It's got everything," she said. "It's spiritual. It's physical. I didn't feel I was an artist in that area yet, but I felt that I could be."

Gitane joined Pompeii 99, a band that released a single and an LP. Musically, they were all over the map, but Williams saw potential. "I'm in my little room in Hollywood writing songs," Gitane said, "when I got a call from Valor, who was the leader of Pompeii 99. He told me he was going to go join Christian Death. Well, Rozz was also interested in having me join as a keyboard player and a backing vocalist. So I met Rozz and I was pulled into Christian Death."

There was just one problem. At the time, Gitane was pregnant with Valor's child. Because of her rock and roll lifestyle, her friends encouraged her not to have the baby, but after having what she described as a paranormal experience in which her son spoke to her, Gitane decided to go through with it. "*You better have me*, he told me. *You better have me*. So I said, I don't care what everybody else is doing. I'm having my kid!"

Gitane started playing shows with Christian Death while she was pregnant, which was shocking to some because the material was very dark, but she wasn't fazed in the least. When Gitane was young, she always wore dark clothing and would ask her mother why she couldn't wear black all the time. Her poetry was focused on death and decay to an almost obsessive degree.

> Since I was a child, I've always been interested in dark, dark things. It was a part of me like, for instance, seeing entities. I was an insomniac and I'd be up all night and I'd see things. I was fascinated by death, by decaying insects and creatures that I would find in the backyard. I had a very dark imagination. I like to hide in the shadows. That sounds like typical kid stuff, but I was into hide and seek and I liked where my imagination took me when I was hiding amongst plants. Very interested in nature and attracted to being a part of nature. I loved the brightness of plants and flowers but there was something that drew me into the decay and the smell of decay.

Gitane and Valor fit in with the new version of Christian Death and immediately began playing shows and writing new material. The band embarked on a lengthy European tour when she was seven months pregnant. Gitane took it all in stride.

"I went on this tour and it was going to be for several months. I figured I would not only be on tour, but I would have my child somewhere. I didn't think about it. All I knew was I didn't want to stay at home pregnant, and I wanted to continue my adventure in music. So I did and it was very difficult. The rest of the band was out doing everything that a band can do at that age and I had to stay in. I had to stay in and take care of myself. I couldn't smoke. I couldn't drink."

Not only did Gitane tour, she recorded the second Christian Death album while pregnant. While Christian Death was in Wales, the band stopped long enough to record *Catastrophe Ballet* and stayed in an old building that was said to be haunted.

"We stayed up on this hill from the studio, and it was full of spirits," Gitane said. "Our drummer saw a little girl sitting on his bed that wasn't there. Rozz woke up one morning and saw his clothes just fly off the clothes rack. I, on the other hand, would walk through a doorway and it would be like clouds of perfume coming at me. I found out this is the spirits' way of welcoming me because I was carrying life."

Gitane at Dingwalls in 1986
Credit: Richard Bellia

Gitane gave birth to her son, but not long afterward Williams left the band and Christian Death continued under different guises. A great deal of controversy and confusion ensued when Williams started using the name Christian Death again in the nineties, and the acrimony continued until his untimely suicide in 1998.

Gitane never stopped creating. Whether she was making art, writing poetry, or creating music, performance is her calling. "I feel like I'm right at home when I get onstage," she said. "I feel more sociable when I'm onstage than I do off!"

Some people see the darker music of Goth as a destructive force in the universe, but I think that's misguided. The acknowledgment of the dark side can bring forth a new way of being in the world and, in some cases, new life.

CHAPTER SEVEN

WE ARE MANY

NINE INCH NAILS

Nine Inch Nails got its start in Cleveland in 1987 when songwriter Trent Reznor was playing keyboards in a synthpop band called the Exotic Birds. This project was managed by John Malm Jr., who befriended Reznor and became his de facto manager for his solo career. At the time, Reznor worked as an assistant engineer and janitor at Right Track Studios, where he was able to record demos between sessions for free. He played all the instruments himself while programming drums as he was not able to play them, an approach that has remained consistent throughout his time as Nine Inch Nails.

After supporting Skinny Puppy in 1988, several labels expressed interest in the demos Reznor had put together. Ultimately, Reznor signed with independent label TVT, who put out his debut album, *Pretty Hate Machine*, on October 20, 1989. The album's synth-focused sound blended industrial and rock sounds with lyrical themes of angst, lust, and betrayal. The album's muscular beats and synth sounds are reminiscent of late eighties Depeche Mode as well as EBM groups like Front 242 but with a darker edge. The album features contributions from producers Adrian Sherwood on "Down in It" and Flood.

In 1990 the group began touring *Pretty Hate Machine*, opening for Peter Murphy and The Jesus and Mary Chain, among others. In 1992, Reznor relocated to the house in Benedict Canyon, Los Angeles, where Sharon Tate was murdered by the Manson Family. He set up a studio in this house and worked on what would become *The Downward Spiral*. His 1994 follow-up to *Pretty Hate Machine* is a concept album detailing the downfall of a man, a kind of antihero's journey. To my mind, this carries on the themes of prototypical Goth antiheroes such as Alan Vega of Suicide.

I was moving from the UK to California when this album came out. In many ways it was the soundtrack to my journey. I had just finished a disastrous court case with my old label and music partner, and my first marriage had fallen apart at the same time. If anyone was on that spiral, it was me. I had been sober for some time but felt untreated. Tracks like "Hurt" spoke to me in another way, not just about the pain of addiction but the chaos of a life torn apart by what that brings into your life. I was learning to live again by confronting some demons. Mostly, as it turned out, those self-centered and self-pitying ones. I sensed underneath all the nihilism and solipsism of *Downward Spiral* there was the beating melancholy heart of darkness that I associated with Goth.

The album expands on the synthpop tendencies of the first LP with a much more industrial and textural focus that proved to be enormously successful. "March of the Pigs" and "Closer" were released as singles; "Hurt" and "Piggy" were issued to radio without a commercial single release but found listeners nonetheless. After this record, Reznor's struggles with addiction, depression, and writer's block would prolong the release of *The Fragile* until 1999.

"Hurt" was famously covered by Johnny Cash in the final years of his career. I was in Nashville a few years back and went to the Johnny Cash Museum. Whilst walking around and looking at the exhibits, I was astonished to see the biggest crowd of people around the presentation of the video for "Hurt" and the red velvet chair featured in that video. The track played continuously at the exhibit, and the audience seemed mesmerized by the power of this song as sung by the original "Man in Black." True Goth.

Some years later, The Cure was selected for induction into the Rock and Roll Hall of Fame. It has to be said there was initial resistance from some members of the band, notably Robert and Simon, who were not convinced about its validity. Having lived in America for a quarter of a century by this time, I had a different viewpoint. I believed that all the Goth kids who loved The Cure and lived in small towns across America would feel validated by The Cure's selection. I felt it was time that The Cure was recognized as a vital part of the history of rock and roll and not apart from it.

Eventually, the others came around and members of The Cure, both past and present, convened in Brooklyn, New York, for the ceremony. I had been asked who I thought should induct us into the Hall of Fame. I suggested Trent as I always loved Nine Inch Nails, *The Downward Spiral* in particular. That album carried me through a dark time in my life. I knew from my own band's experience with *Faith* and *Pornography* that music had the power to save you from the pit of despair by giving you the strength to walk through that pit. I sensed a like-minded soul.

As we sat in the hall, Trent came out to speak to the audience to explain why he felt we should be in the Hall of Fame: "I grew up in a small town—small town USA. Mercer, Pennsylvania, to be precise, where there was nothing to look at but cornfields. It was a primitive time, long before the miracle of the internet arrived to devalue our wonderful art form. Even pre-MTV, with nothing to listen to on the radio and nothing to do but dream and escape . . ."

He continued to talk about what it had meant to finally hear The Cure's music on college radio. "I suddenly felt connected and no longer quite so alone in the world." Hearing those words, I knew we'd picked the right person. I understood all too well what he meant. We came from a small town too—albeit on the edge of a big city—but small towns are the same in the US and the UK. It was the same mindset, the same apathetic people lived there, and the same nothingness would swallow us up if we didn't do something to escape.

After the speech, we trooped up onto the stage to collect our awards. As I walked along the stage front, I went straight over to Trent, and although I had never met him until this very moment, we hugged like long-lost friends. Because, of course, we were.

DRAB MAJESTY

Drab Majesty is a Los Angeles–based new wave/Goth band formed by Deb Demure (real name Andrew Clinco) in 2011. Clinco first developed the idea for Drab Majesty while drumming for the band Marriages.

He conceived a project where he played all the instruments himself. After recording a few songs in his bedroom, Clinco found himself surprised by the recordings, feeling as if they came from another person. Thus, he took on the pseudonym Deb Demure to distinguish himself from the creator of Drab Majesty's music. The music blended the heavily chorused guitar and throbbing sequenced bass and drum machines of post-punk with futurist and cult themes, giving the band the feel of an alien musical group that happened upon Depeche Mode.

Clinco self-released the first EP *Unarian Dances* in a limited run of cassettes and on Bandcamp in 2012 before Lolipop Records reissued it. Drab Majesty signed with Dais Records in 2015, releasing a single "Unknown to the I" before putting out their debut full-length album, *Careless*, that same year. *Careless* was recorded over the preceding two years at Clinco's home studio. The record blends the mechanical rhythms of Depeche Mode with the lush guitar work of Felt and the textures of minimal wave group Martin Dupont.

In 2016 the group expanded into a duo with the addition of keyboardist Mona D for tours of Europe and North America. The group's second album, *The Demonstration*, dealt thematically with concepts of the psychology of mass suicide, particularly Marshall Applewhite and the Heaven's Gate cult. The group toured extensively over the following two years with stops at various festivals.

The group's third album, *Modern Mirror*, was released in 2019. The band adopts a theatrical performance style, donning full whiteface makeup and wigs and sunglasses as well as pseudonyms, giving the group the appearance of religious leaders or extraterrestrials. This theatricality, paired with the astute eighties pop stylings of their music, has earned the band a significant following in the worlds of Goth, post-punk, and other underground music communities.

COLD CAVE

COLD CAVE WAS FORMED IN LOS ANGELES IN 2007 BY WESLEY EISOLD, who had previously sung in hardcore bands Give Up the Ghost and Some Girls. Eisold was born with one hand, which led him to electronic composition. After early releases on Dais, Cold Cave signed with Matador Records to re-release their first album, *Love Comes Close*, in 2009. The album takes inspiration from the synthpop of groups like New Order and Gary Numan as well as the darker sounds of Joy Division.

Matador released the group's follow-up, *Cherish the Light Years*, in 2011 and the band toured extensively, opening for Nine Inch Nails, The Jesus and Mary Chain, and Soundgarden. Cold Cave is essentially a solo project of Eisold, who also runs Heartworm Press, which publishes his own poetry as well as work by the late Mark Lanegan and other projects. Since the second album Cold Cave has opted to release a series of singles, including 2021's *Fate in Seven Lessons*.

BLACK MARBLE

Black Marble was formed in 2011 by Chris Stewart in Brooklyn, New York. He released the debut EP *Weight Against the Door* on Hardly Art in 2012. He released the debut album *A Different Arrangement* later that year. These records harkened back to the coldwave and darkwave genres of the eighties, with icy, minimal drum machines, prominent bass lines, and pulsing sequences. Stewart's deadpan vocals clash perfectly with the warm analog synth and drum machine textures, veering between the nihilistic and nostalgic. Black Marble released its second album, *It's Immaterial*, on electronic label Ghostly International in 2016, followed by *Bigger Than Life* and *Fast Idol*, both on Sacred Bones.

MOLCHAT DOMA

Belarusian post-punk group formed in 2017 in Minsk. Its sound blends Russian rock music from the eighties with coldwave, new wave, and synthpop. Its first album, *S krysh nashikh domov*, was self-released in 2017, followed by *Etazhi* on Detriti Records in Europe in 2018 and re-released by Sacred Bones in 2020 in the US. The band's deadpan, dark, and minimal style has been deemed "doomer" music by online communities, representative of a nihilistic and disaffected youth subculture bereft of opportunity with lyrical themes of loneliness and isolation. The band's song "Судно (Борис

Рыжий)" ("Bedpan [Boris Ryzhy]") has appeared in roughly 225,000 TikTok videos after going viral. The band released their third album, *Monument*, also with Sacred Bones in November 2020. "Doomer" internet culture is a sort of rehashing of Goth in the internet era with similar thematic concerns but without a definitive aesthetic.

LEGIONNAIRES

Since the days of the Eternals, virtually every nation has produced dark and gloomy bands that look to their Goth forebears for insight and inspiration. Forever Grey from LA, Fearing from Oakland, and Cholo Goth from San Diego represent different approaches to Goth within the Golden State. In the US, Goth reigns from Portland, Oregon's Soft Kill to Boy Harsher from Savannah, Georgia. You've got Twin Tribes from Texas, She Past Away from Turkey, and Italy's Ash Code. Goth brings people together in Lebanon Hanover, an English-German band with a Swiss vocalist, and Goth is on the move with Australian artist Kris Baha now residing in Berlin. Silent Servant draws on its roots in Central America and experience in LA and London. Bestial Mouths devours audiences in Berlin via New York and LA. Goth is everywhere, a global phenomenon with adherents in every dark corner of the planet, and it's not going away anytime soon.

CHAPTER EIGHT

BEFORE AND AFTER GOTH

VISUALLY GOTHIC

You only have to look at the cover of The Cure's third album, *Faith*, a grey and misty photo treatment of the ruins of Bolton Priory in northern England, to get it. Intensely connecting the dark and gloomy image on the cover to the somber music inside and thence to the Gothic imagination of our world.

While the sweeping buttresses and cavernous spaces of Gothic cathedrals no doubt informed the aesthetics and general funereal mood of Goth, one can also trace the origins of the Gothic aesthetic to the Symbolist painters and poets of the mid-nineteenth century who sought to portray things not as they were so much but rather through the emotional states they produced. Writers such as Charles Baudelaire, Stéphane Mallarmé, and Paul Verlaine were three leading exponents of this movement.

The connections in music are numerous from Tom Verlaine of the band Television changing his name from Miller to Verlaine in honor of Paul Verlaine to the lyrics for "How Beautiful You Are" on The Cure's album *Kiss Me, Kiss Me, Kiss Me*, which were inspired by the Baudelaire poem "The Eyes of the Poor."

Painters associated with the Symbolist movement include Edvard Munch, Odilon Redon, and Gustave Moreau. These artists used dream and mythological imagery to express both personal and obscure truths.

Expressionist aesthetics in poetry and visual art certainly influenced the development of Goth. The Goth "view" has always been shaped by emotional reactions and feelings, even if it's just the understanding of the absence of these conditions.

Expressionist artists applied their subjective lens in order to present images of the world radically altered by emotional experience. The "meaning" of these pieces is found in the transcription of these individual emotional states. The Expressionist artist builds on inner psychic landscapes to craft works that have more to do with an interior rather than an exterior world. The paintings of artists such as Egon Schiele exemplify this. Schiele's portraits transform his subjects into fragmented, tortured semblances of human beings. The inner chaos he felt is shown in the painful angles and lurid colors of his paintings that influenced the works of later British artists Lucian Freud and Francis Bacon.

It is only appropriate then that the cover of The Cure's most extreme and emotional album, *Pornography*, should bear more than a passing resemblance to a Bacon painting with its violent slash of colors. The image on the outside is a signpost to the meaning of what was found on the actual recording of the album, the lyrics and the music portrayed by the brutal and intense cover.

German Expressionist cinema also figures into the development of Goth, with plots and stories of the Expressionist films often dealing with madness, insanity, betrayal, and other topics triggered by the experiences of World War I. These films, shot in stark black and white, often utilized harsh geometric angles and unrealistic set design to, in a manner similar to Expressionist painting, examine the turbulent emotional world of their subjects. Notable films are *Metropolis*, *The Golem*, and, of course, *Nosferatu*—the vampiric character who has served as an icon for Goths ever since.

I imagine it won't come as a surprise to the reader to learn that on our early tours with The Cure, before the advent of DVDs and streaming services, we carried a small Super 8 projector with which to show silent black-and-white films on the blank walls of our budget hotels. A showing of *Nosferatu* featured regularly in our postshow entertainments.

One of the most striking uses of this vampiric iconography in musical presentation in recent years was Peter Murphy making an astonishing stage entrance hanging *upside down* like a vampire bat while singing "Bela Lugosi's Dead," with Bauhaus at the Coachella music festival in California in 2005.

Goth was influenced by and has influenced numerous adaptations of the Gothic horror novel *Dracula*, published in 1897 by Irish author Bram Stoker. In 1931 Universal Studios made the first sound film adaptation. Who played the lead part in the movie? None other than Bela Lugosi himself. This kicked off a series of imitations, homages, and modern-day retellings of the vampire myth, none more influential on youth culture than 1987's *The Lost Boys*.

By the nineties, Goth culture wasn't a secret anymore, thanks to a pair of films by filmmaker Tim Burton: *Beetlejuice* and *Edward Scissorhands* were dark and strange, but featured Hollywood stars like Winona Ryder and Johnny Depp dressed in Goth-inspired attire. Tim Burton's films reference Goth styles and tropes. He's made no secret of The Cure's influence on his films. "Their music has always been inspirational to me, so somewhere," Burton said, "in anything I've done, always in the back of my mind, it's probably rolling around there somewhere in my soul."

It's a mutual admiration society. In 2011, while I was playing at the Beacon Theatre in New York on the Reflections Tour with The Cure, the familiar face of Tim Burton approached me backstage to talk. Even though we had never met before in person, conversation came easily and I found myself talking with a like-minded soul, and in that Goth connection we understood each other perfectly.

Burton was also responsible for making Batman's Gotham darker and more dangerous. In a tacit acknowledgment of the connections between the Gothic leanings of Batman and Goth music, Burton asked Siouxsie and the Banshees to compose the main song, "Face to Face," for 1992's *Batman Returns*. These movies influenced the look and feel of more mainstream films (and films that would become mainstream) such as *Blade*, *The Crow*, *The Doom Generation*, *The Craft*, and *The Matrix*.

It's worth noting that Tim Pope, who is responsible for directing many of The Cure's music videos as well as the cinematic release of *The Cure in Orange*, directed *The Crow: City of Angels* in 1996. Goth aesthetics continued to inform twenty-first-century films such as *Twilight*, *The Girl with the Dragon Tattoo*, *This Must Be the Place*, and *Only Lovers Left Alive*.

And the legacy lives on. At the end of 2022, Netflix premiered *Wednesday*, a series based on the imagined life of Wednesday Addams. For the role, actress Jenna Ortega studied the dance moves of the original queen of Goths—Siouxsie Sioux.

ELDER GOTHS AND FASHION

GOTH AS A MUSICAL SUBCULTURE HAS BEEN GOING FOR NIGH ON FORTY years. The original Goths from the late seventies and early eighties are now in their sixties. Many of them still adhere to the subculture's rules and, by and large, are the same as they ever were: romantic and melancholic nonconformists who have somehow avoided relinquishing their way of being and becoming more conventional. Rather, they have adapted their lives to honor their Gothness while aging gracefully.

Not too long ago I met with a friend of mine, James Murphy of LCD Sound System, and we had a long conversation about how being part of an artistic movement will keep you young. In the course of Murphy's travels around the world, he's spoken with a great many people. Invariably, when the conversation

Nik Fiend prepares for an Alien Sex Fiend performance at The Venue in 1984.
Credit: Mick Mercer

turned to the passage of life and getting older, Murphy would realize that he's actually much older than the person he's speaking with. He developed a theory that being actively engaged with something creative helps you maintain a more youthful outlook—no matter how old you are.

I tend to agree with this outlook. I know a lot of people in the Goth subculture, and many of them are still doing creative things. It's not just the musicians or the writers, doing what they've always done, but Goths engaged in a wide range of creative pursuits. From producing podcasts to making jewelry to creating visual art. Whatever it is, these people are passionately engaged with their art. Is it a coincidence that so many of these people are adherents of the Goth subculture? Does the Goth mindset help people deal with the problems of aging? Or do creative people in general have a leg up on the rest of the population?

I read an article in the *Washington Post* about Leah Bush, an academic and musician from Baltimore, who wrote a thesis on this phenomenon for her doctorate about how Elder Goths may very well have discovered the secret to aging successfully. My curiosity piqued, I arranged to talk with Leah and ask her about her research.

She told me the origins of her project went back to 2010, when she was in a band. They were hired to play what she thought would be a typical New Year's Eve party, but the people who hired her were far from ordinary.

"We get there and it's a Goth house," Leah said. "Goth adults, Goth kids running around. It was great. We played the next year and they're having a Goth funeral because it's someone's fortieth birthday. It's got a coffin with roses and a portrait and someone delivered a eulogy to her youth. Then the requests started coming in. 'Hey, can you guys play Peter Murphy?' It was hilarious."

That experience stuck with her, and she began to question why someone would do that. What keeps people attached to this particular subculture?

When Leah started to think about studying Goth, she discovered there were all kinds of misconceptions about it—even at the academic level. "There was this preconception that Goths are these depressed people," Leah said, "even among my dissertation committee, 'Oh, Goths, they're very deviant. They're very freaky.'" To which Leah diplomatically responded, "Well, your version of freaky might not be theirs." Initially, Leah got a lot of resistance from people who thought her project was strange. "No," Leah tried to explain, "they're just people."

Part of the problem was so many different behaviors fall under the umbrella of Goth—from the music to the fashion to the fetish scenes—that many people are reluctant to identify as Goth because they don't participate in *all* those scenes. For example, someone who loves listening to Goth might not say they're Goth because they don't wear the kind of makeup associated with it.

Goth, Leah found, is whatever you want it to be, but it requires a commitment to the subculture. Most Elder Goths held on to some aspect of their youthful passion and refused to let go. In other words, they weren't a Goth by accident. They may have stumbled upon the music by happenstance, but their decision to stay in the scene was a choice.

For her study, Leah spoke to a great many musicians and DJs in and around Baltimore, where she lives. The people she talked to were from Maryland, Virginia, and Washington, DC—not exactly hotbeds of fashion like New York, Chicago, and Los Angeles, where people tend to be more image-conscious. Being a musician herself, finding people to talk to was fairly simple. "You just find people and they find you," she told me.

Leah also spoke with people who were connected to Goth through the world of fashion. Some owned boutiques, others made their own clothes, while the majority simply enjoyed buying and wearing Goth clothing. This makes sense since the way Goths dress is one of the most noticeable things about us. Interestingly, for some of these people Goth music was secondary to fashion. "I bought a jacket from someone on Instagram," Leah said, "and I get in there and she has a Goth house filled floor to ceiling with Goth clothes, but I didn't see band posters. What I thought was interesting about her was she didn't feel comfortable giving her age. She said, 'It's well over forty. Let's leave it at that!'"

For many people that Leah talked to, their passionate involvement was brought about by a midlife change that encouraged them to follow their dream. One had to quit their job, which enabled them to be full-time Goth and start a clothing business. After the death of a parent, another participant used their inheritance to make a fresh start. For others, it was a desire to change the course of their life by going back to school. The interest in exploring an alternative path was always there, but an event caused them to examine their life and give it a more purpose-driven direction, one that centered on Goth music, fashion, or culture.

There's something about experiencing a major change in life that makes people more inclined to seize the day. I think getting older makes people think about the time they have left. Maybe they lived outside the mainstream during their youth. Maybe they were punks or Goths when they were teenagers. That earlier experience with the subculture makes it easier for people to go back to it as they get older.

Punk is where it started for me. I feel like when punk came along, it gave me permission to do things and see things in a different way. Before punk I never dreamt of being in a band. It seemed too far above my aspirations. I think one reason people stay in the subculture is because it gives you permission to experiment and do new things, which is a key component of staying young at heart.

Leah found there was a lot of overlap between the music and fashion. Some started out with punk and found Goth, others were drawn to the subculture from the get-go. Both punk and Goth fashion espouse a "fuck you attitude" that was attractive to many of the people Leah talked to for her study. For some, that attitude was more important than the music itself. "There are people who are not even necessarily identifying as Goth," Leah said, "so much as identifying against the status quo. They're saying 'I don't want that. I don't want this. I don't want the f-ing Lexus. I don't want these middle-class things.'"

These were people who rejected the values of middle-class consumer culture and were drawn to a different kind of lifestyle. While some people rejected the idea of living a so-called normal life outright, others found a way to incorporate it into their lives. One individual Leah spoke with had a house and kids. He and his partner took turns looking after the children one night a week while the other one went out to Goth clubs.

Others were able to dedicate their lives to Goth because they didn't have the pressure of a day job that demanded they conform to what someone who works in an office should look like. Many Goths are simply unwilling to work in that environment. They want to do something where they can express themselves through their hairstyle, makeup, and clothing. It takes someone who's willing to assert themself, who isn't afraid of getting strange looks, and may, in fact, even enjoy the attention. "That takes a lot of nerve," Leah said.

Of course, there are always exceptions to the rule. On a recent visit to that most conformist of environs—an IRS office—I found my agent was not only Goth but very much looked the part while working nine to five for the federal government. The times they are a-changing...

People in the Goth lifestyle come from all different backgrounds—from trailer parks to ivy-league schools; what unites them is they've chosen a lifestyle over a career path. One Goth told Leah, "We want to live this way. If I'm going to live in a shack, that's fine, but we live like kings, because we love what we're doing."

Goth is so much more than just the music. Leah found that most of the Goths she talked to were philosophical in nature. One gentleman was formerly a priest in the Anglican church. He left the church because he felt it wasn't progressive enough with regards to the LGBT community. It was a difficult decision to leave, but he followed his values. Ultimately, his commitment to the counterculture was stronger than his faith. "Jesus was the most countercultural figure who ever lived," he told Leah.

People like the Goth priest, however, are outliers. For most people it comes down to the music. First, the counterculture positions you against the mainstream, and then the music closes the deal. "So many people I talked to, that's what did it. 'I heard this Sisters of Mercy record and that did it for me.' It only takes one album; it only takes one song."

During the course of her studies, Leah discovered something that I've known for quite some time: Goths are everywhere. While taking a trip to see a tribute to Courtney Love in upstate New York, Leah stayed at an Airbnb that just so happened to be a Goth house. The host was so happy to have someone she could talk to at length about being a sensitive, fragile soul in a world that pretends to be unconcerned with death. This, I feel, is another hallmark of Goth: a willingness to peer into the dark places of the soul. Goths are very much interested in the light and the dark and are less inclined to be flustered when things take a turn for the worse because, in a sense, we've been preparing for these moments all our lives.

In the end, I feel that being an Elder Goth is about self-determination. It's about feeling comfortable in your own skin. It brings to mind a friend of mine in Los Angeles who owns a store with her husband that sells Goth things. They've had their ups and downs like anyone who owns and operates a small business, but they live a life that mirrors their values. They don't have to come home from their regular jobs and change out of their clothes and start doing this other Goth thing. It's not a costume for them. They are who they are.

Goth is creeping into the mainstream without being mainstream, which is the reason it keeps going, because people will always be attracted to doing things differently and rejecting what everybody else is doing. "At the end of the day," Leah said, "it's about community. It's about people who understand you. It's about people who you can see across the room and know you're one of them, even if you're new."

One realization that Leah heard over and over again was the idea that it's okay to be strange. One woman that Leah spoke with admitted, "I forget that a lot of people don't live like me." That's why community is so important to the Goth subculture. It can get lonely being the only weirdo in town. We all want a tribe to belong to.

WHY GOTH MATTERS

So, after all this, you might ask, Why does Goth matter? After all, it was just part of the story of the eighties, right? One that's been pored over by TV and the internet but only dimly recalled by a few fanatics?

Well, not quite. That's not where the story ends. As a subculture, it's really become part of the fabric of society more than any other recent subculture other than, say, hip-hop. Not only in music and art but also on television, the internet, and in the most reliable indicator of the mainstream—the clothing lines of numerous fashion houses.

The dark and exciting lines of Goth accoutrement abound. Check out Susie Cave's The Vampire's Wife or Adolfo Sanchez's beautiful haute couture Goth wedding dresses. It's mainstream but underground. It's everywhere and nowhere, baby. In every small city across America there are hundreds of Goth kids (even if they don't know it yet) just waiting to be validated by the dark power of Goth. I know they are there for I've seen them on my journeys around the world.

Chad Duell and Courtney Hope wearing clothing designed by Adolfo Sanchez. "The message or feeling I want to convey in my clothing is power and confidence. When I put a suit on, it feels like I'm adding armor to my body. It even changes the way I stand and carry myself. This is exactly the way I want someone to feel in my designs." —Adolfo Sanchez
Credit: Joanna Miriam

While promoting my memoir, *Cured*, I encountered many of the demimonde. The young and the older Goths at every small and not-so-small bookstore and record store across the US and the continent of Europe. They are true believers after all these years, and new ones are just coming into the fold. They all feel connected to the genre, and even though life has rolled on ever forward, they still believe in the power that helped them traverse the most delicate part of a young (or not-so-young) person's life.

It's not just a fashion for these people, not just a subculture they identify with, so much as a way of dealing with the world that acknowledges the sad and the melancholy and, most importantly, validates their worldview. It is an outsider group that's bigger than the Deadheads and been going almost as long. The brilliance of the idea is in its acceptance of everyone: the structure of their association encourages all whilst holding true to their initial experiences. If you say you're in, you are. That duality of purpose works beautifully.

Meanwhile, new purveyors of bleak abound. Recently, in the Silverlake area of Los Angeles, I witnessed the continuation of the old urge at Zebulon with my son Gray's band, Topographies. The dark and claustrophobic tendrils in

Wedding gown and veil designed by Adolfo Sanchez for Kat Von D. "I have such a passion for the Victorian era like so many others who love Goth—Kat Von D's wedding gown and veil were such a treat to bring to life. It's like seeing your painting, but instead of a wall, it's wrapped around a body." —Adolfo Sanchez
Credit: Look FotoGrafia

their new music both familiar and ancient. I also saw Godspeed You! Black Emperor just before the pandemic, and they played their droning, oppressive canvases of noise partially inherited from the old vision to a full house of followers who mostly dressed in de rigueur black. They might call it experimental, but I know Goth when I see it!

Yes, yes, I hear you say, but why should it matter now? Why does Goth matter?

Well, unless you've been living under a rock these last few years, you can't help but notice the terrible slide our world is taking toward oppressive authoritarianism. Just like before, these severe forms of government will seek to stifle the unhindered flow of thoughts and ideas under the guise of "freedom." Art and open expression will be controlled to facilitate those ends subtly or not so subtly. It's happening already with the weaponizing of fake news.

That's where, to my mind, Goth comes in as the last true alternative outsider subculture. As a type of cultural resistance, it will push something good forward on that beautiful, bleak wave of art, the wave that started for me that night long ago in a darkened room in August 1977 and has yet to break.

And that's why it matters.

AFTERWORD

At first, I approached the subject matter of *Goth: A History* in a more traditional way; I felt I should write a comprehensive encyclopedia of the times. I thought hard and long on this for a year or so. I finally realized I am no historian and neither do I want to be one. It's too persnickety for me, with absolutes that shouldn't be absolutes. Always just one person or one culture's view. You can see where this has got us, right?

I believe that this traditional narrative would not help anyone—least of all myself—make sense of what occurred in the world to bring about this psychic and cultural change. The revolution after the revolution, so to speak.

I am also acutely aware that writing such a book will never make everyone happy. Someone will protest that I didn't include their favorite figure, and they will be absolutely correct. I will inevitably leave out artists or people or events that they deem vital to the understanding of the subject. It's not my intention to die on that particular cross. I truly feel that someone else will make good that strange labor of love and enjoy doing it. Not I.

I determined my best course was to write a historical memoir of sorts, the memoir of a subculture, if you will. After my life-changing experience with my first book, *Cured*, I realized what I enjoy writing about is not just the stories but the connections from those stories that lead to an understanding of the memories we have experienced with this music and genre.

There were obstacles to this undertaking. Although we have photos and clips of certain things, we didn't have the internet because it wasn't there, back in the seventies and eighties, but you're in luck: I was there! As were many I've talked to for this book. I've produced a combination of stories, interviews, opinions, and extensive research, in which I was ably assisted by my son Gray, to weave that arbitrary tapestry into a coherent set of essays that present a totality of my experiences. I was also aided by Jim Ruland, who managed to keep this project on course and make sense despite the author's best attempts to derail it from time to time! Both Gray and Jim were my invaluable collaborators and partners in the making of *Goth*.

Many readers have told me that the social anthropology they got from *Cured* was both interesting and instructional in that it transcended the actual facts to become a geographical textbook of how to be post-punk. The map of the territory, if you like. It showed how we drew the many and various threads of the art and our circumstance together. This helped us discover our own raison d'être and break down the stifling walls of conformity of a postwar world. The fact that most of the world had suffered extensively from the early to the middle part of the twentieth century through two worldwide conflagrations meant that society had turned inward for the preservation of what little there was left to navigate in those broken times. There was a lot of wall building going on, both materially and in a more metaphysical sense, in that postwar era, which had to be broken down.

What we young punks found was that underneath all this mayhem and misery was a strong, even essential, desire to change the world that we were born into. Before punk, post-punk, and Goth, there were only a handful of outliers that included a gender fluidity or androgynous aspect to their shows or presentations. Bowie was there, but it wasn't *really* acknowledged until the revolution that was punk. By the early seventies, rock music, for all its anti-establishment spirit, was put into the cupboard, where it became part of the normal fabric of society, by and large. There was disco and prog for sure, but there were precious few artists that promoted the exploration of the kind of space that independent post-punk artists started to inhabit. My God, it was about feelings, and not just the phallic ones that hard rock promoted, but feelings of alienation and vulnerability, yes, vulnerability as an actual thing. Also, as I hope I have shown, the driving force was not only music and fashion. We drew from literature and the visual arts as well. Imaginations were set free from the bonds of wartime deprivation.

I determined, as in my previous book, that I would draw together my experience with this music, my stories, and observations to provide a sense of what it was like to live back then. What was needed for this undertaking was a view of the forces that made this happen, an attempt to connect the dots across the arc of the arts that produced Goth.

I'm sure some will have heard stuff went down a different way, but this is my version—how I perceived things. For better or worse, it's my reality inhabiting these pages, showing how the atmosphere of the times fused all this together, reflecting on the societal changes, and demonstrating why we need to hold on to the good transformations even more than ever.

Every generation rebels against the previous one. When I was younger, I saw life as a series of events occurring in a linear fashion. I got to the top of one mountain and saw another to climb, but as I've gotten older I realize it's

The author in 2023
Credit: Louis Rodiger

not that way at all. Rather, it is akin to a set of concentric circles where we jump from ring to ring, circling around and back again and again. You learn from your mistakes and jump up to the next circle or you drop back down to repeat them again. That's pretty much how I see life. But I've discovered it is more than that. I feel it's been a complete rewiring of what it means to be in the thrall of music and art, realized by the hand of Goth, if you will.

As I walk into the latter part of my life, I feel I might best contribute to my own and others' understanding by putting it down in black and white. Talking to many friends and various others these past few years since *Cured* was released, I've found that those I've spoken to on my travels enjoy that part of my writing that conveys the actual *experience*. That's the thing they want. It is, in a way, the community I never had growing up as a child, which we have all forged together since. It's given me my understanding of the world and my life; and this is a homage to that community. Long may it live!

Lol Tolhurst
California, December 21, 2022

ACKNOWLEDGMENTS

COLLABORATORS

Jim Ruland, project manager, whose wrangling of the various photos, ephemera, and general structures make *Goth: A History* reality. Thanks again for your constructive guidance and help in refining my work into a voice worth hearing. Gray Tolhurst, research writer, whose meticulously detailed inquiries and thoughts for *Goth* formed a perfect template for my various recollections, stories, and opinions. Ben Schafer, editor, whose calm and intelligent passion for music culture and its muses helped us make a better book together. I'm also grateful to the photographers—Richard Bellia, Edward Colver, Michael Costiff, Dina Douglass, Tracy Fahey, Mick Mercer, Louis Rodiger, Tom Sheehan, and Cindy Tolhurst—whose work helps bring the Gothic culture to life. Also, thank you to JC Moglia for the flyers, clippings, and other assorted oddments. Thank you, Rob Steen, for enhancing some of the photos.

WITH LOVE

Cindy Tolhurst, my wife, whose cheerleading and belief are the reasons I was able to write this book. I love you, always x. Budgie, my creative partner and friend, whose hope, belief, and artistry give me wings every day, so grateful to be trudging the road of happy destiny together x.

Acknowledgments

THANK YOU

Mark Kates and Sophie Wilde Spare, at Fenway Recordings Artist Management. Luis Valencia at Fenway, and Olivia Horowitz at Atwater Village Music. Marjy Taylor, personal assistant, the impossible made possible, daily. Jonathan Larr, legal skills. Max Bean at Scout Ranch for the writing room—again! Peter McGuigan, Ultra Literary, thank you for the initial concept for this book. Caspian Dennis, literary agent, at Abner Stein UK. Richard Milner at Quercus, UK publishers. Jason Heller for your valuable input. Leah Bush. Gitane DeMone. Tracy Fahey. Kevin Haskins. Wayne Hussey. David J. Jo Jones. Julianne Regan. Adolfo Sanchez. Steve Forrester, my man in Blighty. Joe Wong, first reader and friend. Mario Ponce at Shure. David Pilotte, making dreams come true. Mike Kehoe, thanks for making it happen.

Anyone else that helped me realize this book in any way, if I've forgotten you, please accept my apologies and thanks.

> "I write entirely to find out what I'm thinking,
> what I'm looking at, what I see and what it means.
> What I want and what I fear."
> In memoriam Joan Didion
> December 5, 1934—December 23, 2021

The author at the Elephant Fayre in 1983
Credit: Tom Sheehan

SOURCES

CHAPTER ONE
Mohr, Tim. *Burning Down the Haus—Punk Rock, Revolution, and the Fall of the Berlin Wall.* Algonquin Books (September 2018).

CHAPTER TWO
Groom, Nick. *The Gothic: A Very Short Introduction.* Oxford University Press (September 2012).
Halberstam, Jack. *Skin Shows: Gothic Horror and the Technology of Monsters.* Duke University Press (August 1995).
Aldiss, Brian W. *The Detached Retina: Science Fiction and Fantasy.* Syracuse University Press (May 1995).
Sunstein, Emily. *Mary Shelley: Romance and Reality.* Little, Brown (January 1989).
Williams, Gilda. *The Gothic.* MIT Press (August 2007).
Traversi, Derek A. "Wuthering Heights After a Hundred Years." *Dublin Review* (Spring 1949).
Eliot, T. S. *Sacred Wood* (1920).
Tearle, Oliver. "A Short Analysis of T. S. Eliot's 'East Coker.'" *Interesting Literature* (February 2007).

CHAPTER FOUR
Reynolds, Simon. *Rip It Up and Start Again: Postpunk 1978–1984.* Penguin Books (2006).

CHAPTER SIX
Bag, Alice. Interview with Dinah Cancer. www.alicebag.com (November 2004).

CHAPTER SEVEN
Burton, Tim. BBC News (February 2009).

INDEX

Adam and the Ants, 101
Adams, Craig, 160–161, 163
addiction, 51–52, 64, 67, 208
The Adverts, 17
alcoholism, 104, 155
Aldiss, Brian W., 25
Alexander, Larry, 161
Alien Sex Fiend, 183, 216 (photo)
All About Eve, 171–179, 171 (photo), 173 (photo), 176 (photo)
   Elizabeth Fraser, 151–155, 151 (photo), 153–155 (photo)
   Touched by Jesus, 173
"All Cats Are Grey," 136–138, 137 (photo), 140
Almond, Marc, 187
Alomar, Carlos, 64–65
And Also the Trees, 167–171, 168 (photo)
Andy, Horace, 154
Applewhite, Marshall, 210
Ariel (Plath), 34, 38
Ash, Daniel, 92, 94–95, 97
Atkins, Martyn, 87
"Atrocity Exhibition," 87–88

Bacon, Francis, 18, 124, 146, 186, 214
Bailey, Steve. *see* Severin, Steven
Ballard, J. G., 102
Ballion, Susan. *see* Siouxsie Sioux
Bang, Lester, 47
Banshees. *see* Siouxsie and the Banshees
Barefoot in the Head (Aldiss), 25
Barrett, Syd, 167
Bascombe, 195
Basildon, 193–194

The Batcave, 23, 23 (photo), 181–190, 181 (photo), 185 (photo), 187 (photo)
Batman, 96, 174, 184, 215
Baudelaire, Charles, 26, 51, 95, 213
Bauhaus, 24, 43, 90–99, 90 (photo), 96 (photo), 183, 201
   "Bela Lugosi's Dead," 92–95, 186, 190, 215
   Burning from the Inside, 95–96
   In the Flat Field, 94
   Mask, 94
   in New York (1980), 97–99
   The Sky's Gone Out, 94
Bean, Mikey, 199
Beetlejuice (film), 215
"Bela Lugosi's Dead," 92–95, 186, 190, 215
The Bell Jar (Plath), 37–38, 142
Bingenheimer, Rodney, 15
The Birthday Party, 24, 183
Black Flag, 197, 199
Black Marble, 211
Blake, William, 29
Blaustein, Marcy, 200
"Blue Monday," 190
Bolan, Marc, 60–63, 162
Bolles, Don, 198
The Bonaparte's, 44–45
Bowie, David, 61, 63–68, 71, 94–95, 98, 131–132, 162, 190, 226
Boy George, 187, 195
Boys Don't Cry, 132
Brel, Jacques, 95
Bricheno, Tim, 161, 172–173, 175
Brixton, 52–53
Brontë, Emily, 26–27, 91
Brotherdale, Steve, 72
Bruhn, Andreas, 161

235

Buckley, Tim, 154
Budgie, 79, 103–104, 114, 117–119, 118 (photo), 143, 147, 156, 163, 187
Burke, Edmund, 178
Burning Down the Haus—Punk Rock, Revolution, and the Fall of the Berlin Wall (Mohr), 13
Burning from the Inside, 95–96
Burton, Tim, 215
Bush, Kate, 26–27
Bush, Leah, 217–221
Buskin, Richard, 131
Buzzcocks, 71, 73, 80, 85

Cale, John, 51–52
Camden Palace, 12, 187–188
Camus, Albert, 30–33, 122
Can, 66, 86, 102, 129, 147, 157
Cancer, Dinah, 198–200
"Candidate," 85
Captain Sensible, 166
Careless, 210
Carruthers, John Valentine, 118 (photo)
The Cars, 48
Cash, Johnny, 208
The Castle of Otranto (Walpole), 21
Catholic/Catholicism, 28–29, 31, 36, 111, 124–128, 134–136, 143–144, 172
Cave, Nick, 183, 183 (photo)
Ceccagno, Marc, 119–120
Cheever, John, 102
Cherish the Light Years, 211
Child, June, 61–62
Christian Death, 185 (photo), 189 (photo), 198–199 (photo), 199, 201–205, 201 (photo)
　Catastrophe Ballet, 204
　Only Theatre of Pain, 201–202
The Clash, 9, 11, 14, 195–196
　concerts/touring, 48, 53
　"The Guns of Brixton," 48
　influence of, 16–17, 90–91
The Clash: Westway to the World, 196
Clinco, Andrew, 209–210
Closer, 73, 87–90
　"A Means to an End," 88–89
　"Atrocity Exhibition," 87–88
　"Colony," 88
　"Decades," 89–90

　"The Eternal," 89
　"Heart and Soul," 89
　"Isolation," 88
　"Passover," 88
　"Twenty Four Hours," 89
clothing. *see* fashion/clothing
Club Lingerie, 200
Cocteau Twins, 151–156, 153–154 (photo)
"Cold," 144, 146
Cold Cave, 210–211
college radio, 15, 209
"Colony," 88
community, Goth, 221, 228
confessional poetry, 35, 39
conflict, 22
Cooper, Alice, 54–57, 201
Cope, Julian, 58, 105
Corbijn, Anton, 197
Cousin, Andy, 172
The Cramps, 201
Crash, Darby, 199–200
Crawley, 3 (photo), 4, 48, 56, 100, 105, 108, 110, 119, 125, 134, 136, 169, 188, 193–194
Creasy, Martin, 120
The Creatures, 104
Crossing the Water (Plath), 36
Culture Club, 187, 195
Cured (Tolhurst), 22, 129, 141, 172, 222, 225–226, 228
The Cure
　"A Strange Day," 144
　"All Cats Are Grey," 136–138, 137 (photo), 140
　Boys Don't Cry, 132
　"Cold," 144, 146
　Disintegration, 123, 196
　"The Drowning Man," 138–139
　Faith, 5, 29, 65, 80, 113, 123–124, 132–140, 136 (photo), 157, 209, 213
　fans, 5, 15, 81, 140 (photo)
　"The Figurehead," 143
　"A Forest," 127, 129, 132
　"The Hanging Garden," 142
　"How Beautiful You Are," 213
　Join Hands Tour, 79–80, 103, 105, 107–117, 107 (photo), 123, 130
　"Killing an Arab," 32, 122
　Kiss Me, Kiss Me, Kiss Me, 213
　Manchester show (1979), 74–77

"One Hundred Years," 141
origins/early years, 4–5, 53, 119–123
on Peel show, 15
"Play for Today," 123, 128
Pornography, 5, 29, 44, 65, 117, 124, 132, 140–146, 143 (photo), 157, 190, 209, 214
Primary Tour, 167–168
psychedelic influence, 132, 134
punk influence, 16–18, 134
record store appearances, 81–83
Reflections Tour, 215
Rock and Roll Hall of Fame, 208–209
Seventeen Seconds, 5, 29, 65, 80, 113, 123–124, 126–132, 157
"Siamese Twins," 142–143
with Siouxsie and the Banshees, 105–118, 109 (photo), 123, 125
at Smith College, 35
themes of lyrics, 27, 29
Three Imaginary Boys, 4, 122, 132
touring, 13–15, 44, 80–84, 82 (photo), 125, 134, 136
with Wire, 156–158, 158 (photo)
The Cure flyers
   in Brussels, 190 (photo)
   Eric's, 122 (photo)
   Faith Tour, 136 (photo)
   first American tour, 82 (photo)
   Friars, 109 (photo), 158 (photo)
   in Ghent, 126 (photo)
   Hanover Rotation, 133 (photo)
   Lyceum, 158 (photo)
   Marquee, 78 (photo), 121 (photo), 127 (photo)
   Picture Tour, 135 (photo)
   Rainbow Theatre, 14 (photo)
The Cure in Orange, 215
Curtis, Deborah, 72–74
Curtis, Ian, 71–74, 77–80, 84–89, 190
Cutler, Paul, 198

The Damned, 24, 62, 165–166 (photo), 165–167
   Damned Damned Damned, 167
Danceteria, 99
Dark Entries: Bauhaus and Beyond (Stennett), 93
David J, 90–92, 94–97, 96 (photo), 186
Davis, Dennis, 65–66, 131

"Day of the Lords," 85
Deathrock, 197–202
"Decades," 89–90
DeMone, Gitane, 189 (photo), 201 (photo), 202–205, 204 (photo)
The Demonstration, 210
Dempsey, Michael, 165
   books, 30
   early life, 119–120
   falling out with Robert Smith, 123, 130
   with Siouxsie and the Banshees, 110, 112–114
   T. Rex album, 60
   Three Imaginary Boys, 4
   travel to gigs, 74
Demure, Deb, 209–210
Densmore, John, 41–42
Depeche Mode, 193–196, 207, 210
   "Enjoy the Silence," 196
   "Personal Jesus," 195–196
   Violator, 196–197
depression, 37–38, 80, 131, 193, 196, 208
Detached Retina: Science Fiction and Fantasy (Aldiss), 25
Disintegration, 123, 196
"Disorder," 85
The Doors, 41–43, 89
The Downward Spiral, 208–209
Drab Majesty, 209–210
Dracula (Stoker), 215
Drake, Nick, 131–132
dream pop, 152
The Drift, 58–59
drums as signature of Goth, 146–147
Duell, Chad, 222 (photo)

Echo and the Bunnymen, 41, 105, 173
Edward Scissorhands (film), 215
Egan, Rusty, 187
Eisold, Wesley, 210–211
Eldritch, Andrew, 160–161, 163
Electric Warrior, 60–62
Eliot, T. S., 28–30
Emerson, Ralph Waldo, 26
"The End," 43
"Enjoy the Silence," 196
Eno, Brian, 64–67, 159
Erasmus, Alan, 85
Eric's, 122 (photo), 156, 163

"The Eternal," 89
existentialist, 30–31, 33, 35, 45, 122, 164
Expressionist artists, 214

Factory Records, 73, 84–85
Fahey, Tracy, 21–24, 26–27, 124
Faith, 5, 29, 65, 80, 113, 123–124, 132–140, 136 (photo), 157, 209, 213
The Fall, 33
fashion/clothing
　at Batcave, 186, 187 (photo)
　glam, 61
　Goth, 123, 218–219, 221–223, 226
　at Palace, 188
　punk, 219
Fenton, Peter, 101
Fiction, 93 (photo), 94, 122, 152
Fiend, Nik, 183 (photo), 216 (photo)
films, 214–215
Five Leaves Left, 131
Fletcher, Andy, 193–194, 196–197
Flood, 195, 207
The Flowers of Evil (Baudelaire), 26
"A Forest," 127, 129, 132
forgiveness, 135
45 Grave, 198–199, 201
4AD, 94, 155
The Fragile, 208
Frankenstein (Shelley), 24, 128
Fraser, Elizabeth, 151–155, 151 (photo), 153–155 (photo)
Freud, Lucian, 214
Friars club, 108–109, 109 (photo), 111, 158 (photo)

Gahan, Dave, 196
Gaiman, Neil, 24
Gallup, Ric, 81
Gallup, Simon, 44, 44 (photo), 130–132, 138–139, 171, 208
Gargoyle Club, 182–183
Gary (friend of author), 52–54, 141
Gene Loves Jezebel, 171–172
Germs, 197–199
ghost train, 54–55
glam, 56, 61–62, 64, 94–95, 100, 164, 167
Glass, David, 185 (photo)
The Golem, 214
Gore, Martin, 193, 195–197

Gormenghast (Peake), 138, 192
Goth
　community, 221, 228
　drums as signature of, 146–147
　elder Goths, 216–221
　Eldritch as Godfather of, 161
　fashion/clothing, 123, 218–219, 221–223, 226
　in literature, 21–39
　post-punk as cousin to, 6, 12
　subculture, 5–6, 161, 172, 190, 216–219, 221–222, 224–225
　visual influences/expressions, 213–216
　why it matters, 221–224
Graves, Robert, 172, 198
Gresty, Martin, 71
Gretton, Rob, 72–73, 78
Grey, Robert, 156–157, 159
Gunn, Ben, 160
Guthrie, Robin, 152–154, 154 (photo)

Halberstam, Jack, 24
Hannett, Martin, 73, 84, 87
Hansa Records, 67, 120, 159
Harmonia, 66–67
Hartley, Matthieu, 83, 130–132
Haskins, Kevin, 91–92, 94–99, 98 (photo), 147
Havas, Graham, 168–169, 168 (photo)
Havas, Nick, 168–169, 168 (photo)
"Heart and Soul," 89
Heaven, 189–190
Heaven's Gate cult, 210
Hedges, Mike, 122, 131–133, 195
Heggie, Will, 152
Heylin, Clinton, 102
"Hong Kong Garden," 102, 105
Hook, Peter, 71, 77, 86–87
Hooley, Terri, 111
Hope, Courtney, 222 (photo)
"How Beautiful You Are," 213
Hume Crescents, 74–77
"Hurt," 208
Hussey, Wayne, 160–165
"Hybrid," 146
Hynde, Chrissie, 166

"I Remember Nothing," 86
Iggy Pop, 98–99

Iggy Pop and the Stooges, 47, 72, 95
In the Flat Field, 94
"Insight," 85
internet, 11–12, 81, 165, 209, 212, 221, 225
"Interzone," 86
"Isolation," 88

Jaki L, 147
James, Brian, 166
James, Tony, 161
The Jesus and Mary Chain, 207, 211
Joan of Arc, 80
Join Hands Tour, 79–80, 103, 105, 107–117, 123, 130
Jones, Brian, 51–52
Jones, Gloria, 62
Jones, Justin "Jo," 168–171, 168 (photo)
Jones, Simon Huw, 168–170, 168 (photo)
Joy Division, 27, 30, 41, 71–90, 78 (photo), 183
  Closer, 73, 87–90
  "Transmission," 73, 85
  Unknown Pleasures, 73, 84–86

Kafka, Franz, 29–30, 130
Kand, Valor, 202–203
Kat Von D, 223 (photo)
Kevorkian, François, 195
Kijak, Stephen, 58–59
"Killing an Arab," 32, 122
Kiss Me, Kiss Me, Kiss Me, 213
Klucynski, Mick, 93 (photo)
krautrock, 64, 67, 86, 147
Krieger, Robbie, 41–42

La Folie, 153
LA Woman, 43
Letts, Don, 186
Lewis, Graham, 156–157
Lewis, Matthew, 23
Liebegott, Paul, 47
Liebezeit, Jaki, 85, 129, 147, 157
"Life's a Gas," 62–63
Lilywhite, Steve, 102
literature, Goth in, 21–39
  Albert Camus, 30–33
  Anne Sexton, 38–39
  Emily Brontë, 26–27
  John-Paul Sarte, 30–33

Mary Shelley, 24–25
Sylvia Plath, 33–38
T. S. Eliot, 28–30
The Little Red Schoolbook, 33
The Lost Boys (film), 215
Love and the Rockets, 97
Love Comes Close, 211
Low, 64–68, 131
Lunch, Lydia, 200
Lydon, John, 103 (photo)

MacCulloch, Ian, 105
MacDonald, Hamish, 186
Mackenzie, Billy, 138
Madonna, 187–188
Magazine, 102–103
Malice, 120
Malm, John, Jr., 207
Manzarek, Ray, 41–42
map paradigm, 11
Marquee Club, 78, 78 (photo), 106, 121 (photo), 127 (photo), 162 (photo), 171 (photo), 176 (photo)
Martyn, John, 132
Marx, Gary, 160
Mary Shelley: Romance and Reality (Sunstein), 25
Mask, 94
Mason, Nick, 167
Mason, Terry, 71
Massive Attack, 154
Maus, John, 58
McClaren, Malcolm, 100
McGeoch, John, 103–104
McKay, John, 42 (photo), 79, 101–103, 110, 112–114
McLaren, Malcolm, 167
"A Means to an End," 88–89
mental health issues, 37, 80, 131, 191, 193, 196–197
Metropolis, 214
Mezzanine, 154
Miller, Daniel, 195
The Misfits, 201
The Mission, 161–165, 162 (photo)
  God's Own Medicine, 164
Modern Mirror, 210
Mohr, Tom, 13
Molchat Doma, 211–212

Mona D, 210
The Monk (Lewis), 23
Morris, Kenny, 79, 95, 101–103, 110, 112–114, 147
Morris, Stephen, 72, 85–86, 88–89, 95, 147
Morrison, Jim, 30, 41–46, 85
motorik beat, 85, 129, 147, 157
Murphy, James, 216–217
Murphy, Peter, 43, 90 (photo), 92–93, 95, 97, 99, 207, 214–215, 217
music, as lingua franca of the world, 12–13
Music for the Masses, 195
music magazines, 14
Mute Records, 159, 195

Nausea (Sartre), 31–32
Neu!, 65, 67
"New Dawn Fades," 85–86
New Order, 73–74, 190, 211
Newman, Colin, 156, 159
Nico, 50–54
Nietzche, Friedrich, 179
nihilism, 6, 17–18, 52, 60, 124, 141, 146, 179, 208, 211
Nine Inch Nails, 147, 207–209, 211
Noferatu (film), 214
Notting Hill Carnival, 9–11
Numan, Gary, 211

100 Club, 90–91, 100–101, 113
"One Hundred Years," 141
O'Toole, Peter, 120
"Outdoor Miner," 156
The Outsider (Wilson), 179

The Palace (Camden), 12, 187–188
Parry, Chris, 77–78, 93 (photo), 94, 111, 121–122
"Passover," 88
Peake, Mervyn, 138, 192
Pearson, Deanne, 109
Peel, John, 13–15, 48, 73–74, 94, 101–102, 170
"People Are Strange," 43
"Personal Jesus," 195–196
Phantoms (Bean), 199
PIL, 103, 103 (photo), 199
pirate radio stations, 13
Pirroni, Marco, 100–101

Plath, Sylvia, 33–38, 142, 147, 191
"Play for Today," 123, 128
Poe, Edgar Allan, 25–26, 95
Polsky, Ruth, 99
Pompeii 99, 202–203
Pope, Tim, 215
Pornography, 5, 29, 44, 65, 117, 124, 132, 140–146, 143 (photo), 157, 190, 209, 214
post-punk. *see also specific bands*
 Bauhaus, 93–94, 99
 The Bonaparte's, 44–45
 at Camden Palace, 188
 The Cure, 17–18, 48, 79, 226
 deathrock compared, 198
 as Goth's cousin, 6, 12
 Joy Division, 72, 84, 87
 Molchat Doma, 211
 origins in UK, 102, 104
 Pompeii 99, 202
 Siouxsie and the Banshees, 102, 104
 Sisters of Mercy, 161
 subculture, 211
 Wire, 156
Presley, Elvis, 4
Pretty Hate Machine, 207
The Priory, 191–194, 196–197
psychedelic influences on The Cure, 132, 134
psychic geography, 9–19
punk, 17–19
 at Camden Palace, 188
 drummers, 147
 fashion, 219
 influence on The Cure, 16–18, 134
 nihilism of, 6, 17–18
 nonconformist impulse,—65
 spiritual birth of, 10–11

radio, 13–15, 15, 209
Rat Scabies, 165–167
Raymonde, Simon, 152
The Rebel (Camus), 30–31
record stores, 36, 81–83, 112, 222
Redon, Odilond, 213
Regan, Julianne, 138–139, 171–179, 173 (photo), 176 (photo)
Rev, Martin, 17, 47–48
Reynolds, Simon, 49, 132
Reznor, Trent, 207–209

Rimbaud, Arthur, 30
Rock and Roll Hall of Fame, 208–209
Ruland, Jim, 226

Sanchez, Adolfo, 222–223 (photo)
Sarte, John-Paul, 30–33, 45
Saville, Peter, 84, 87
Schiele, Egon, 214
"School's Out," 56–57
"Secrets," 127
Sergeant, Will, 105
Seventeen Seconds, 5, 29, 65, 80, 113, 123–124, 126–132, 157
Severin, Steven, 100, 104–105, 110, 112–114, 116, 118 (photo), 187
Sex Pistols, 17, 71, 90–91, 100, 106, 166
Sexbeat, 183, 186
Sexton, Anne, 35, 38–39
"Shadowplay," 86
Shelley, Mary, 24–25
Sherwood, Adrian, 207
"She's Lost Control," 86
"Siamese Twins," 142–143
Siouxsie and the Banshees, 24, 41, 42 (photo), 52, 79, 95, 100–119, 107 (photo), 109 (photo), 123, 125, 130, 146, 152, 161, 183, 187, 215
  "Hong Kong Garden," 102, 105
  Hyaena, 104
  "Hybrid," 146
  Join Hands, 102, 115
  Join Hands Tour, 79–80, 103, 105, 107–117, 123, 130
  Juju, 104
  Kaleidoscope, 103
  A Kiss in the Dreamhouse, 104
  The Rapture, 118
  The Scream, 102
Siouxsie Sioux, 42 (photo), 100–101, 100–101 (photo), 104–105, 107 (photo), 108–110, 112–113, 115, 117, 118 (photo), 151–152, 187, 216
Sisters of Mercy, 160–161, 163, 220
  First Last and Always, 160
Skin Shows: Gothic Horror and the Technology of Monsters (Halberstam), 24
The Slits, 103, 186
Small Wonder Records, 92–94
Smith, Patti, 30, 95

Smith, Robert
  archnophobia, 55
  The Clash in concert, 4, 16–17
  in concert, 32 (photo), 144 (photo)
  early life, 119–120, 124, 126
  Faith, 134–136, 138
  falling out with Michael Dempsey, 123, 130
  football, 162
  influential books, 30, 32
  London apartment, 152
  as lyricist, 129
  Pornography, 141–145
  Pornography Tour, 44
  on "Secrets," 127
  Seventeen Seconds, 127, 129–131
  with Siouxsie and the Banshees, 79, 103–105, 110, 112–114, 116–117
  sound check song, 54
  source of angst, 126–127
  Suicide in concert, 48
  T. Rex album, 60
  Three Imaginary Boys, 4
The Smiths, 27, 39, 53
So It Goes (TV program), 72–73, 101
Soft Cell, 183, 187
Solid Air, 132
"Song to the Siren," 154–155
Sounds, 14, 72, 94
The Sound, 41
Southern Death Cult, 182 (photo), 183
The Specials, 49
Specimen, 183, 184 (photo)
Starr, Ringo, 147
Stennett, Peter, 93
Stewart, Chris, 211
Stickney, John, 41
Stoker, Bram, 25, 215
"A Strange Day," 144
Strange Days, 43
The Stranger (Camus), 30, 32, 122
Strummer, Joe, 9, 14, 16–17, 16 (photo), 195–196
subculture, 5–6, 161, 172, 190, 216–219, 221–222, 224–225
Suicide, 17, 18 (photo), 46–50, 46 (photo), 161, 208
Sumner, Bernard, 71, 77, 86–87
Sunstein, Emily, 25

Symbolist painters, 213
Syndrum, 85–86, 156
synthpop, 49, 207–208, 211

T. Rex, 60–62, 95, 162, 167
Tabac, Tony, 71–72
The Teardrop Explodes, 105
Tearle, Oliver, 29
Thatcher, Margaret, 4, 9, 17, 111, 121, 188
"The Drowning Man," 138–139
"The Figurehead," 143
"The Hanging Garden," 142
The Sky's Gone Out, 94
theatricality, 22, 54, 197, 210
They Eat Scum, 198
This Mortal Coil, 155
Thompson, Porl "Pearl," 10, 120, 196
Thornalley, Phil, 141–142, 144
Thorne, Mark, 156
Three Imaginary Boys, 4, 122, 132
Throbbing Gristle, 198
Tolhurst, Gray, 225–226
Tolhurst, John, 33
Tolhurst, Lol
  mother's illness and death, 133–134, 136–138, 140, 156
  photographs, 68 (photo), 107 (photo), 140 (photo), 145–146 (photo), 177 (photo), 227 (photo)
  at The Priory, 191–194, 196–197
Top of the Pops, 15
  Bauhaus, 95–96
  Bolan, 61
  Bowie, 64
Topographies, 222–223
Tower Records, 81
T.S.O.L., 197, 199, 201
Turmel, Jean-Pierre, 83, 87
"Twenty Four Hours," 89

Unknown Pleasures, 73, 84–86
  "Candidate," 85
  "Day of the Lords," 85
  "Disorder," 85
  "I Remember Nothing," 86
  "Insight," 85
  "Interzone," 86
  "New Dawn Fades," 85–86

"Shadowplay," 86
"She's Lost Control," 86
"Wilderness," 86

Vanian, Dave, 63 (photo), 165–166 (photo), 166–167
Vega, Alan, 17, 18 (photo), 46 (photo), 47–50, 50 (photo), 208
Velvet Underground, 50–51, 93, 95, 102
Verlaine, Paul, 213
Verlaine, Tom, 213
Vicious, Sid, 101, 113
violent gigs, 109
violent gigs/clubs, 189–190
Virgin Records, 58, 71, 81
Visconti, Tony, 61, 64–65, 67, 131

Walker, Scott, 58–60, 95
Walpole, Horace, 21
Warhol, Andy, 51
Warsaw, 71–72
Watts, Charlie, 147
Watts-Russell, Ivo, 155
Wednesday, 24, 216
Whisky, 200
The White Goddess (Graves), 172
Wilde, Oscar, 45, 74
"Wilderness," 86
Williams, Gilda, 22, 27
Williams, Rozz, 198, 198 (photo), 201–203, 201–205, 205
Wilson, Tony, 72–73, 85, 101
Wire, 156–160, 158 (photo)
  Chairs Missing, 156
  influence on The Cure, 157–158
  154, 159
  "Outdoor Miner," 156
  Pink Flag, 156
Wisdom, Olli, 182–183, 185
Wong, Joe, 119
Woods, Dave, 112, 114
Wuthering Heights (Brontë), 26–27, 91, 128

Yeats, W. B., 26, 177, 177 (photo)
Young, James Edward, 50–51

Zedd, Nick, 198
"Ziggy Stardust," 95